THE KING'S *Beast* 麗

4

STORY & ART BY

Rei Toma

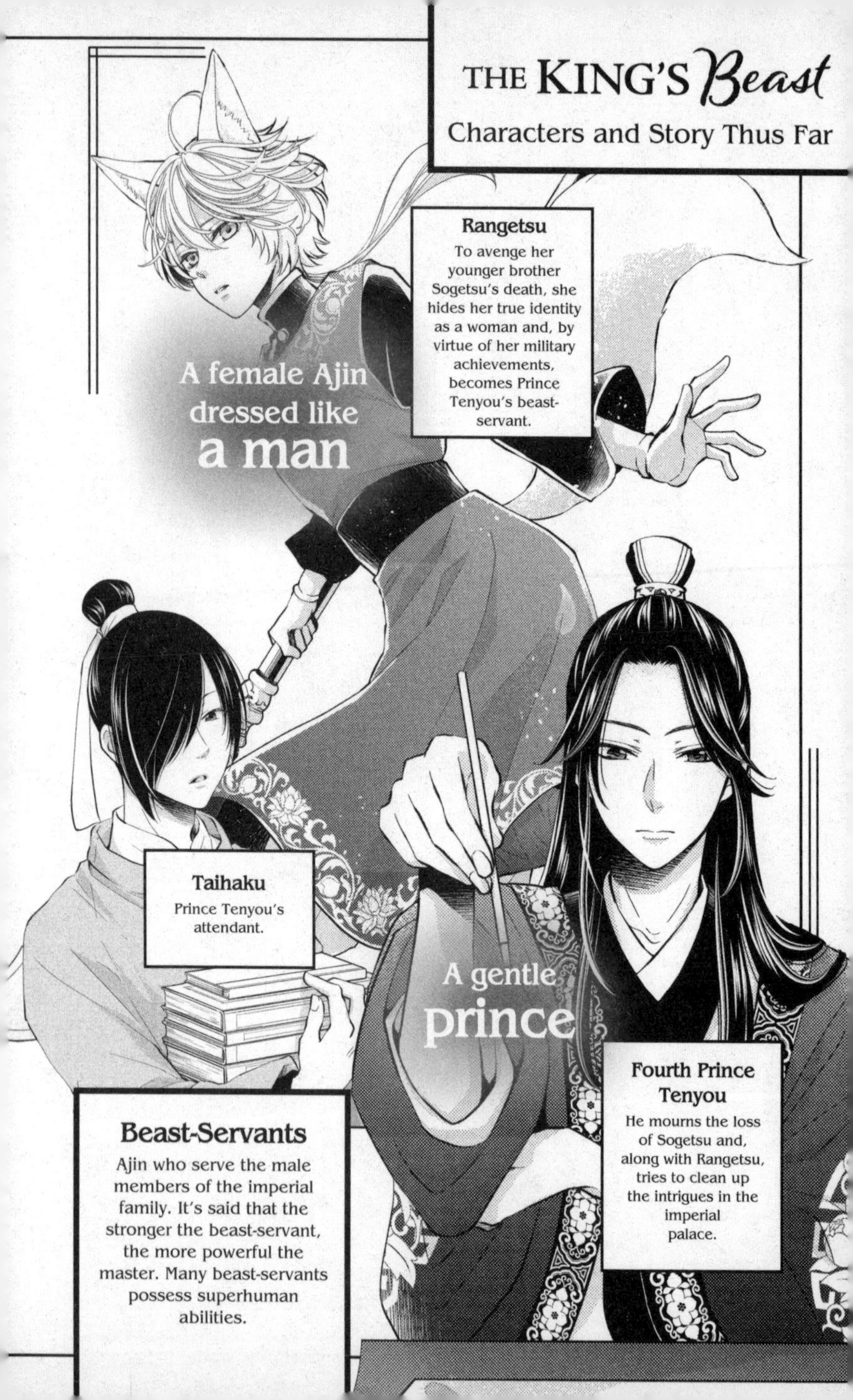
THE KING'S Beast
Characters and Story Thus Far
Rangetsu
To avenge her younger brother Sogetsu's death, she hides her true identity as a woman and, by virtue of her military achievements, becomes Prince Tenyou's beast-servant.
A female Ajin dressed like a man
Fourth Prince Tenyou
He mourns the loss of Sogetsu and, along with Rangetsu, tries to clean up the intrigues in the imperial palace.
A gentle prince
Taihaku
Prince Tenyou's attendant.
Beast-Servants
Ajin who serve the male members of the imperial family. It's said that the stronger the beast-servant, the more powerful the master. Many beast-servants possess superhuman abilities.

Prince Tenyou's Brothers and Their Beast-Servants

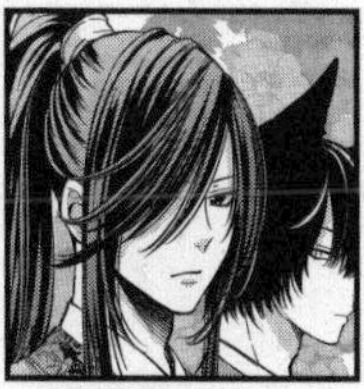

Kougai
The third prince. Still shrouded in mystery.

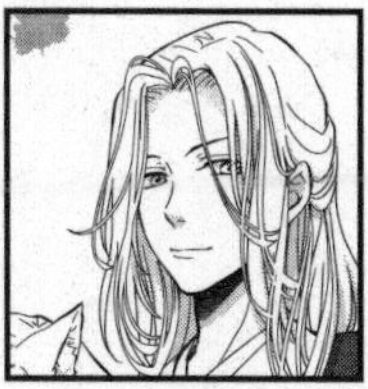

Reiun
The second prince. Intelligent and bored by his own idleness.

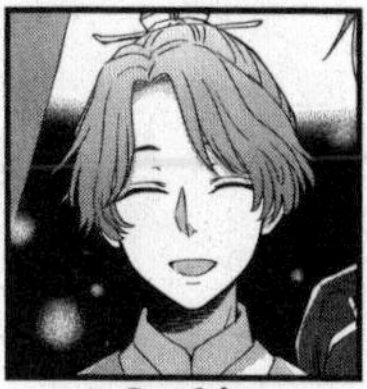

Oushin
The first prince. Sickly and passive.

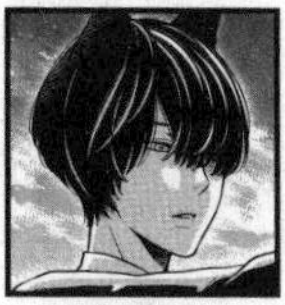

Boku
Prince Kougai's beast-servant.

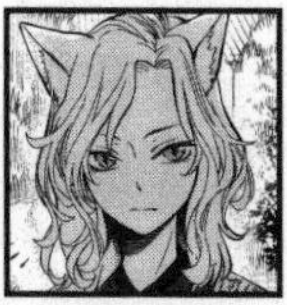

Youbi
Prince Reiun's beast-servant.

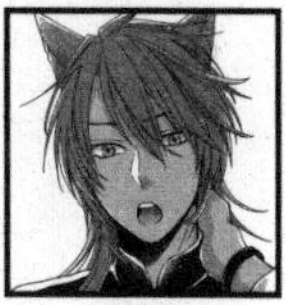

Teiga
Prince Oushin's beast-servant.

The Assassination of Sogetsu

Sogetsu, Rangetsu's twin, was brought to the imperial palace to serve Prince Tenyou as his beast-servant after it was discovered that he had special abilities. He was brutally killed soon after.

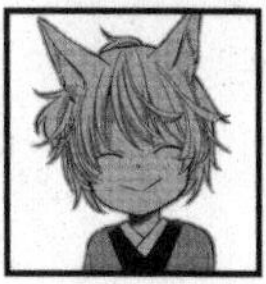

Sogetsu

CONTENTS

◆◆◆

In a world where humans rule the half-beast Ajin, Rangetsu disguises herself as a man to become Fourth Prince Tenyou's beast-servant. Although initially believing the prince to be responsible for her brother's death, Rangetsu soon sees his true nature and vows to help him rule with virtue. As Rangetsu and Prince Tenyou prepare for the coming succession battle, Third Prince Kougai and his beast-servant Boku make their presence felt...

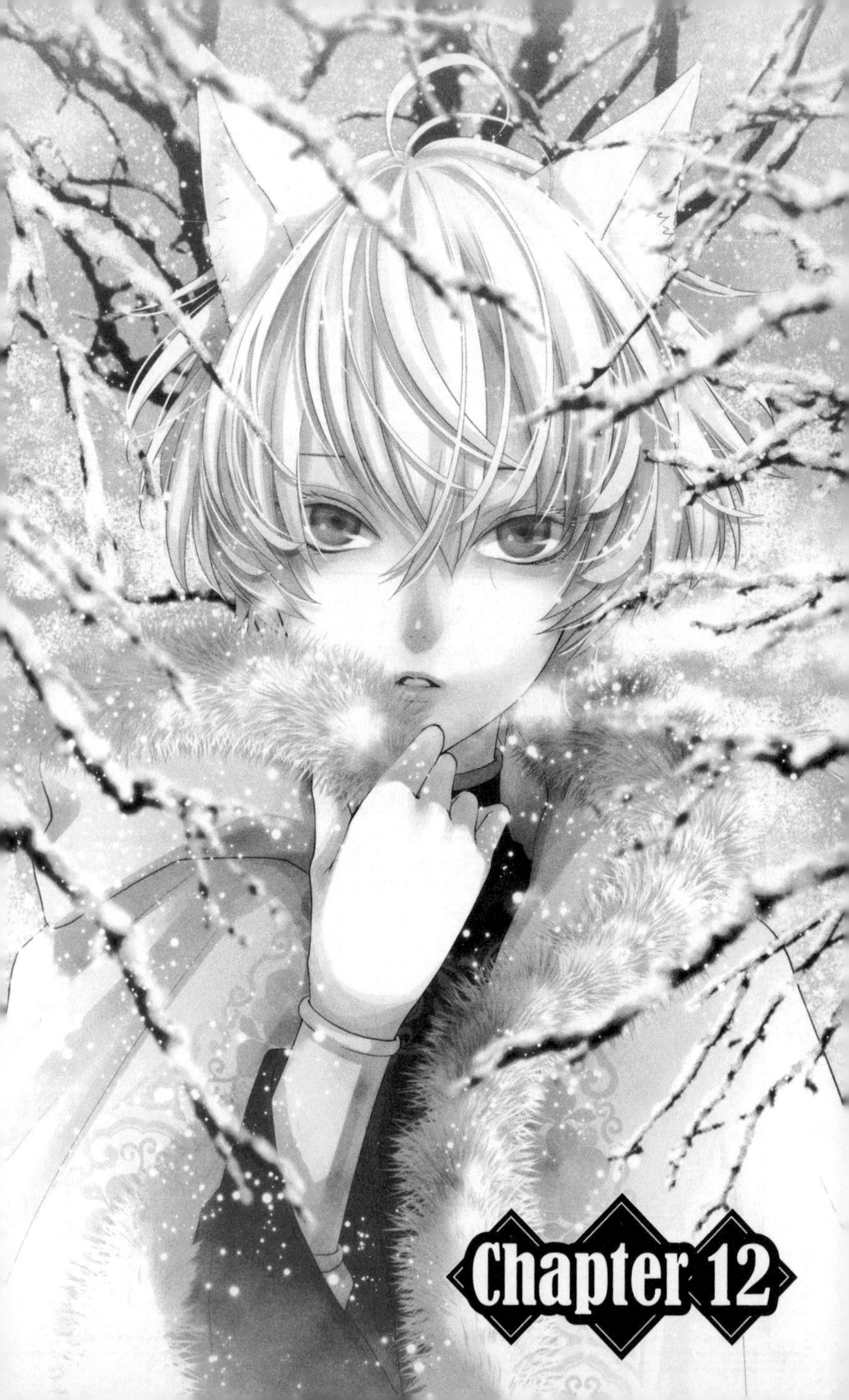
Chapter 12

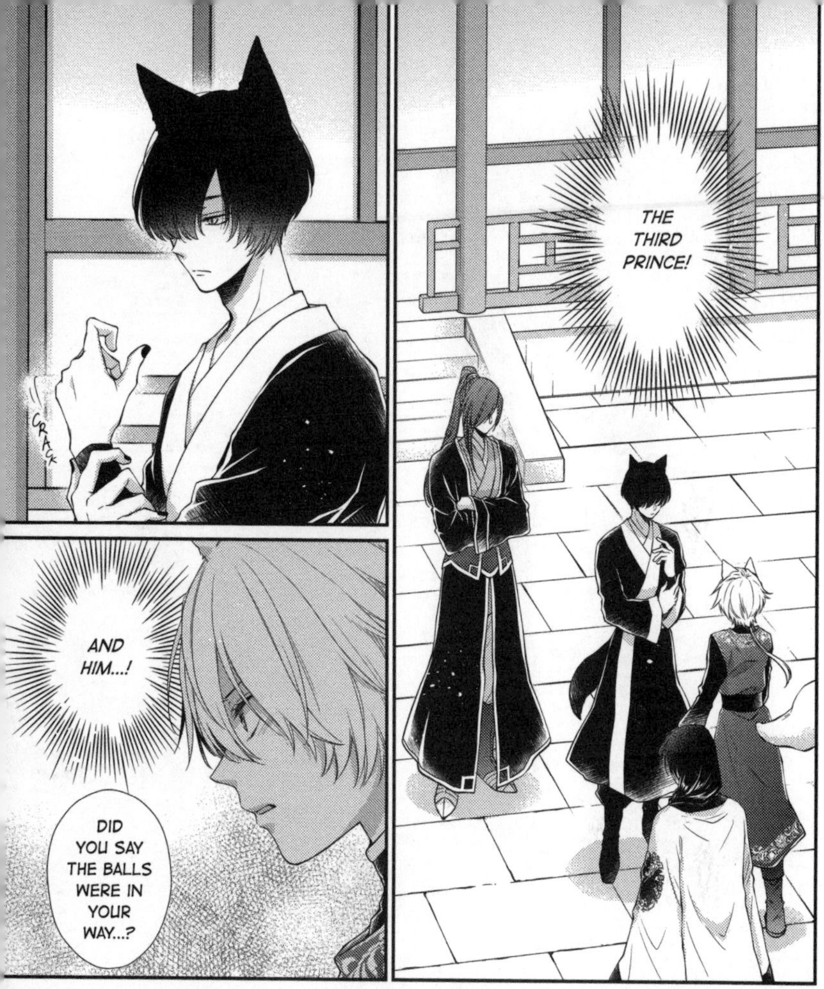
THE THIRD PRINCE!
CRACK
AND HIM...!
DID YOU SAY THE BALLS WERE IN YOUR WAY...?

THE KING'S *Beast*

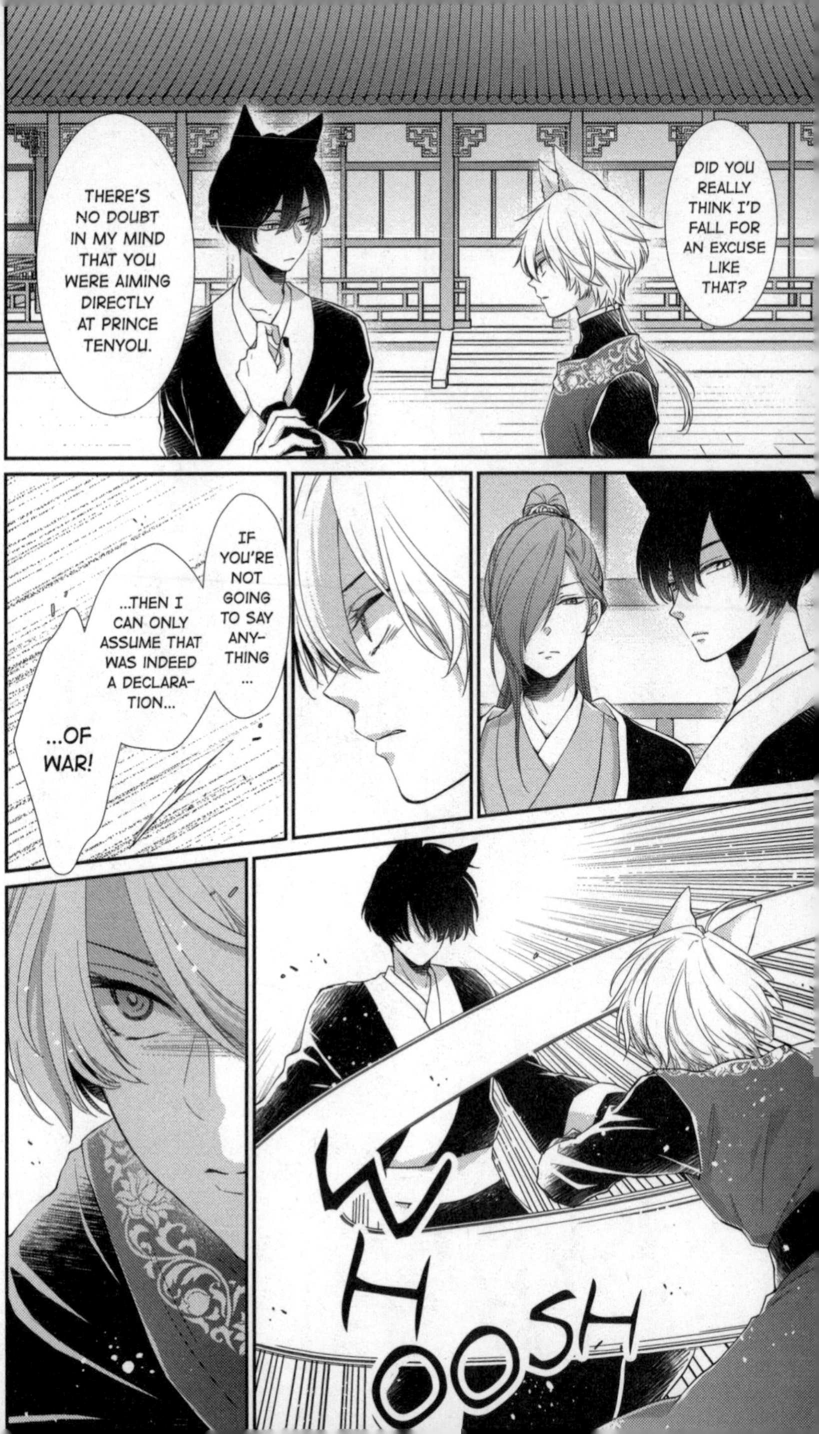
DID YOU REALLY THINK I'D FALL FOR AN EXCUSE LIKE THAT?
THERE'S NO DOUBT IN MY MIND THAT YOU WERE AIMING DIRECTLY AT PRINCE TENYOU.
IF YOU'RE NOT GOING TO SAY ANYTHING...
...THEN I CAN ONLY ASSUME THAT WAS INDEED A DECLARATION...
...OF WAR!
WHOOSH

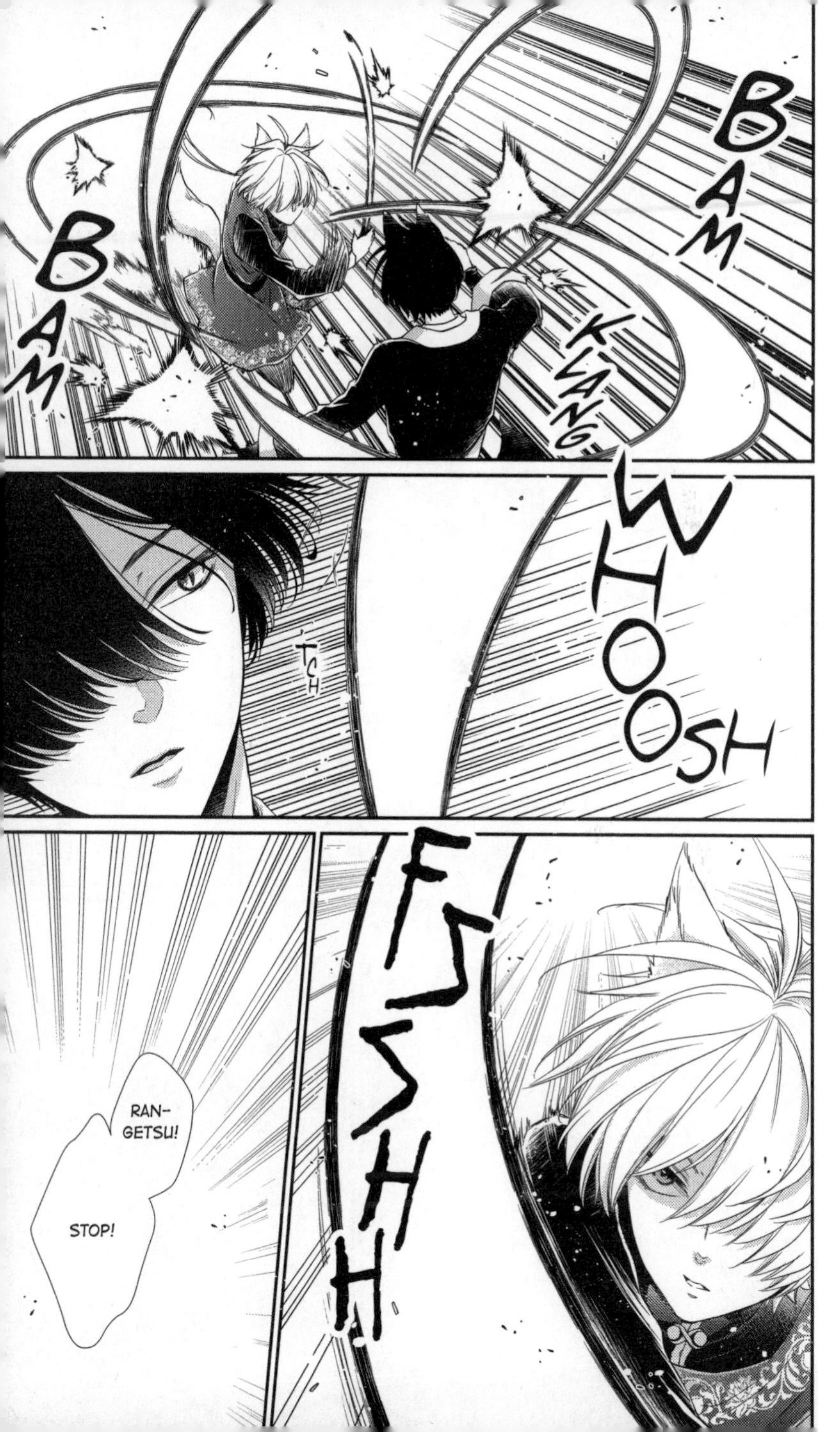
BAM
BAM
KLANG
BAM
WHOOSH
TCH
FSSHH!
RAN-GETSU!
STOP!

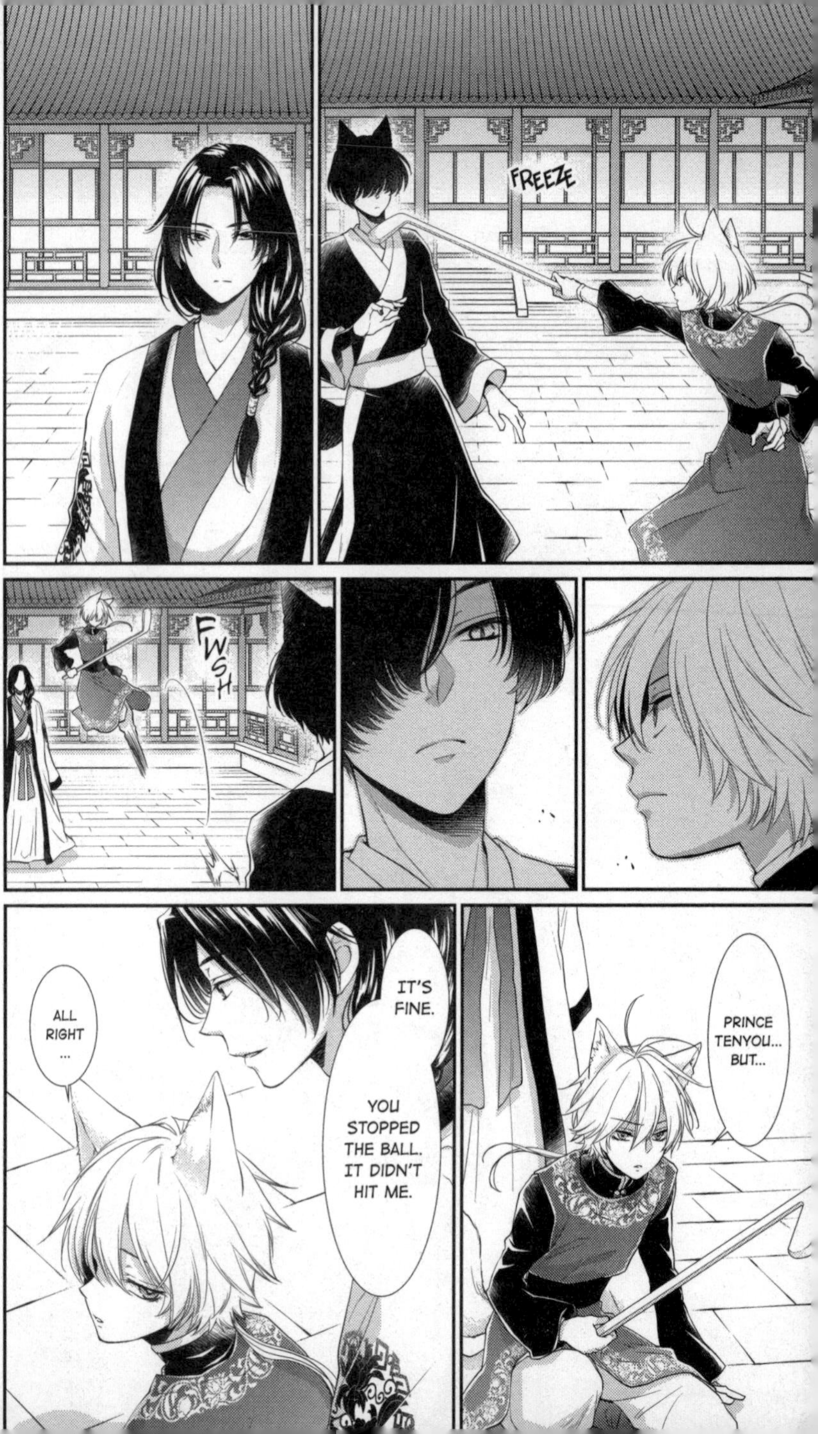
FREEZE
FWSH
PRINCE TENYOU... BUT...
IT'S FINE.
YOU STOPPED THE BALL. IT DIDN'T HIT ME.
ALL RIGHT ...

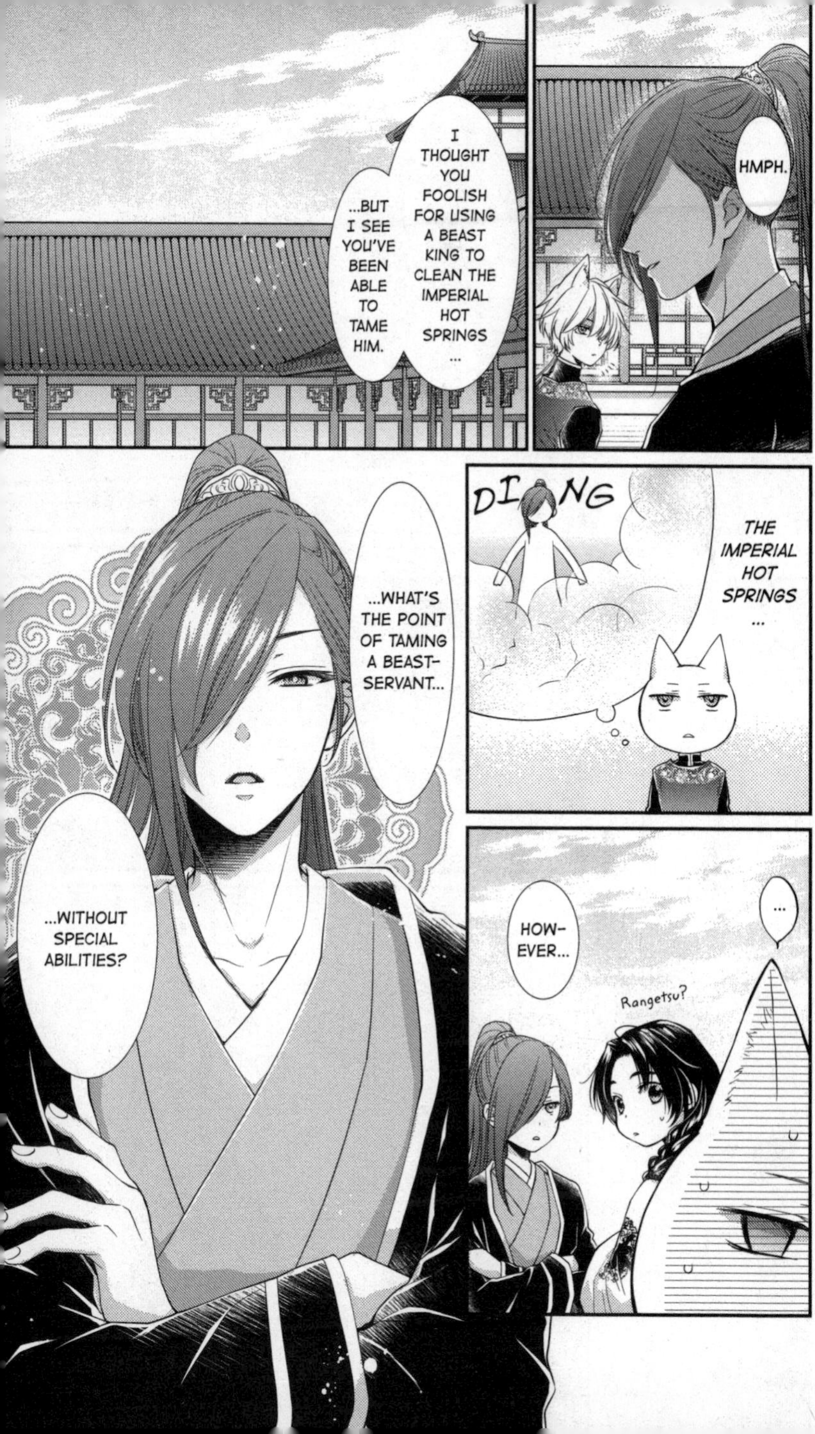
HMPH.
I THOUGHT YOU FOOLISH FOR USING A BEAST KING TO CLEAN THE IMPERIAL HOT SPRINGS...
...BUT I SEE YOU'VE BEEN ABLE TO TAME HIM.
THE IMPERIAL HOT SPRINGS...
DING
...
HOW-EVER...
Rangetsu?
...WHAT'S THE POINT OF TAMING A BEAST-SERVANT...
...WITHOUT SPECIAL ABILITIES?

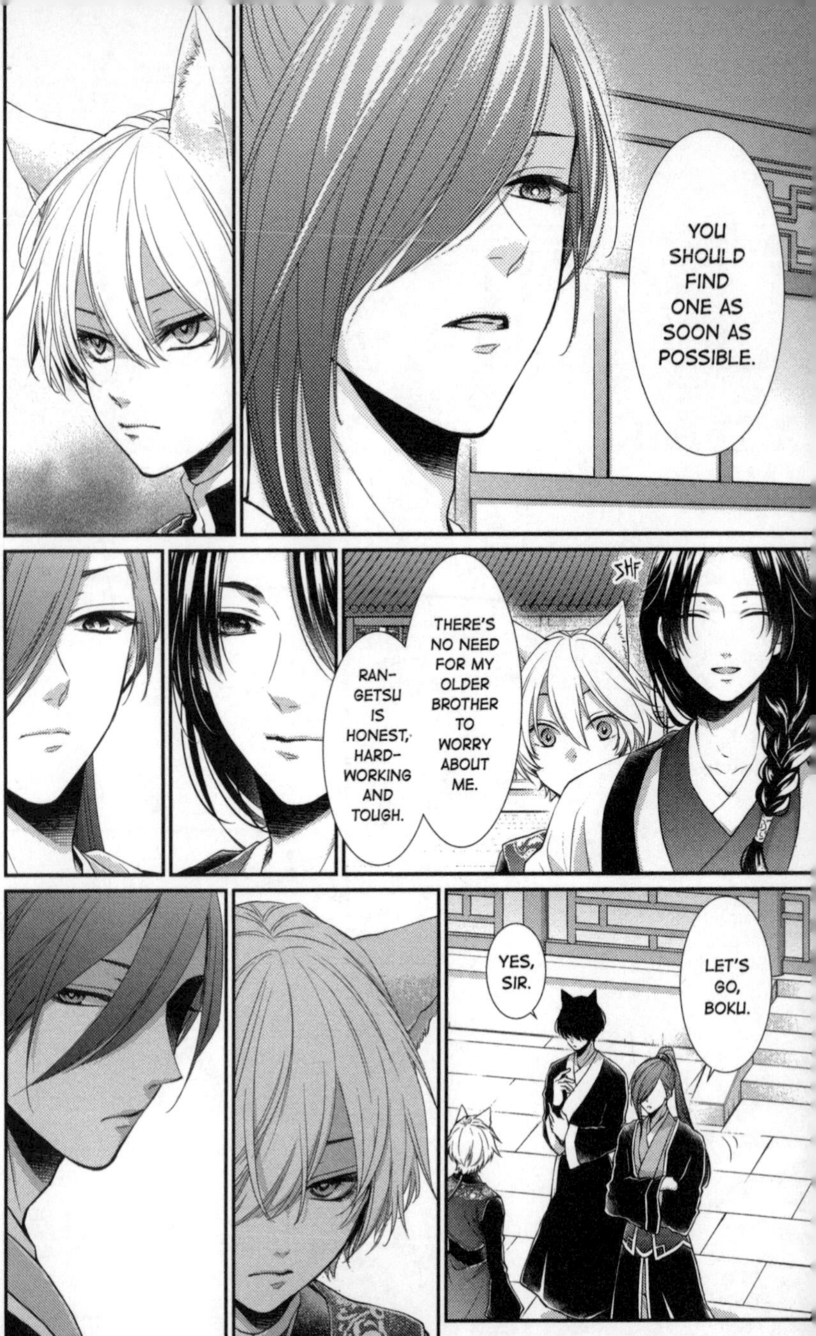
YOU SHOULD FIND ONE AS SOON AS POSSIBLE.
SHF
THERE'S NO NEED FOR MY OLDER BROTHER TO WORRY ABOUT ME.
RAN-GETSU IS HONEST, HARD-WORKING AND TOUGH.
LET'S GO, BOKU.
YES, SIR.

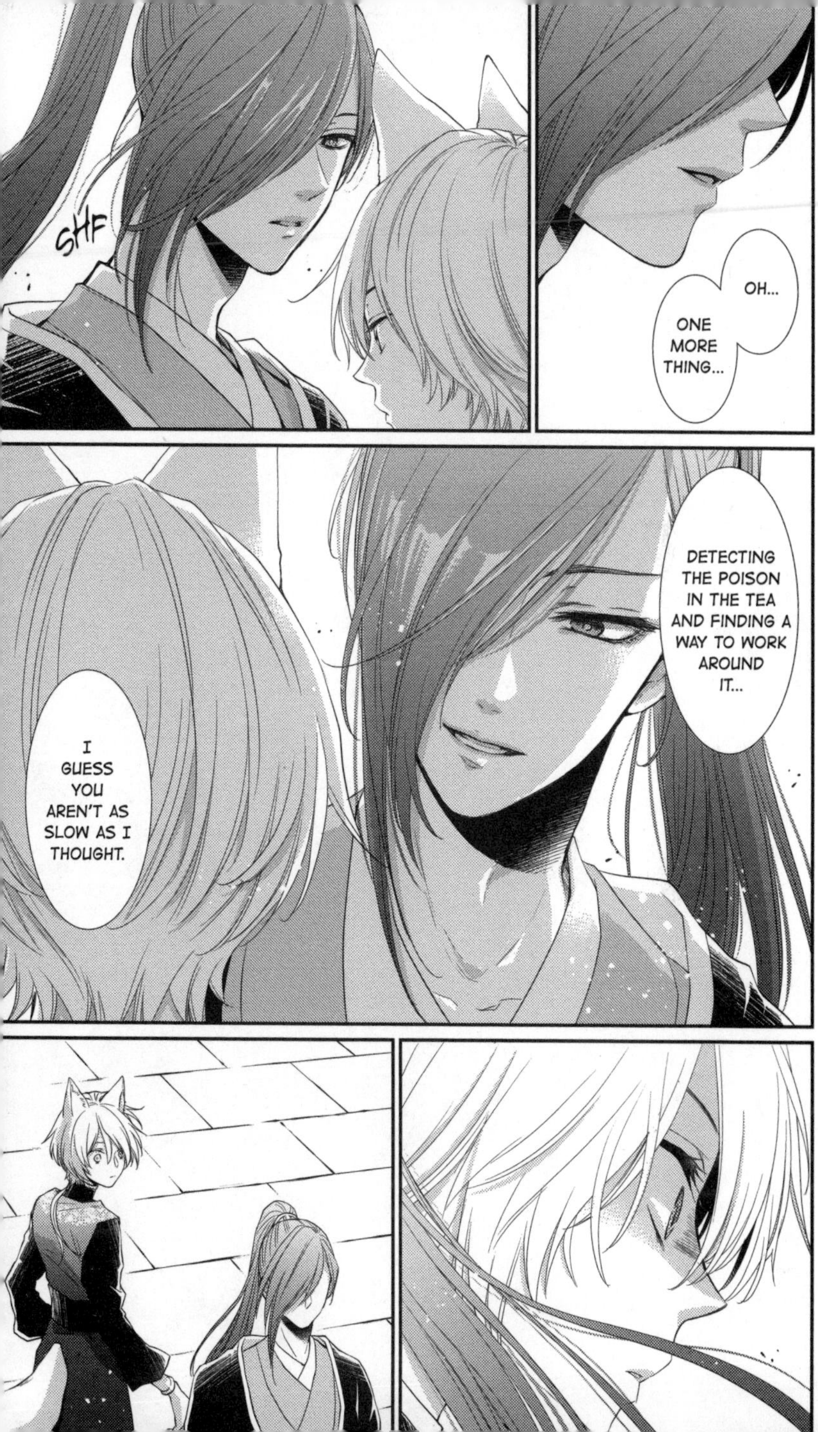
SHF
OH...
ONE MORE THING...
DETECTING THE POISON IN THE TEA AND FINDING A WAY TO WORK AROUND IT...
I GUESS YOU AREN'T AS SLOW AS I THOUGHT.

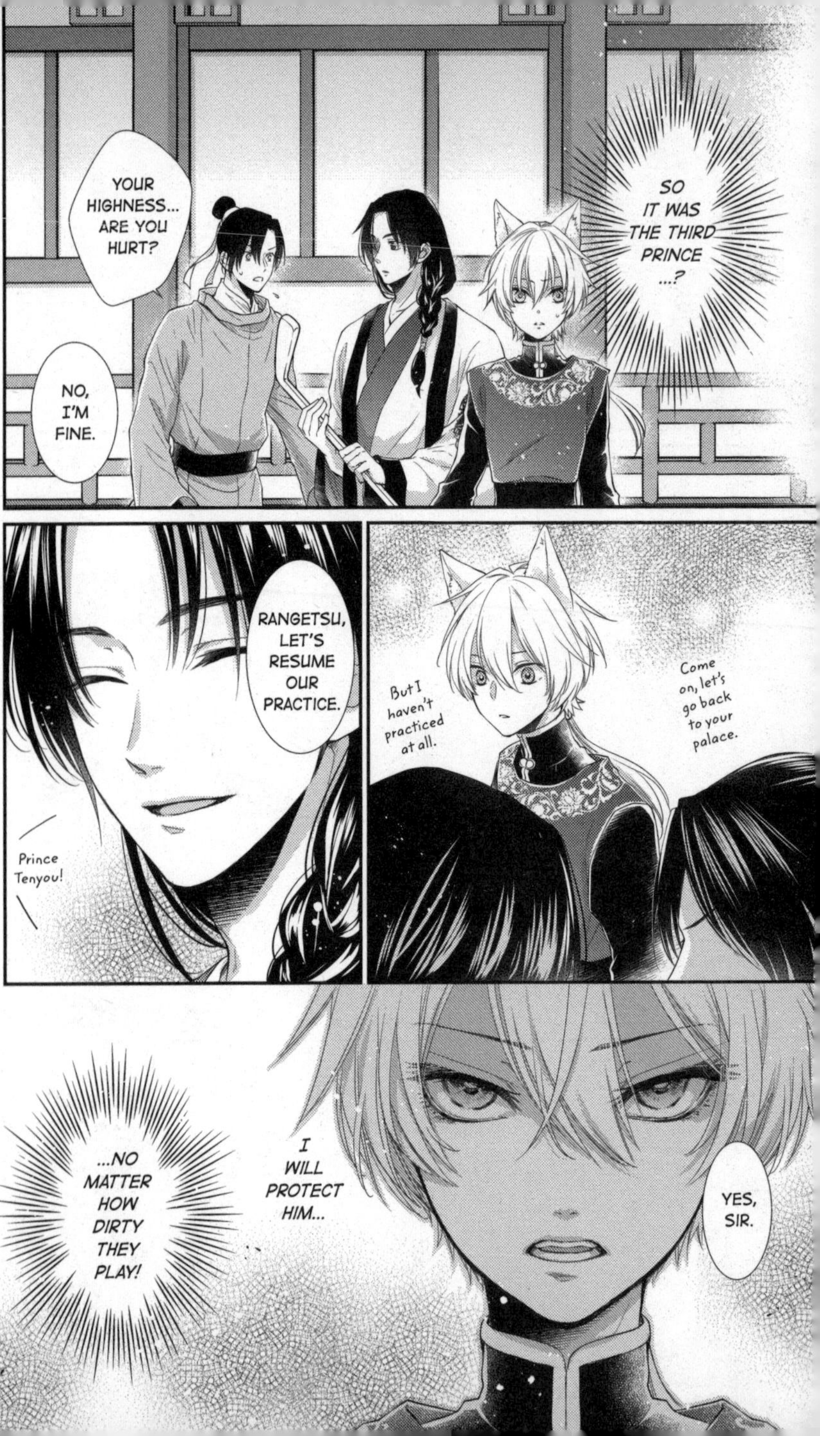
SO IT WAS THE THIRD PRINCE ...?
YOUR HIGHNESS... ARE YOU HURT?
NO, I'M FINE.
Come on, let's go back to your palace.
But I haven't practiced at all.
RANGETSU, LET'S RESUME OUR PRACTICE.
Prince Tenyou!
YES, SIR.
I WILL PROTECT HIM...
...NO MATTER HOW DIRTY THEY PLAY!

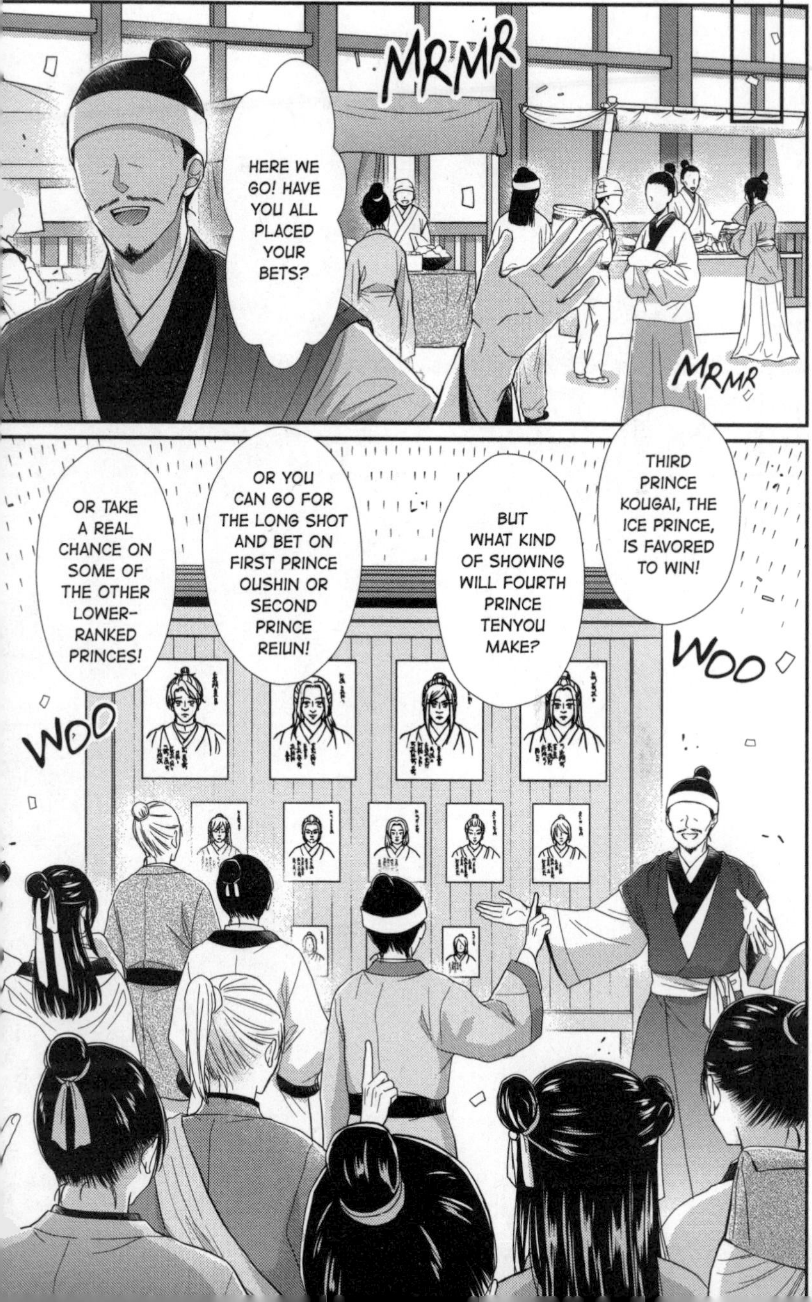
MRMR
HERE WE GO! HAVE YOU ALL PLACED YOUR BETS?
MRMR
THIRD PRINCE KOUGAI, THE ICE PRINCE, IS FAVORED TO WIN!
BUT WHAT KIND OF SHOWING WILL FOURTH PRINCE TENYOU MAKE?
OR YOU CAN GO FOR THE LONG SHOT AND BET ON FIRST PRINCE OUSHIN OR SECOND PRINCE REIUN!
OR TAKE A REAL CHANCE ON SOME OF THE OTHER LOWER-RANKED PRINCES!
WOO
WOO

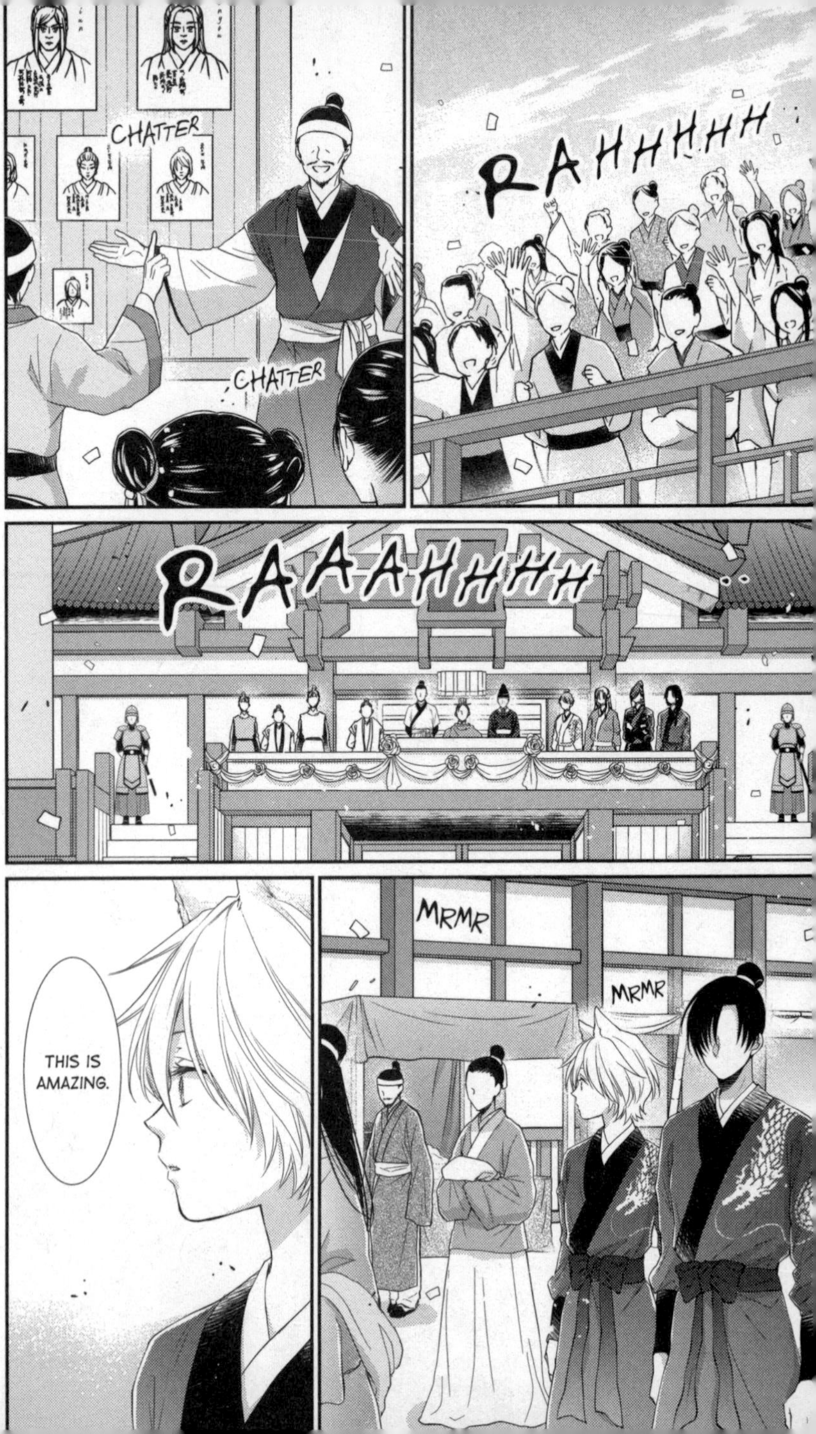
RAHHHHHH
CHATTER
CHATTER
RAAAHHHH
MRMR
MRMR
THIS IS AMAZING.

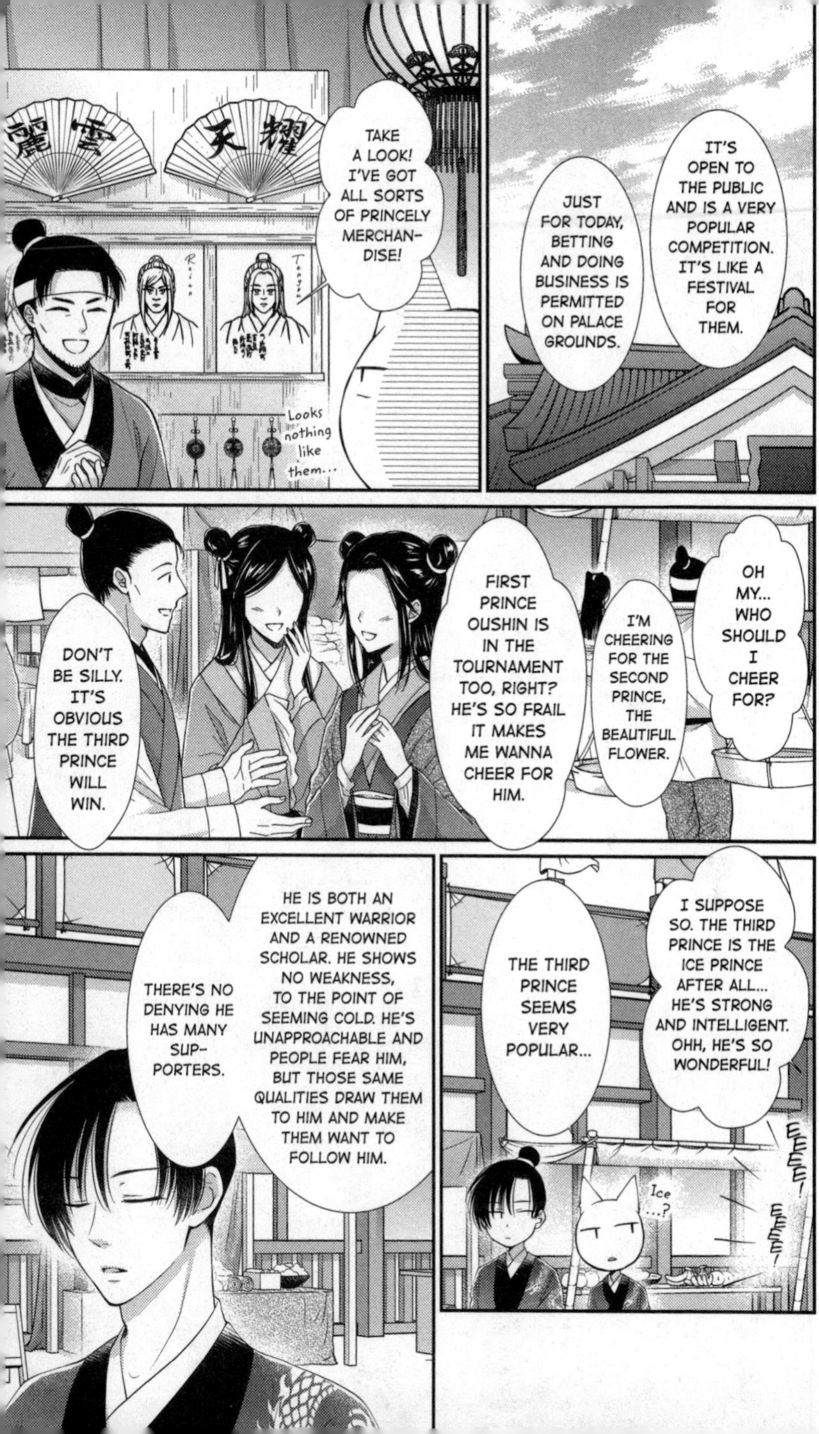
IT'S OPEN TO THE PUBLIC AND IS A VERY POPULAR COMPETITION. IT'S LIKE A FESTIVAL FOR THEM.
JUST FOR TODAY, BETTING AND DOING BUSINESS IS PERMITTED ON PALACE GROUNDS.
天耀
麗雲
TAKE A LOOK! I'VE GOT ALL SORTS OF PRINCELY MERCHAN-DISE!
Looks nothing like them...
OH MY... WHO SHOULD I CHEER FOR?
I'M CHEERING FOR THE SECOND PRINCE, THE BEAUTIFUL FLOWER.
FIRST PRINCE OUSHIN IS IN THE TOURNAMENT TOO, RIGHT? HE'S SO FRAIL IT MAKES ME WANNA CHEER FOR HIM.
DON'T BE SILLY. IT'S OBVIOUS THE THIRD PRINCE WILL WIN.
I SUPPOSE SO. THE THIRD PRINCE IS THE ICE PRINCE AFTER ALL... HE'S STRONG AND INTELLIGENT. OHH, HE'S SO WONDERFUL!
THE THIRD PRINCE SEEMS VERY POPULAR...
EEEE!
EEEE!
Ice ...?
HE IS BOTH AN EXCELLENT WARRIOR AND A RENOWNED SCHOLAR. HE SHOWS NO WEAKNESS, TO THE POINT OF SEEMING COLD. HE'S UNAPPROACHABLE AND PEOPLE FEAR HIM, BUT THOSE SAME QUALITIES DRAW THEM TO HIM AND MAKE THEM WANT TO FOLLOW HIM.
THERE'S NO DENYING HE HAS MANY SUP-PORTERS.

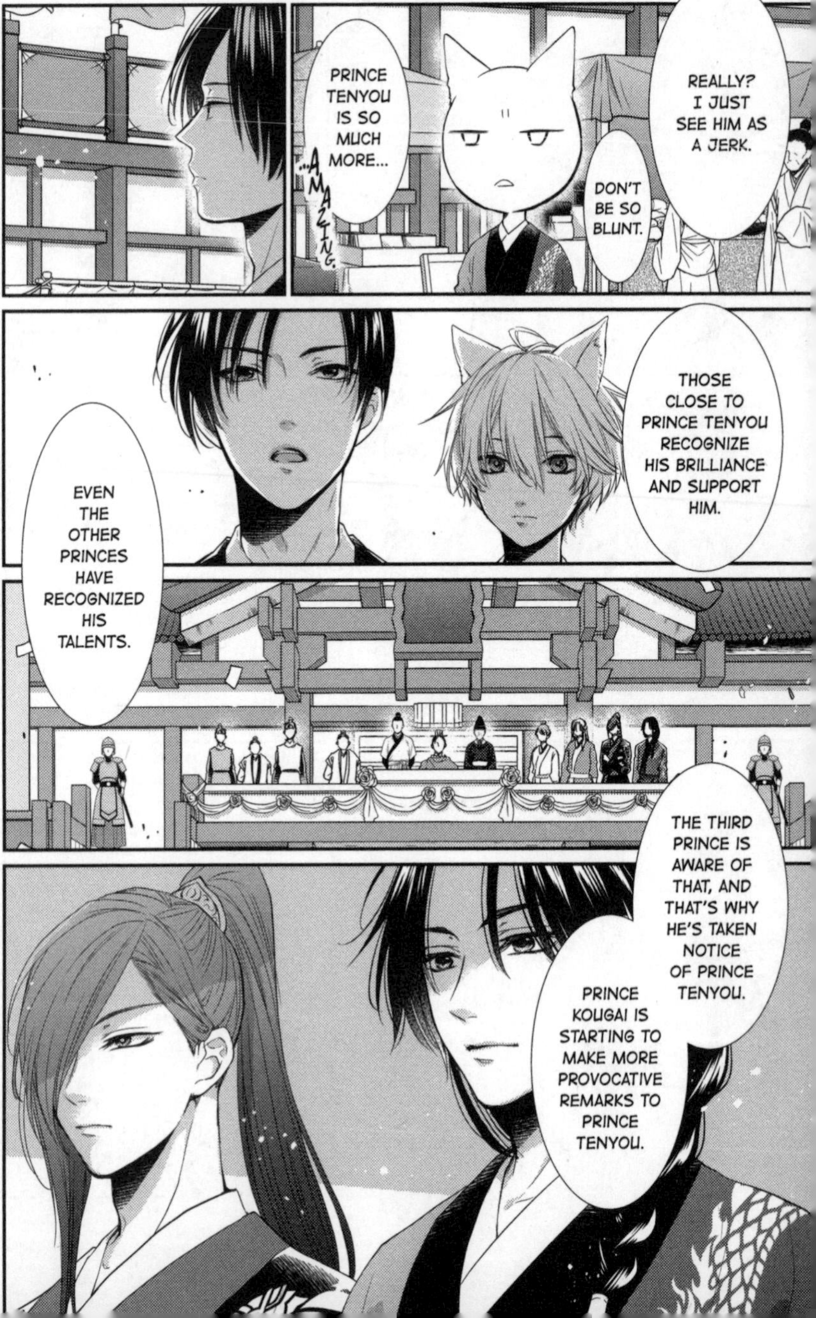
PRINCE TENYOU IS SO MUCH MORE...
...AMAZING.
REALLY? I JUST SEE HIM AS A JERK.
DON'T BE SO BLUNT.
THOSE CLOSE TO PRINCE TENYOU RECOGNIZE HIS BRILLIANCE AND SUPPORT HIM.
EVEN THE OTHER PRINCES HAVE RECOGNIZED HIS TALENTS.
THE THIRD PRINCE IS AWARE OF THAT, AND THAT'S WHY HE'S TAKEN NOTICE OF PRINCE TENYOU.
PRINCE KOUGAI IS STARTING TO MAKE MORE PROVOCATIVE REMARKS TO PRINCE TENYOU.

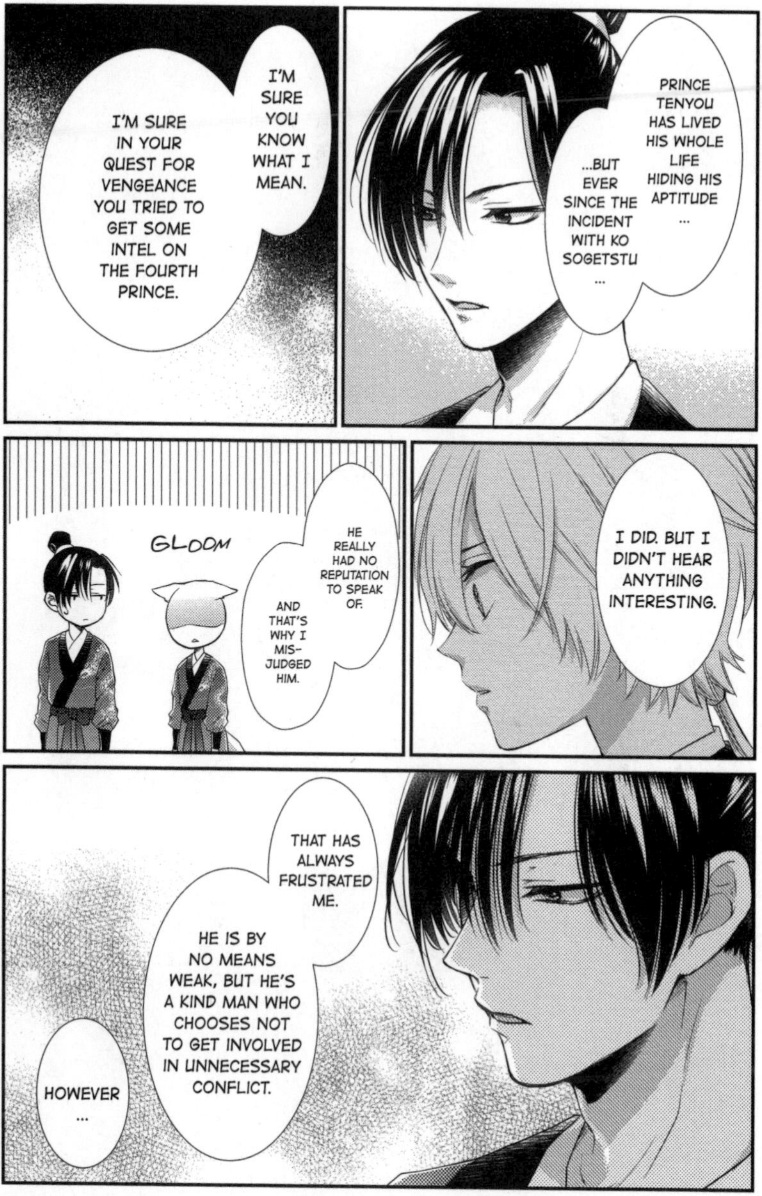
PRINCE TENYOU HAS LIVED HIS WHOLE LIFE HIDING HIS APTITUDE ...
...BUT EVER SINCE THE INCIDENT WITH KO SOGETSU ...
I'M SURE YOU KNOW WHAT I MEAN.
I'M SURE IN YOUR QUEST FOR VENGEANCE YOU TRIED TO GET SOME INTEL ON THE FOURTH PRINCE.
I DID. BUT I DIDN'T HEAR ANYTHING INTERESTING.
HE REALLY HAD NO REPUTATION TO SPEAK OF.
AND THAT'S WHY I MIS-JUDGED HIM.
GLOOM
THAT HAS ALWAYS FRUSTRATED ME.
HE IS BY NO MEANS WEAK, BUT HE'S A KIND MAN WHO CHOOSES NOT TO GET INVOLVED IN UNNECESSARY CONFLICT.
HOWEVER ...

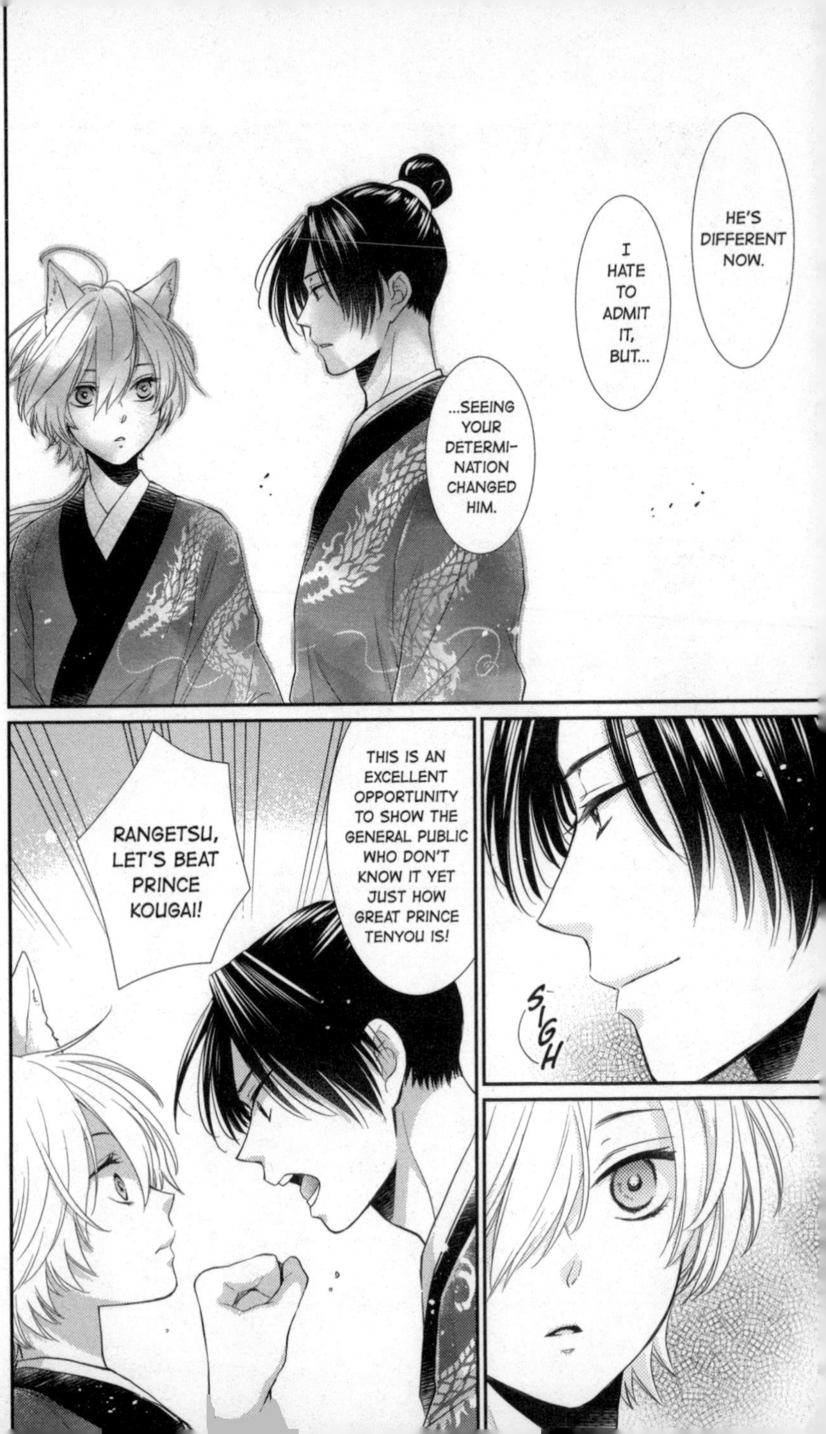
HE'S DIFFERENT NOW.
I HATE TO ADMIT IT, BUT...
...SEEING YOUR DETERMINATION CHANGED HIM.
SIGH
THIS IS AN EXCELLENT OPPORTUNITY TO SHOW THE GENERAL PUBLIC WHO DON'T KNOW IT YET JUST HOW GREAT PRINCE TENYOU IS!
RANGETSU, LET'S BEAT PRINCE KOUGAI!

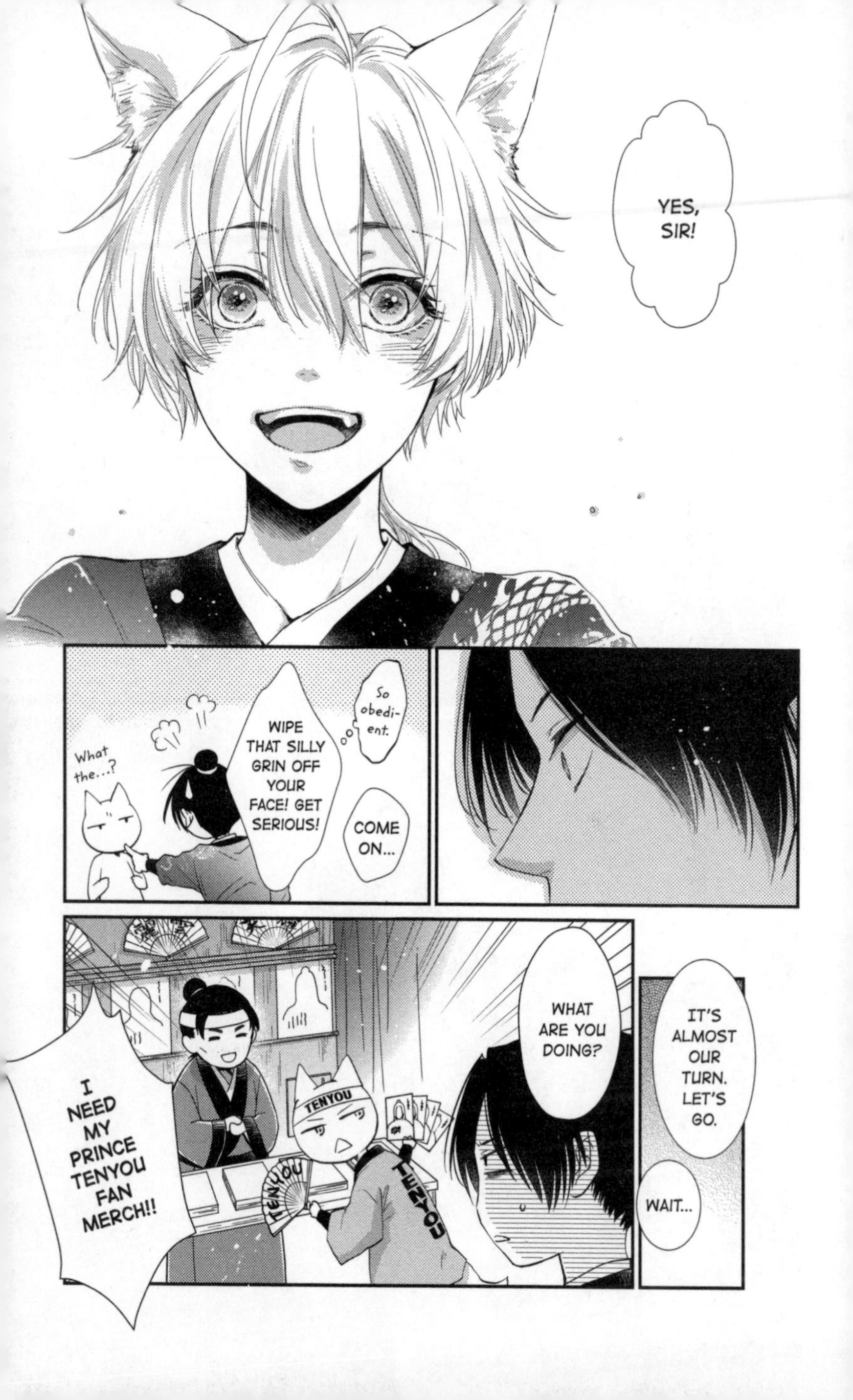
YES, SIR!
So obedi-ent.
WIPE THAT SILLY GRIN OFF YOUR FACE! GET SERIOUS!
COME ON...
What the...?
IT'S ALMOST OUR TURN. LET'S GO.
WAIT...
WHAT ARE YOU DOING?
TENYOU
TENYOU
TENYOU
I NEED MY PRINCE TENYOU FAN MERCH!!

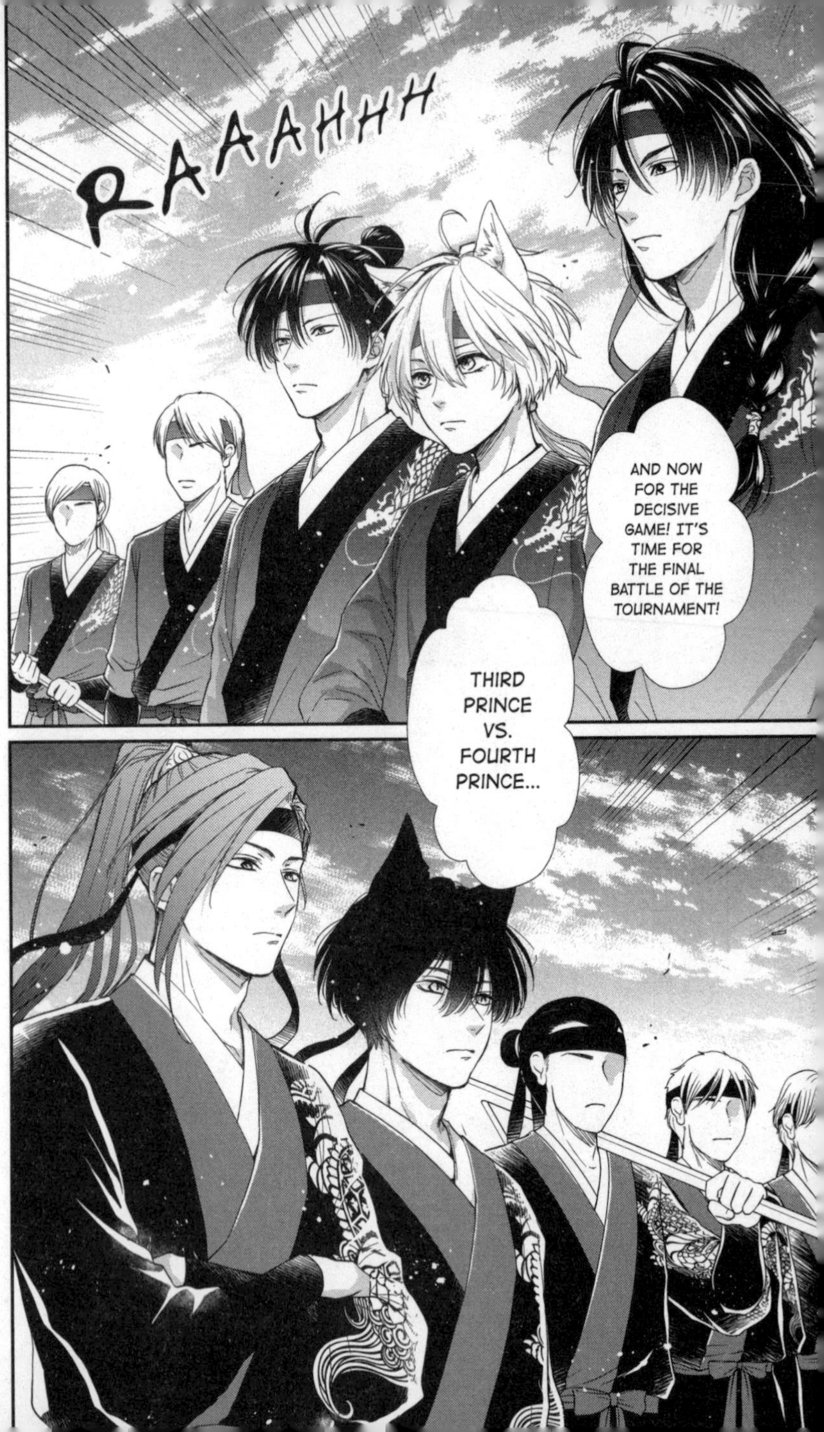
RAAAHHH
AND NOW FOR THE DECISIVE GAME! IT'S TIME FOR THE FINAL BATTLE OF THE TOURNAMENT!
THIRD PRINCE VS. FOURTH PRINCE...

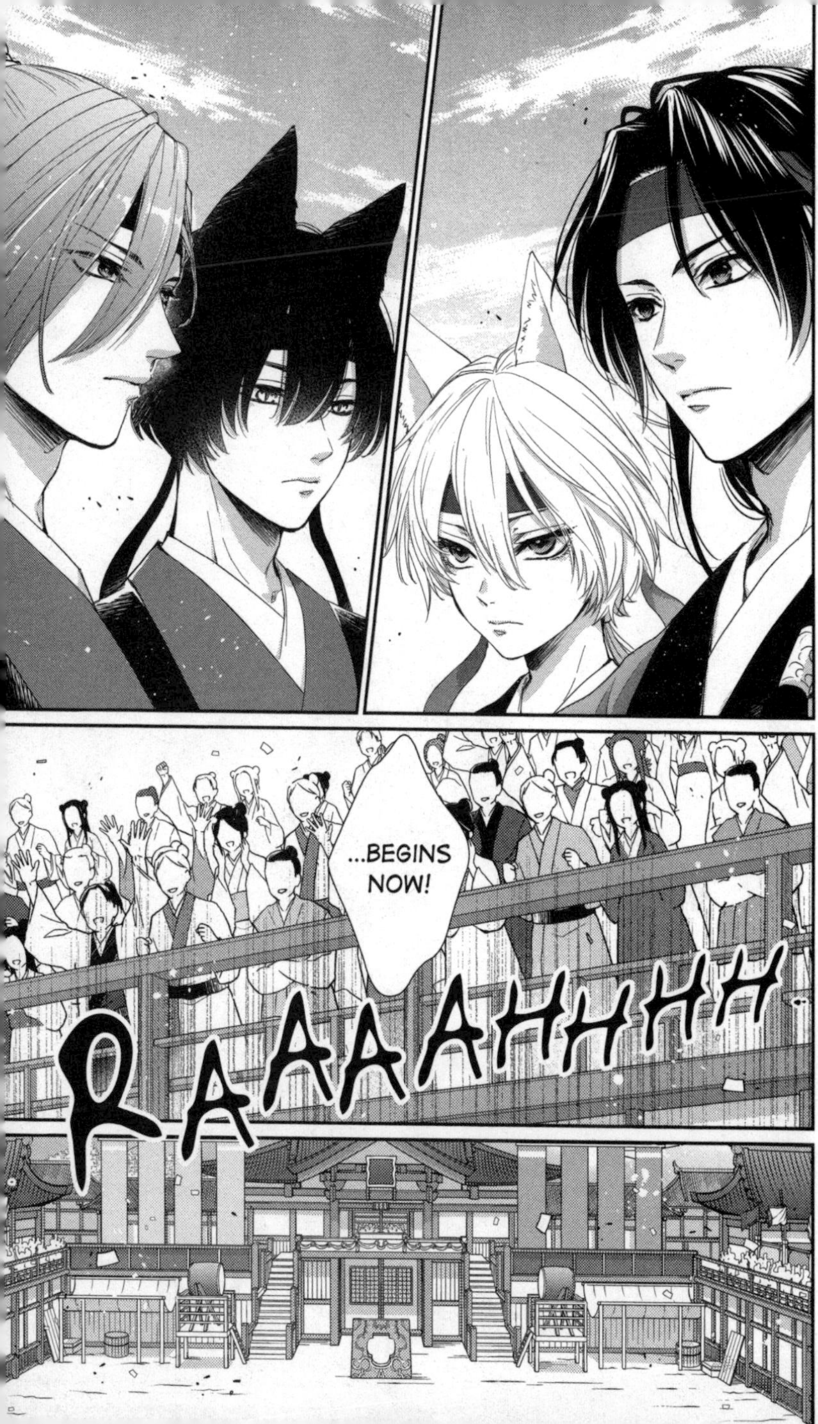
...BEGINS NOW!
RAAAAHHHH

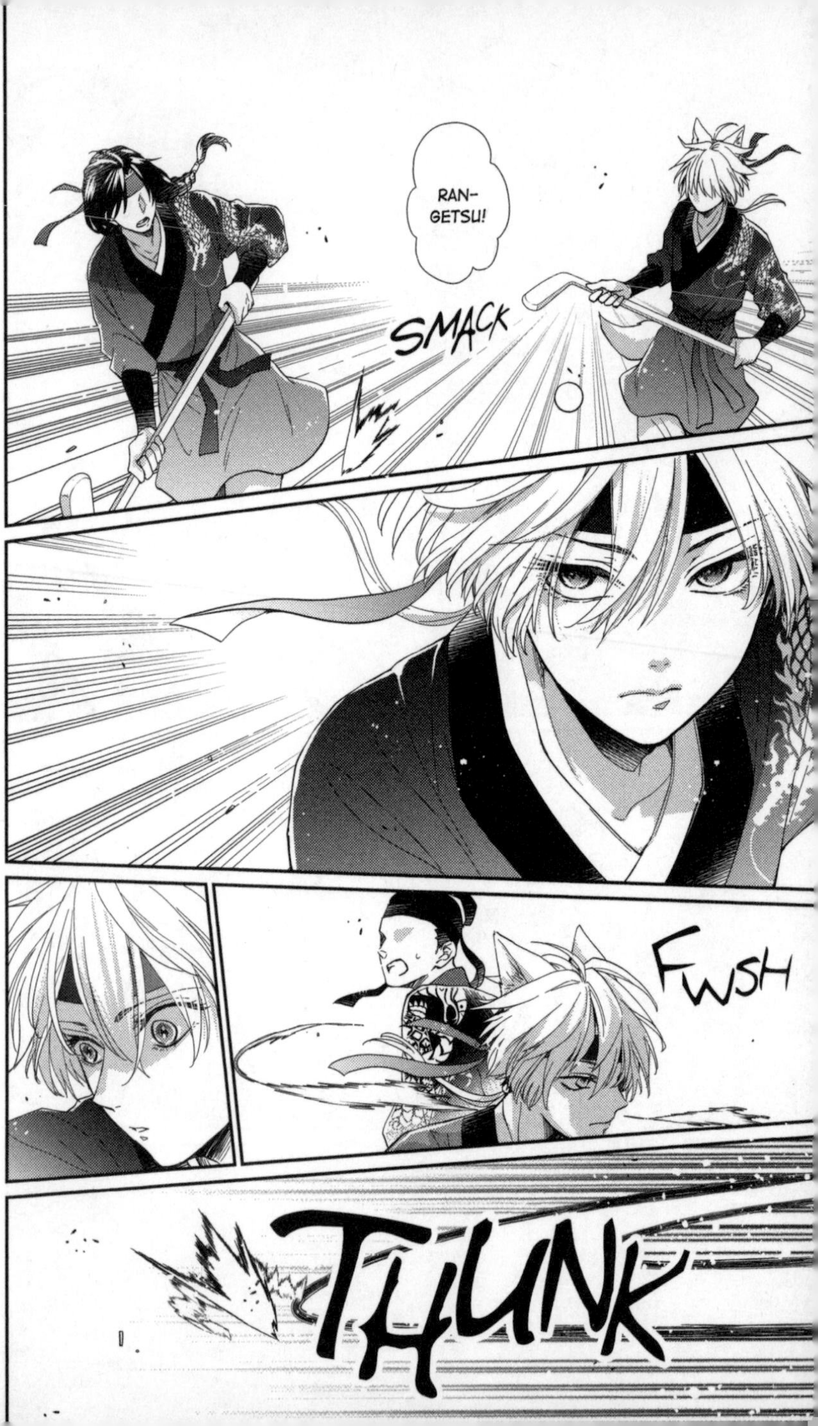
RAN-
GETSU!
SMACK
FWSH
THUNK

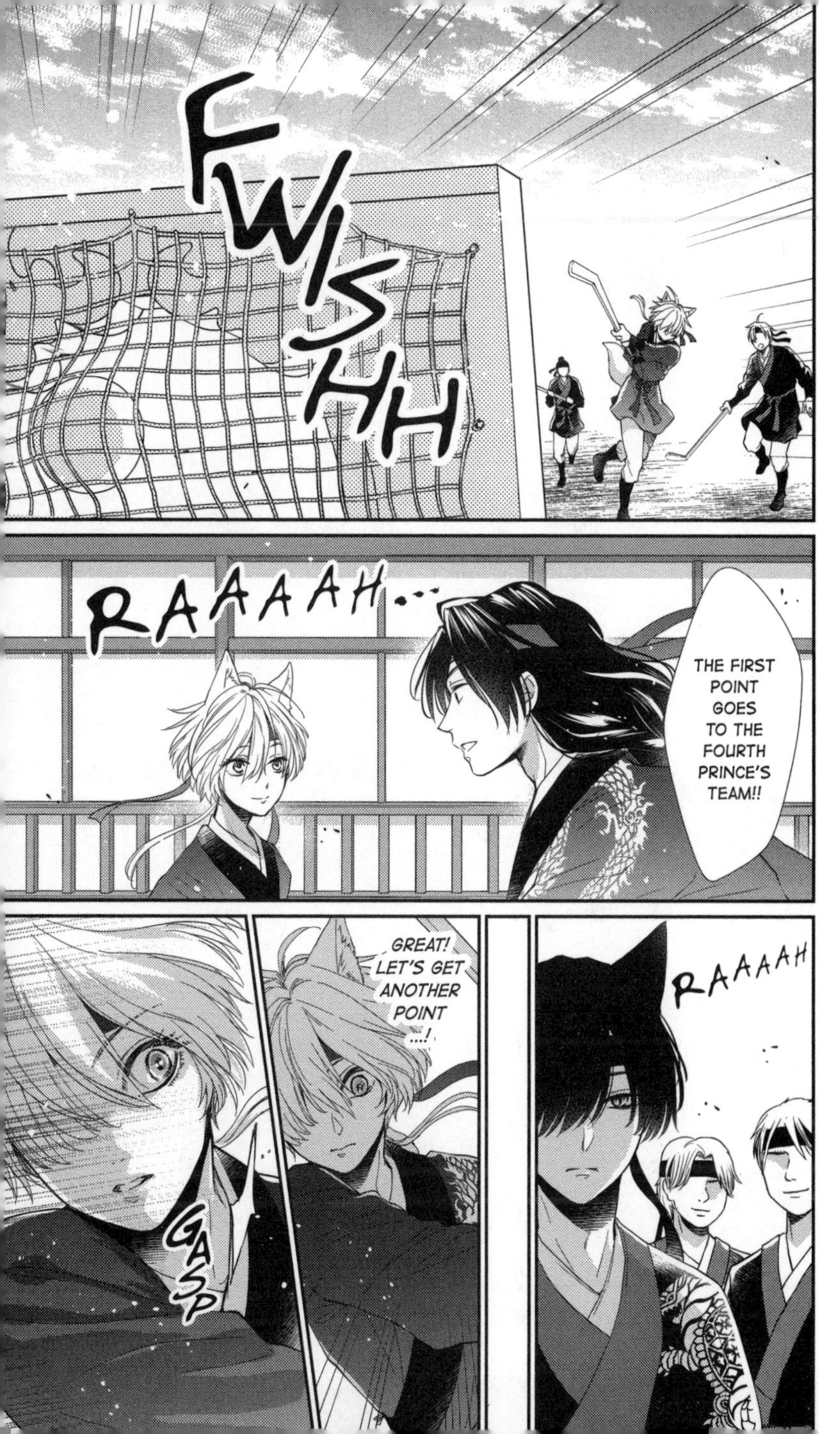
FWISHH
RAAAAH...
THE FIRST POINT GOES TO THE FOURTH PRINCE'S TEAM!!
RAAAAH
GREAT! LET'S GET ANOTHER POINT ...!
GASP

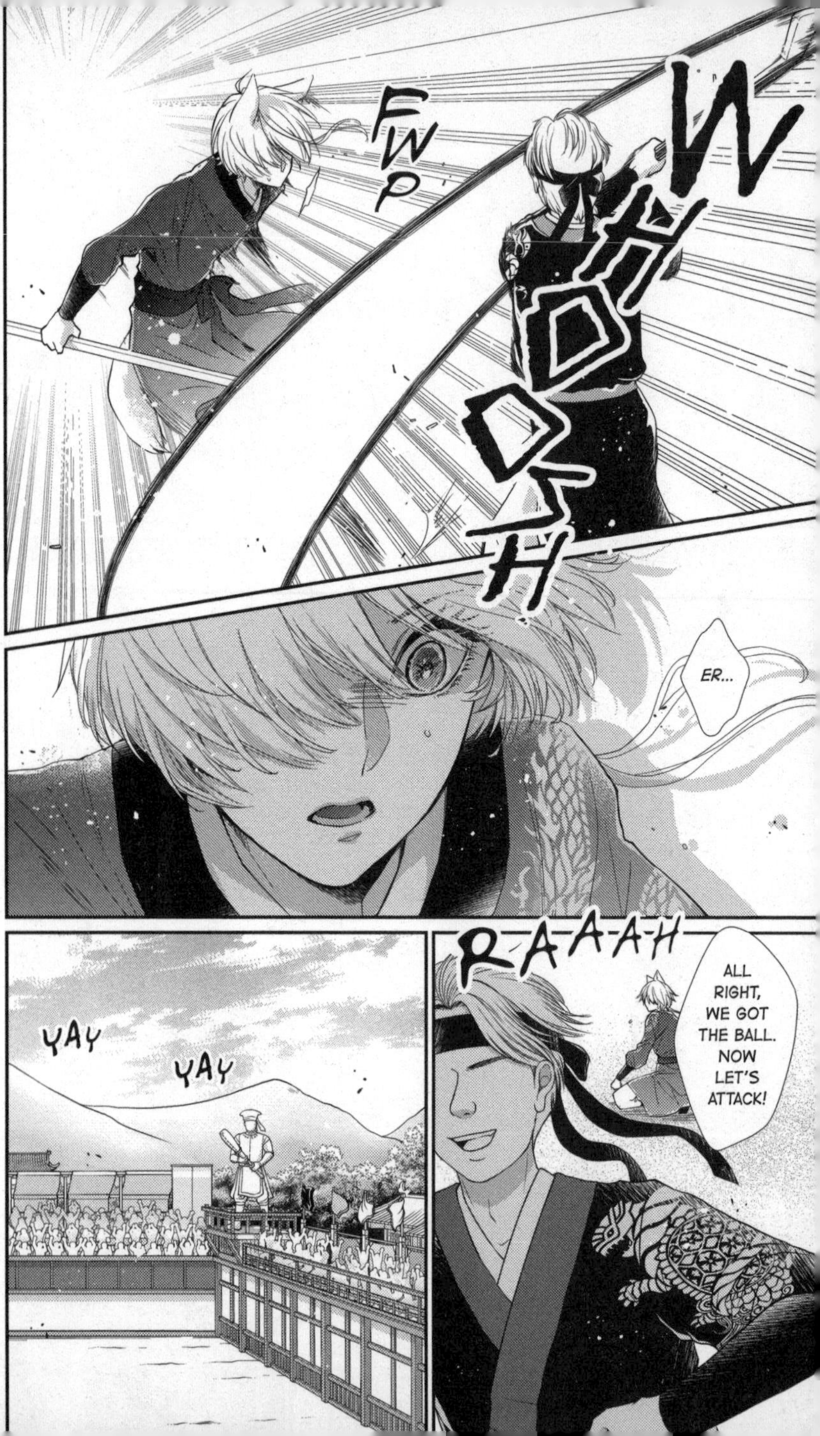
WHOOSH
FWP
ER...
RAAAH
ALL RIGHT, WE GOT THE BALL. NOW LET'S ATTACK!
YAY
YAY

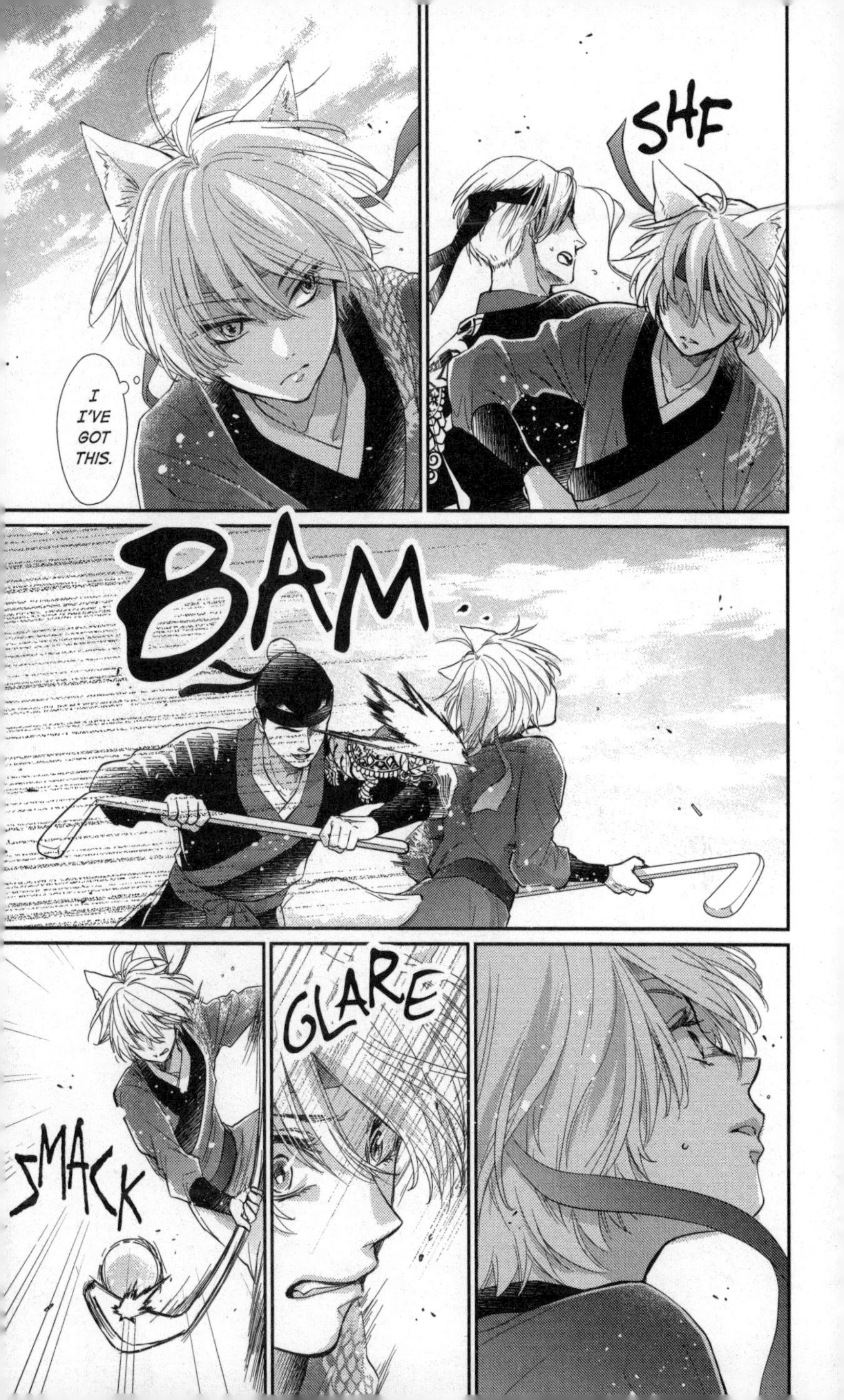
SHF
I I'VE GOT THIS.
BAM
GLARE
SMACK

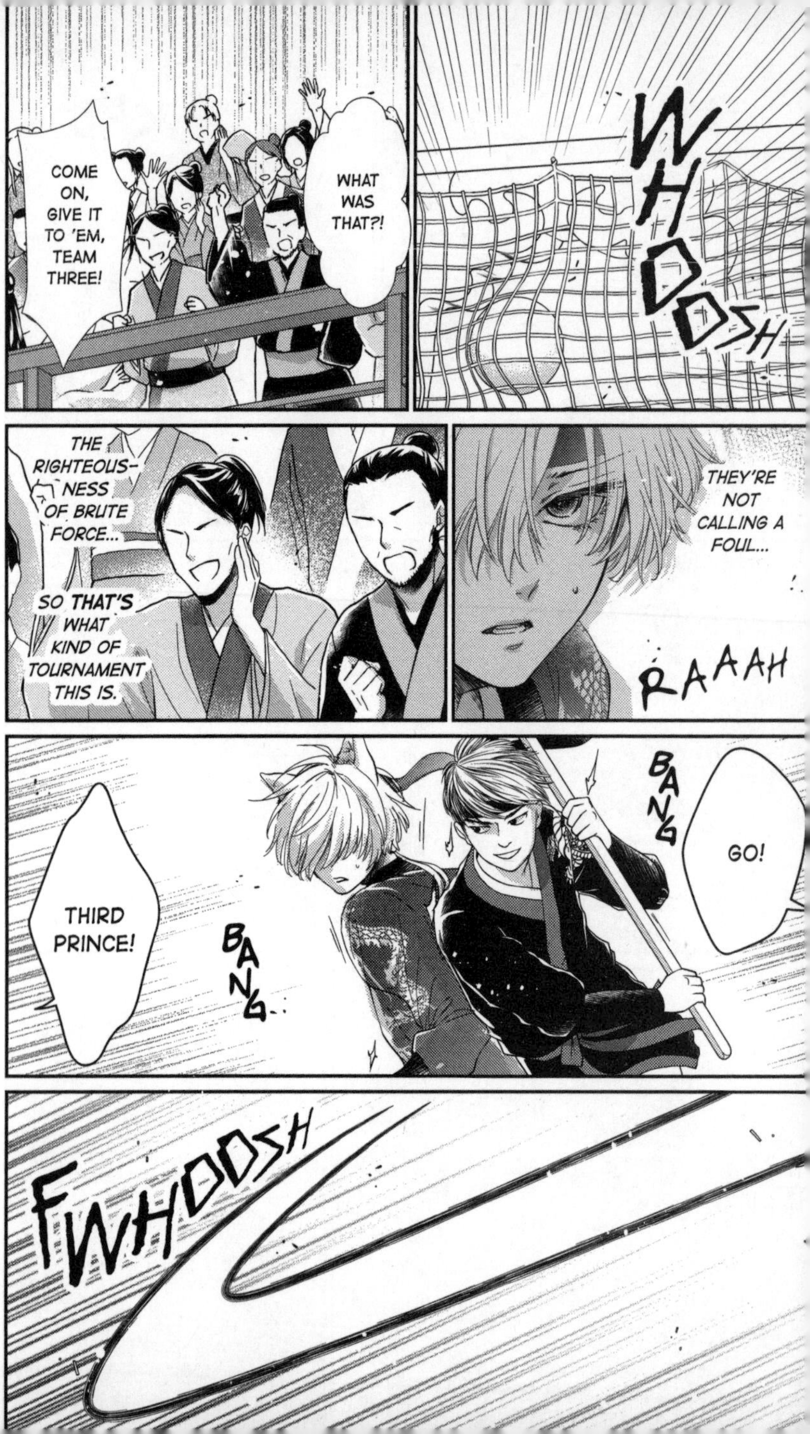
WHOOSH
WHAT WAS THAT?!
COME ON, GIVE IT TO 'EM, TEAM THREE!
THEY'RE NOT CALLING A FOUL...
RAAAH
THE RIGHTEOUS-NESS OF BRUTE FORCE...
SO THAT'S WHAT KIND OF TOURNAMENT THIS IS.
BANG
GO!
BANG
THIRD PRINCE!
FWHOOSH

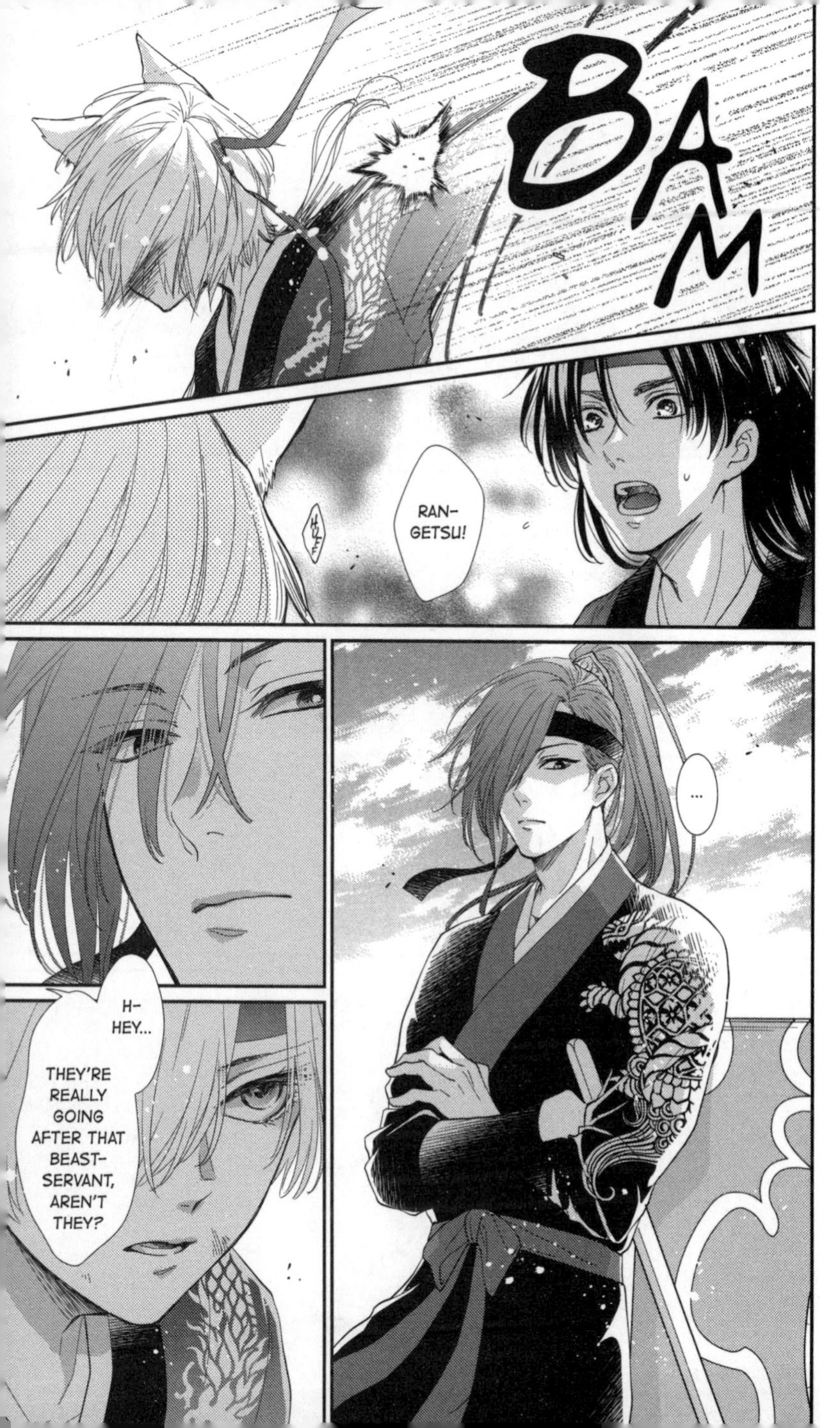
BAM
RAN-GETSU!
HUFF
...
H-HEY...
THEY'RE REALLY GOING AFTER THAT BEAST-SERVANT, AREN'T THEY?

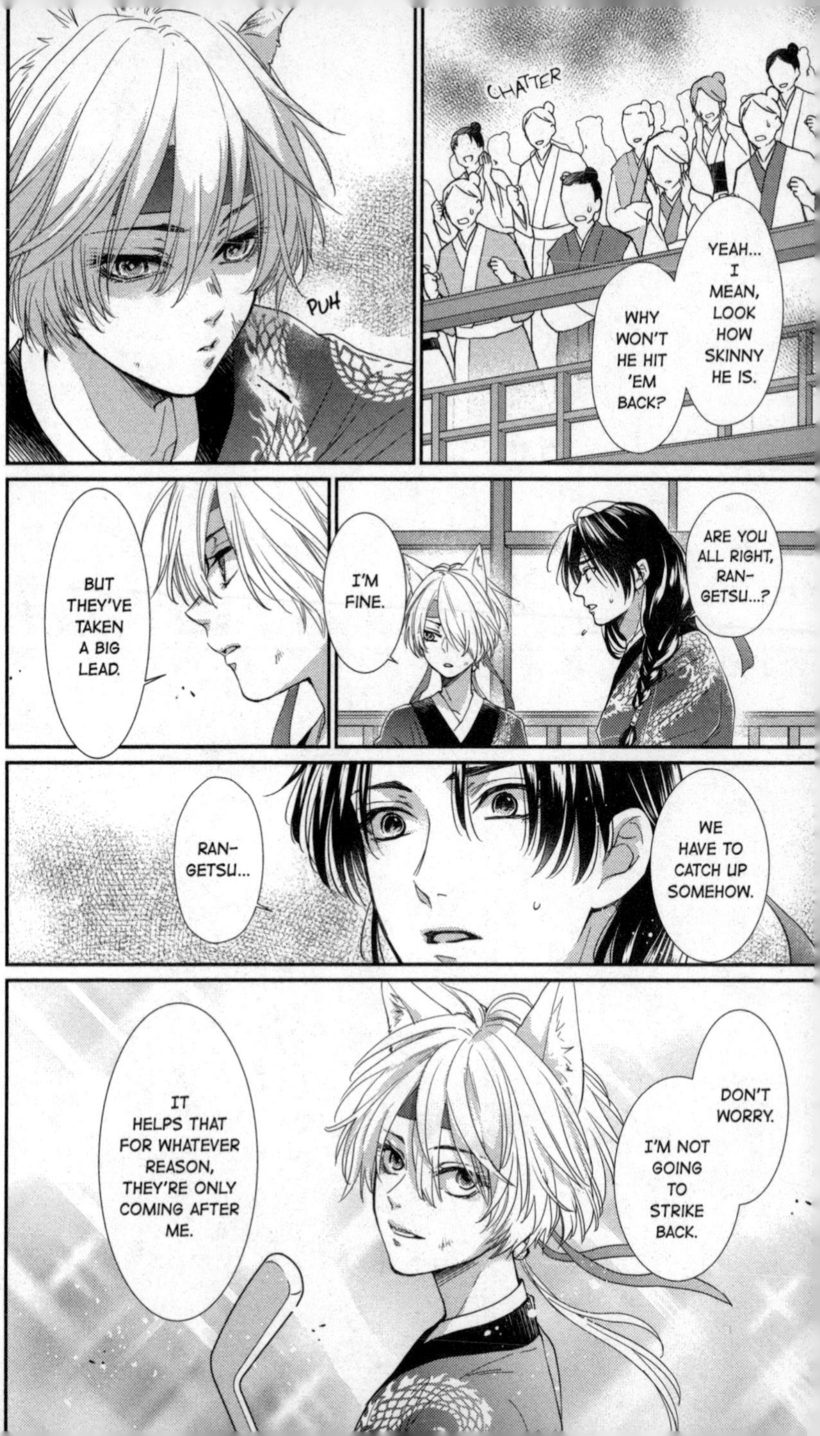
CHATTER
YEAH... I MEAN, LOOK HOW SKINNY HE IS.
WHY WON'T HE HIT 'EM BACK?
PUH
ARE YOU ALL RIGHT, RAN-GETSU...?
I'M FINE.
BUT THEY'VE TAKEN A BIG LEAD.
WE HAVE TO CATCH UP SOMEHOW.
RAN-GETSU...
DON'T WORRY.
I'M NOT GOING TO STRIKE BACK.
IT HELPS THAT FOR WHATEVER REASON, THEY'RE ONLY COMING AFTER ME.

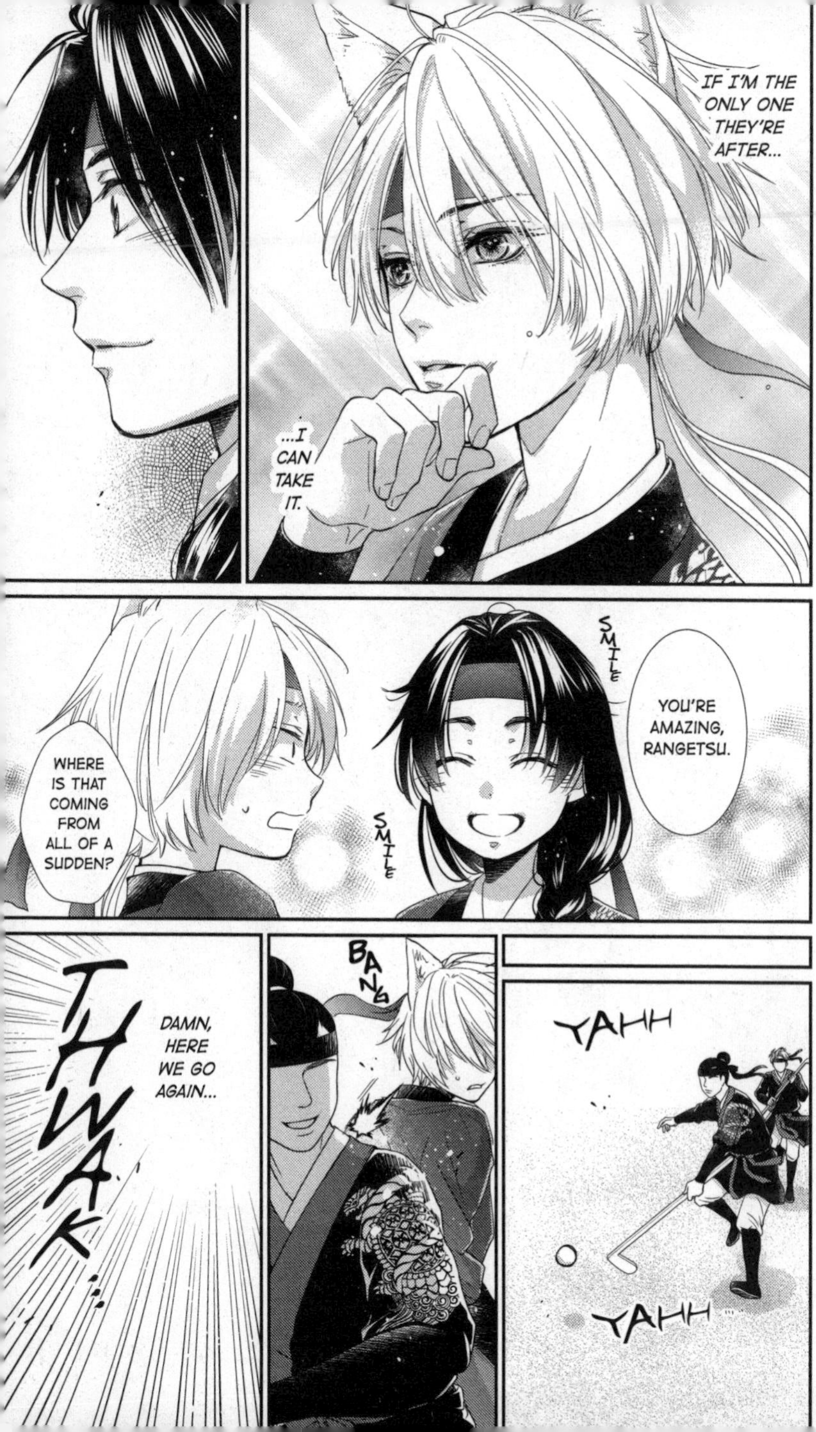
IF I'M THE ONLY ONE THEY'RE AFTER...
...I CAN TAKE IT.
SMILE
YOU'RE AMAZING, RANGETSU.
SMILE
WHERE IS THAT COMING FROM ALL OF A SUDDEN?
YAHH
YAHH
BANG
DAMN, HERE WE GO AGAIN...
THWAK

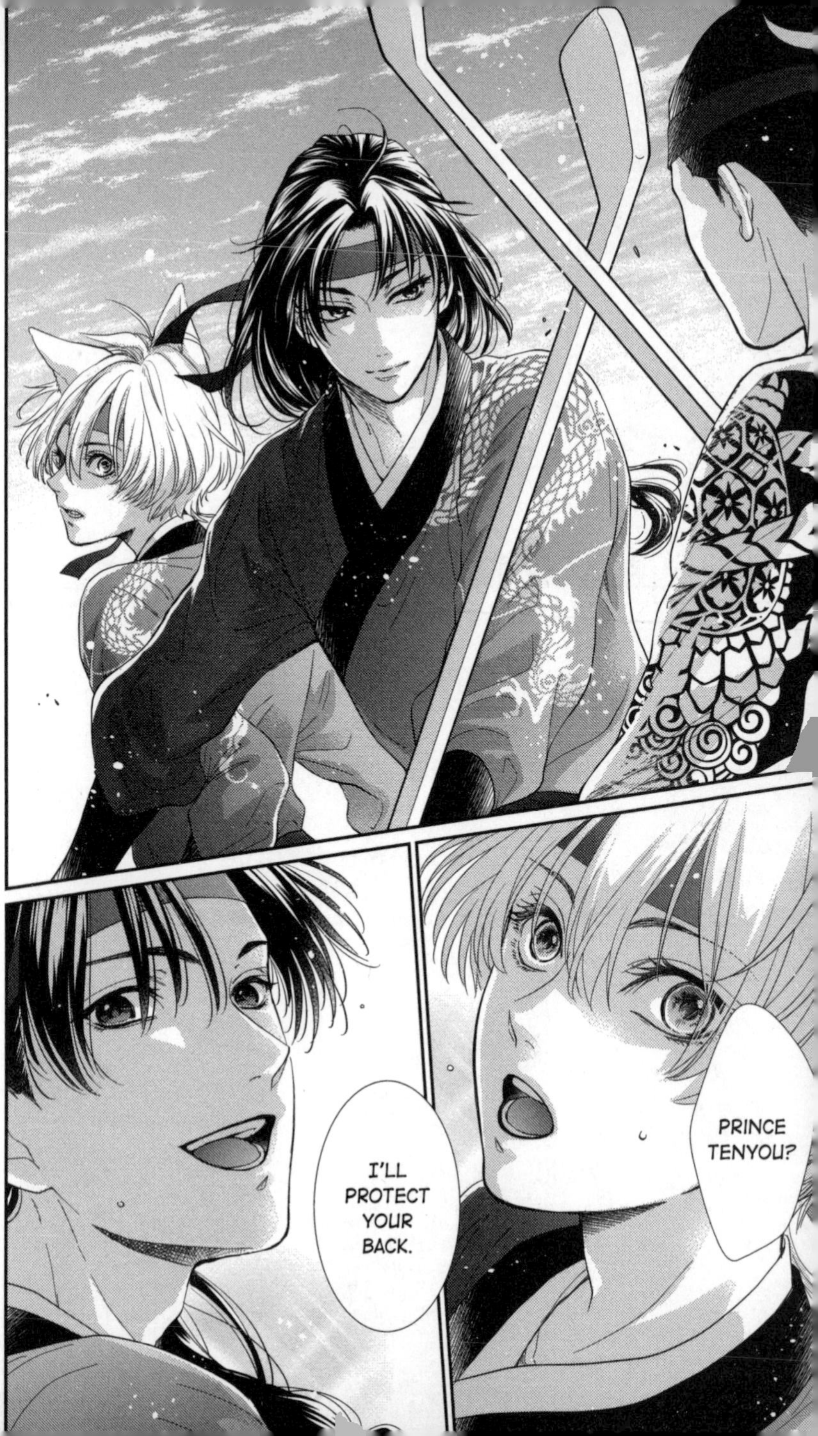
PRINCE TENYOU?
I'LL PROTECT YOUR BACK.

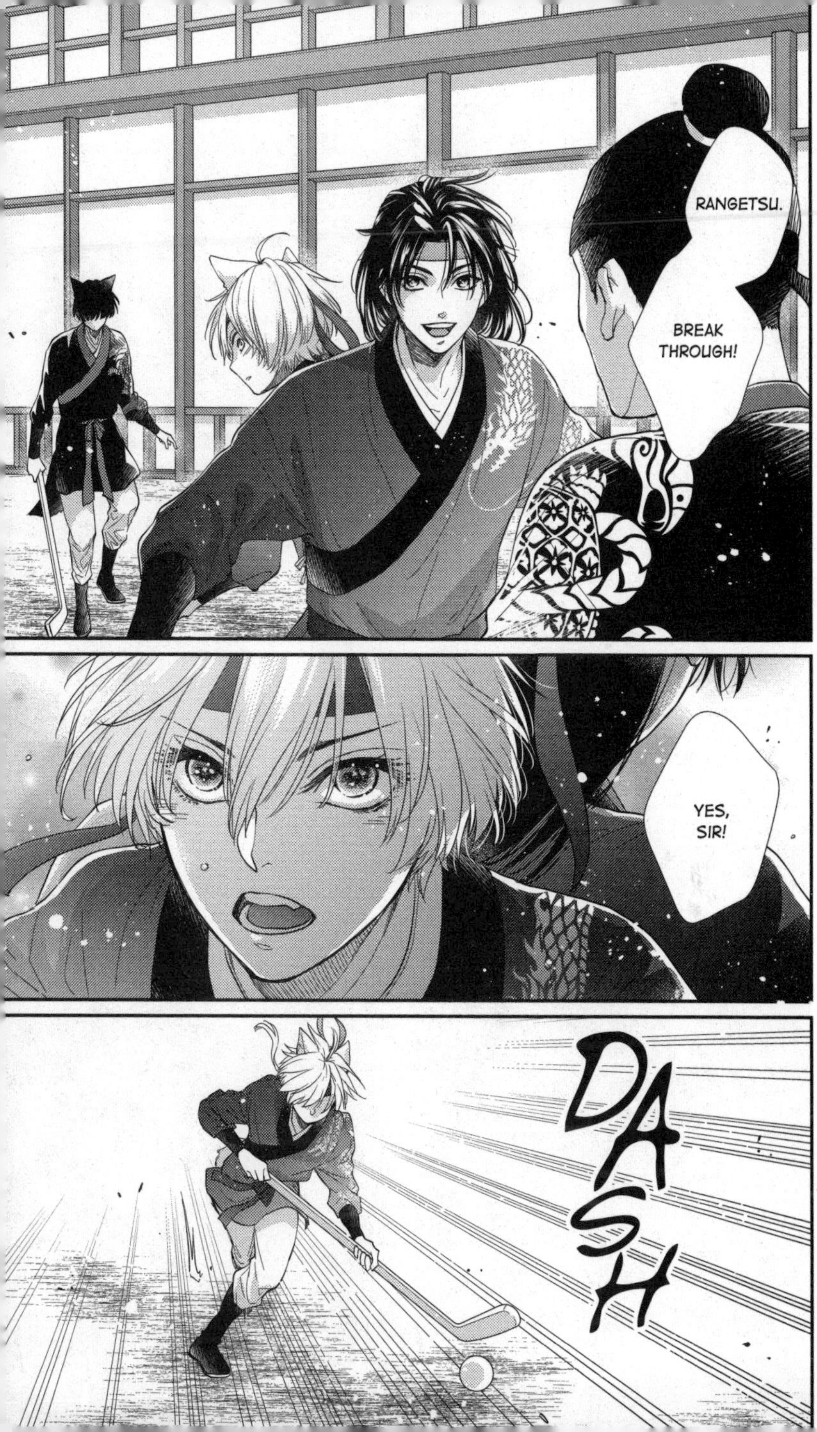
RANGETSU.
BREAK THROUGH!
YES, SIR!
DASH

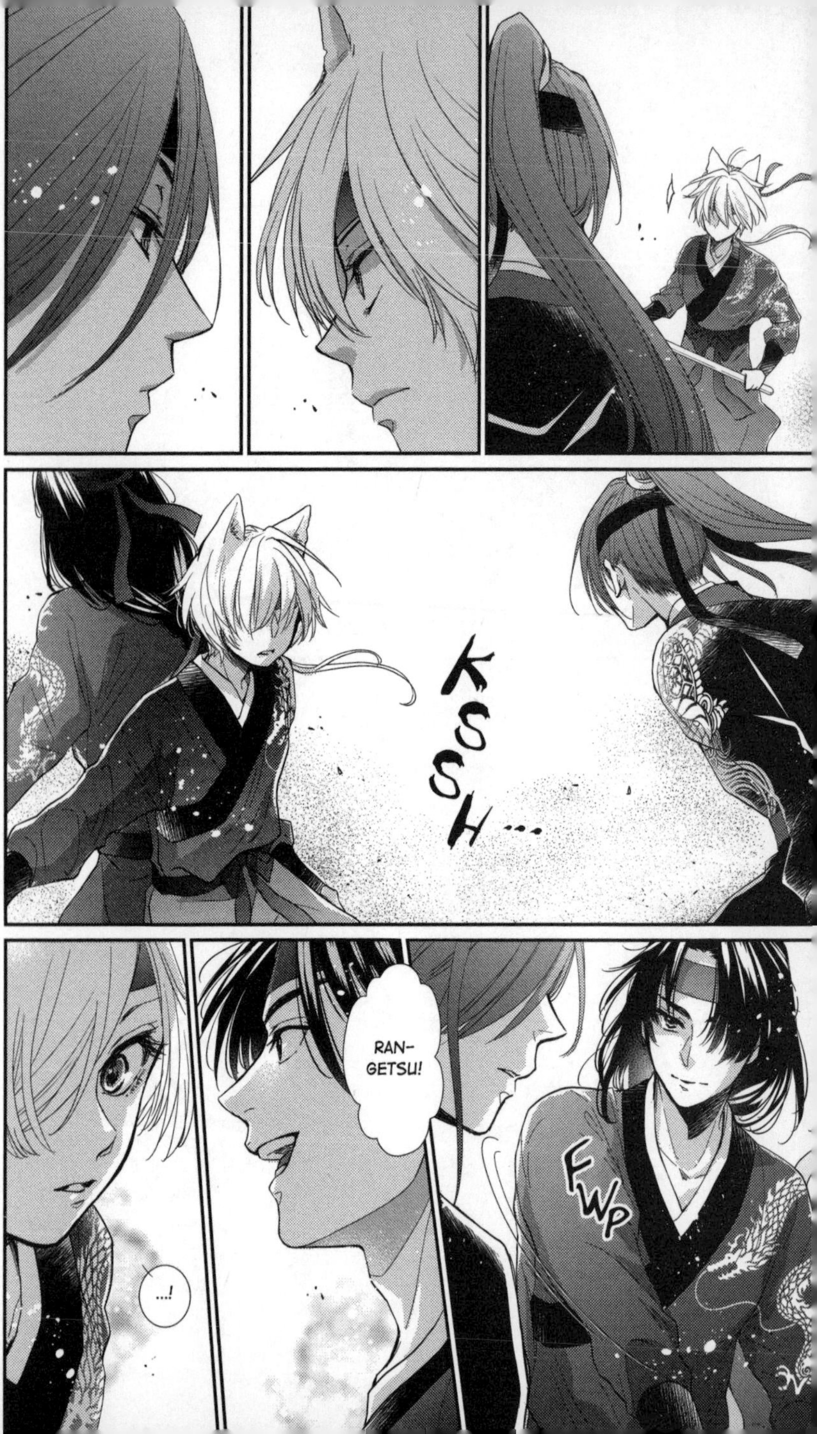
KSSH...
FWP
RAN-GETSU!
...!

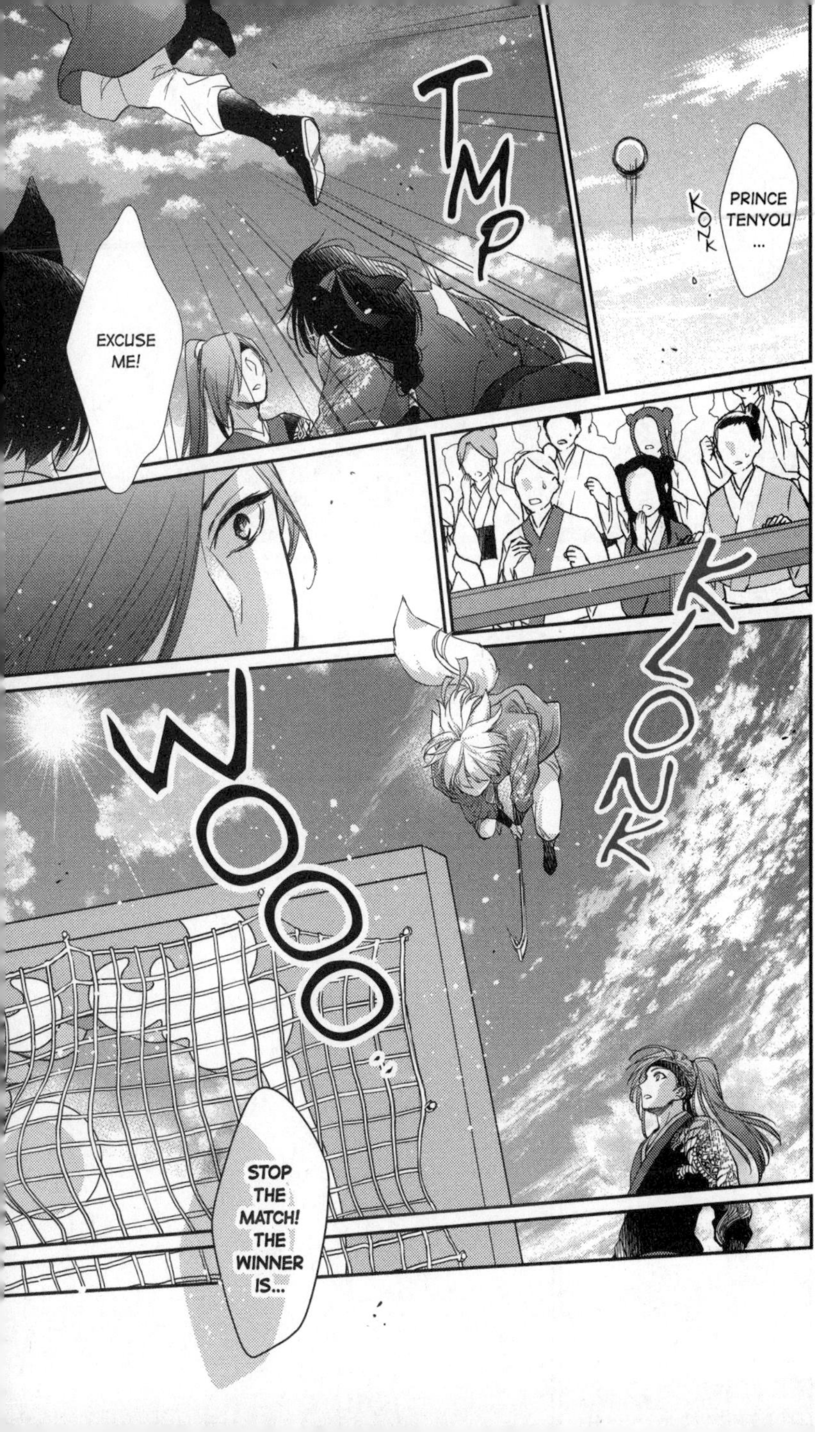
PRINCE TENYOU...
KONK
TMP
EXCUSE ME!
KLONK
WOOOO
STOP THE MATCH! THE WINNER IS...

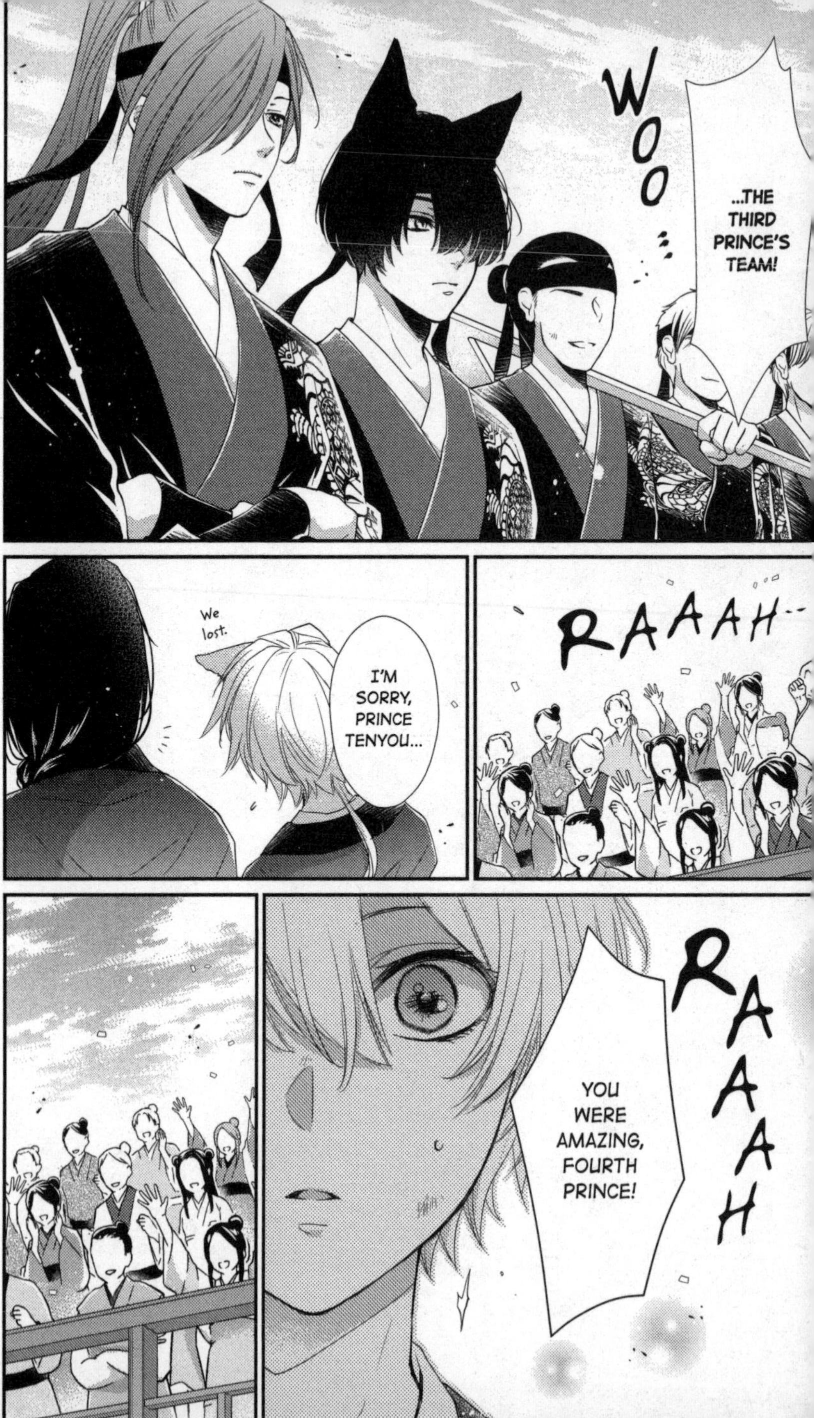
...THE THIRD PRINCE'S TEAM!
WOOO
RAAAH
I'M SORRY, PRINCE TENYOU...
We lost.
RAAAH
YOU WERE AMAZING, FOURTH PRINCE!

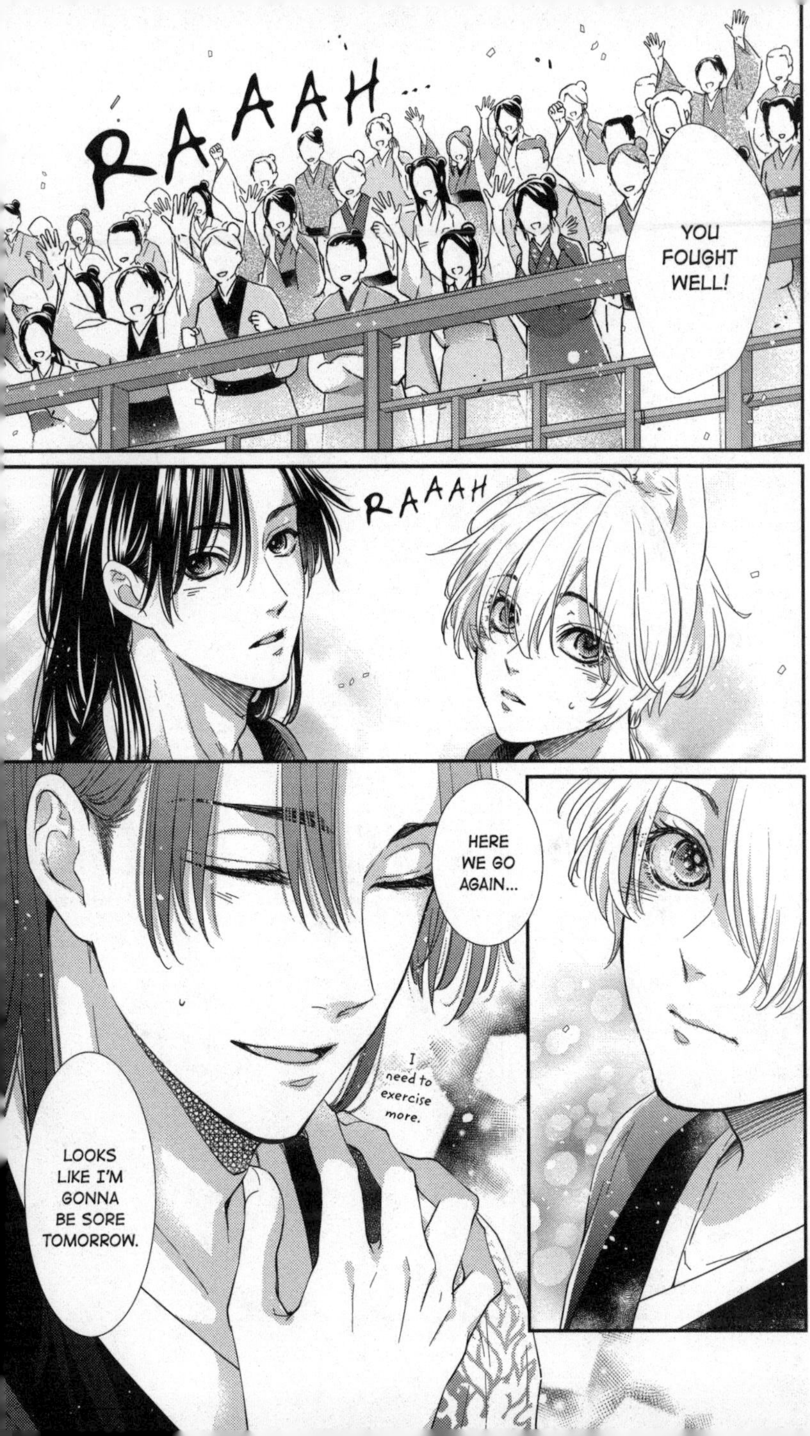
RAAAH...
YOU FOUGHT WELL!
RAAAH
HERE WE GO AGAIN...
I need to exercise more.
LOOKS LIKE I'M GONNA BE SORE TOMORROW.

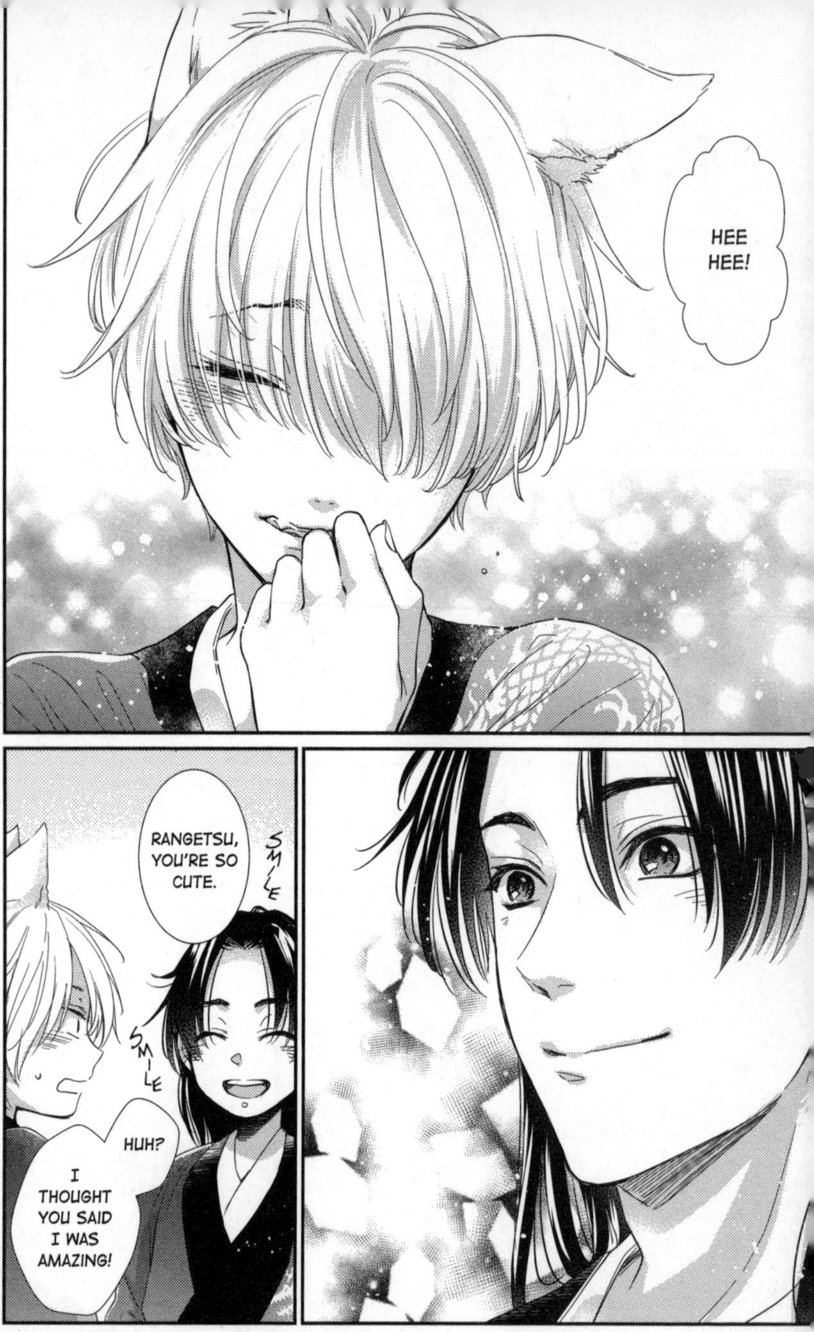
HEE HEE!
RANGETSU, YOU'RE SO CUTE.
SMILE
SMILE
HUH?
I THOUGHT YOU SAID I WAS AMAZING!

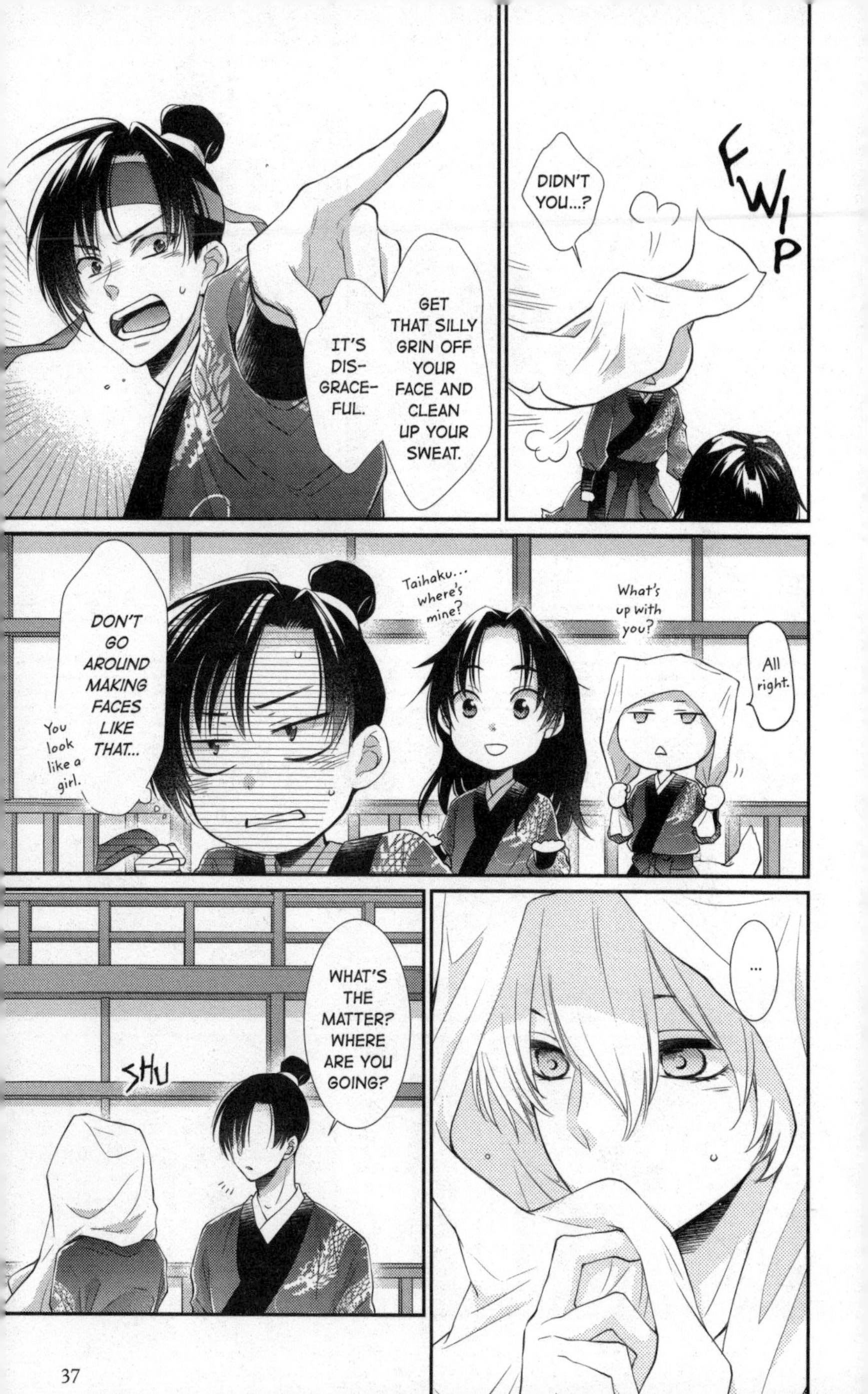
FWIP
DIDN'T YOU...?
GET THAT SILLY GRIN OFF YOUR FACE AND CLEAN UP YOUR SWEAT.
IT'S DIS-GRACE-FUL.
All right.
What's up with you?
Taihaku... where's mine?
DON'T GO AROUND MAKING FACES LIKE THAT...
You look like a girl.
...
WHAT'S THE MATTER? WHERE ARE YOU GOING?
SHU

I NEED TO CHECK SOMETHING.

URGH...

FLINCH

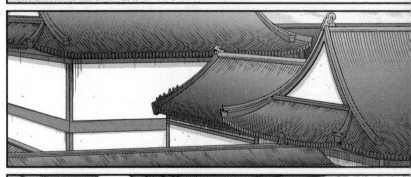

OHHH...

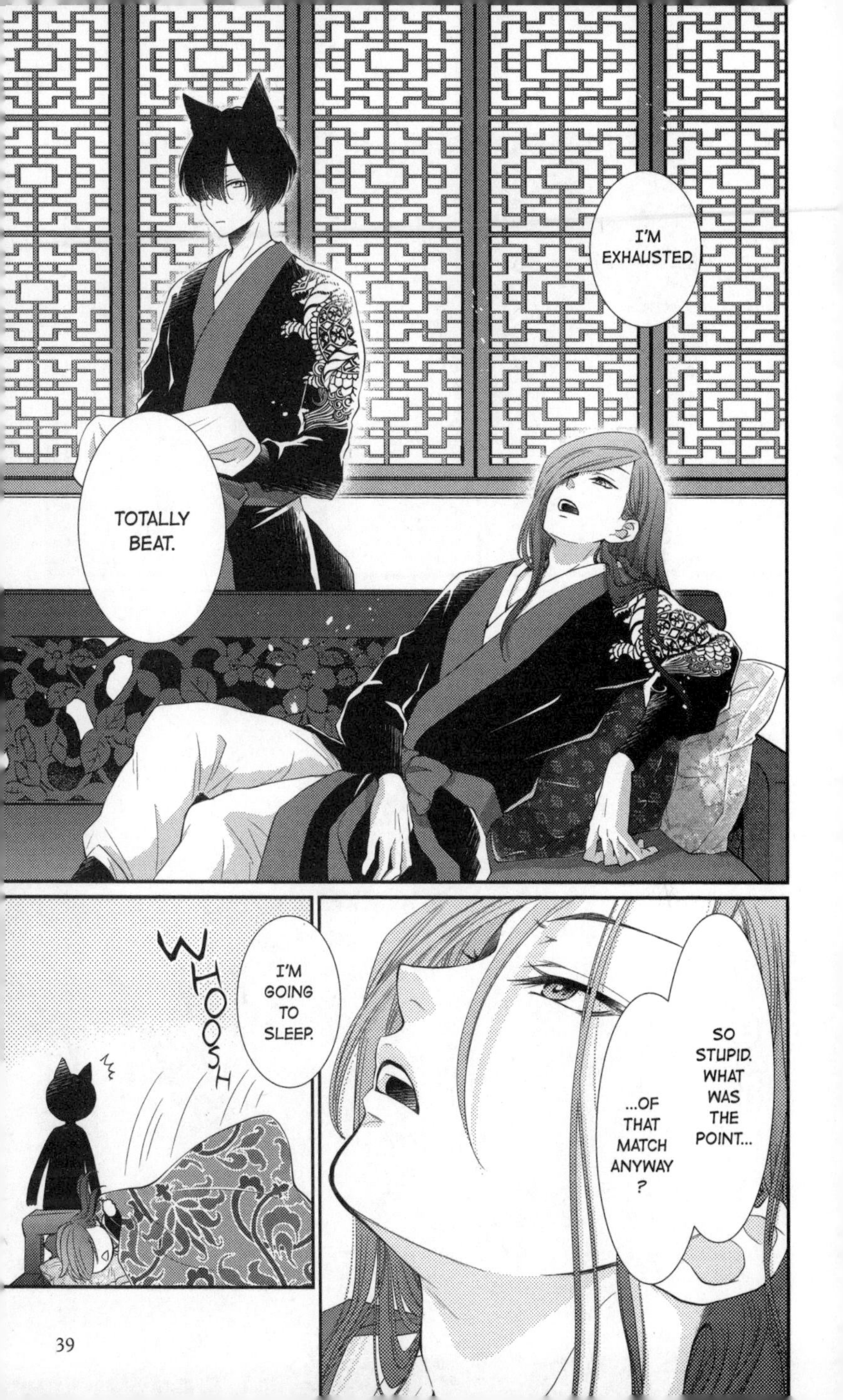
I'M EXHAUSTED.
TOTALLY BEAT.
SO STUPID. WHAT WAS THE POINT...
...OF THAT MATCH ANYWAY?
I'M GOING TO SLEEP.
WHOOSH

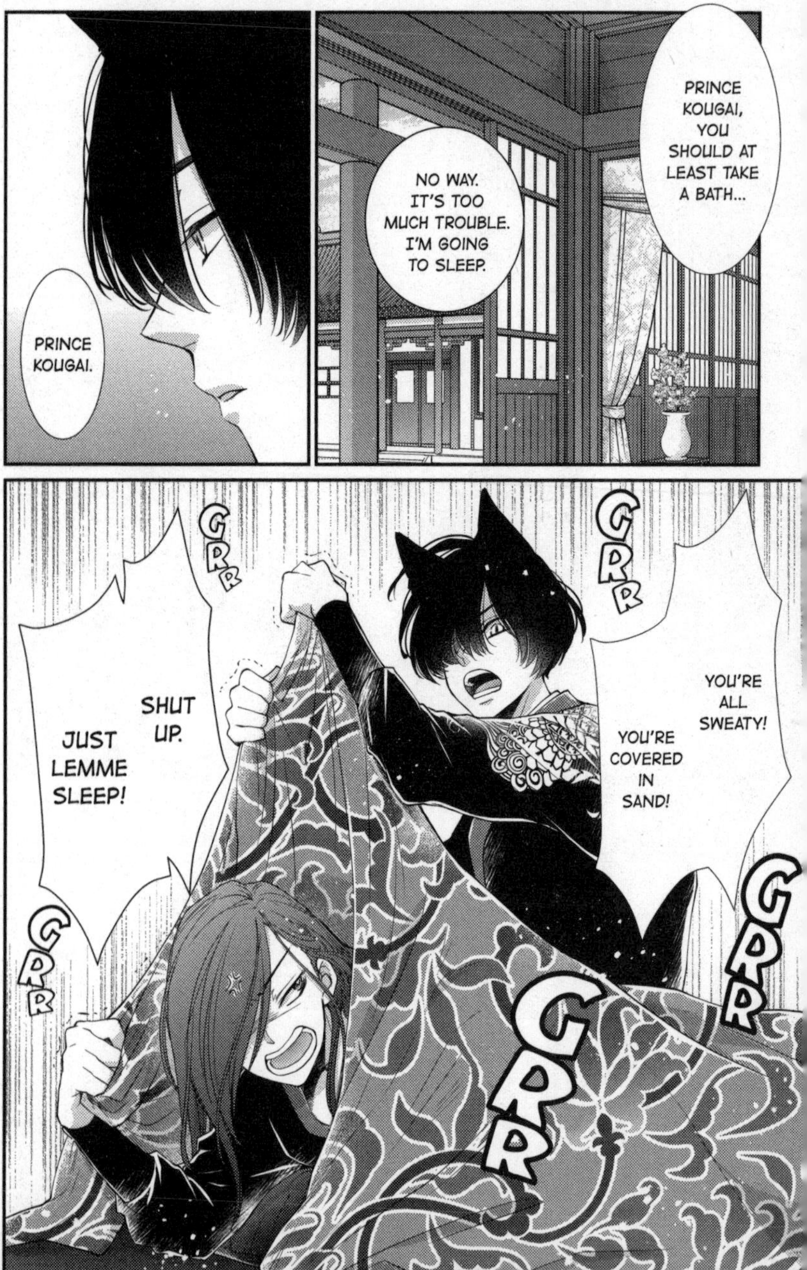
PRINCE KOUGAI, YOU SHOULD AT LEAST TAKE A BATH...
NO WAY. IT'S TOO MUCH TROUBLE. I'M GOING TO SLEEP.
PRINCE KOUGAI.
GRR
YOU'RE ALL SWEATY!
YOU'RE COVERED IN SAND!
GRR
SHUT UP.
JUST LEMME SLEEP!
GRR
GRR
GRR

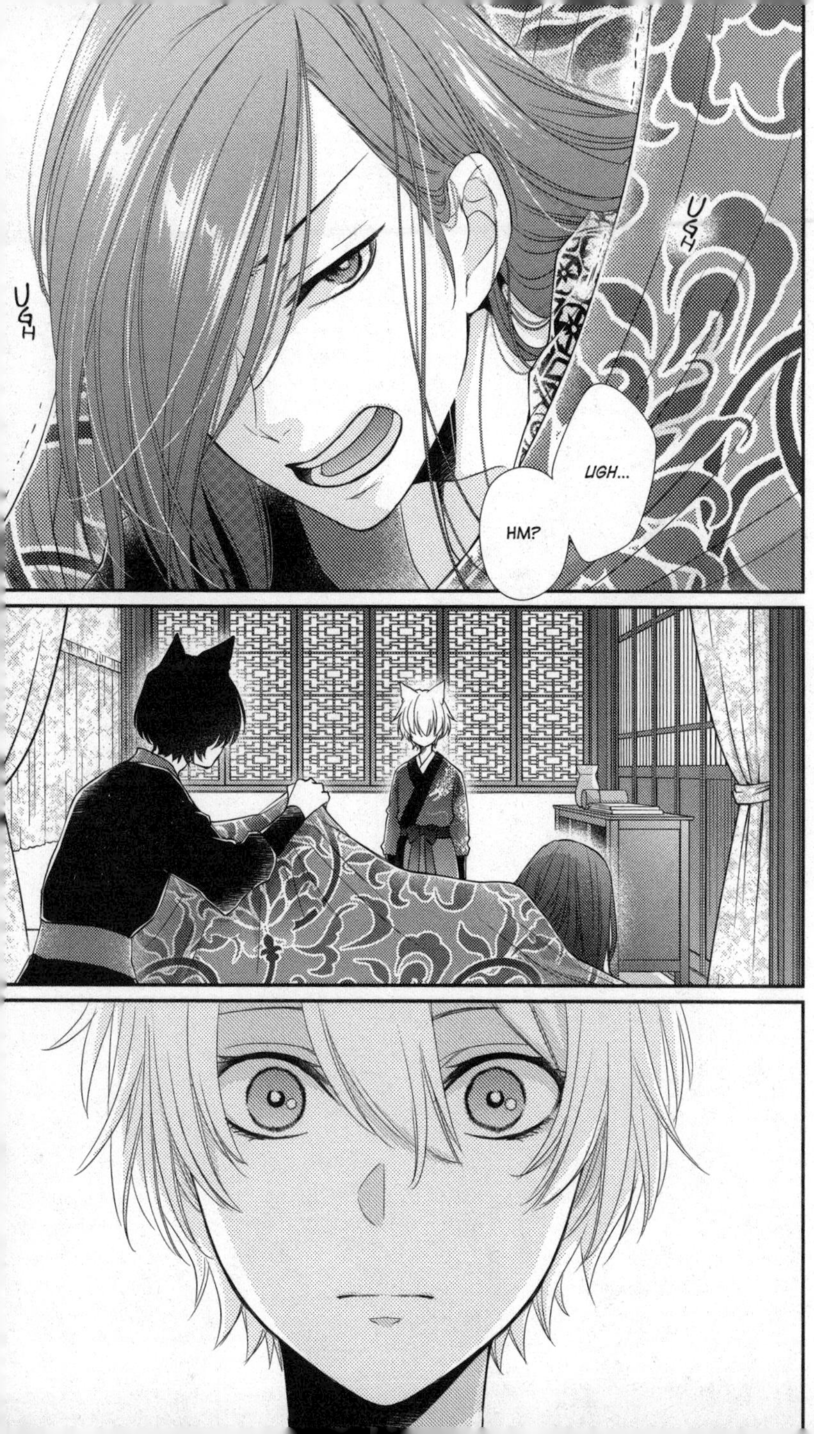
UGH
UGH...
HM?
UGH

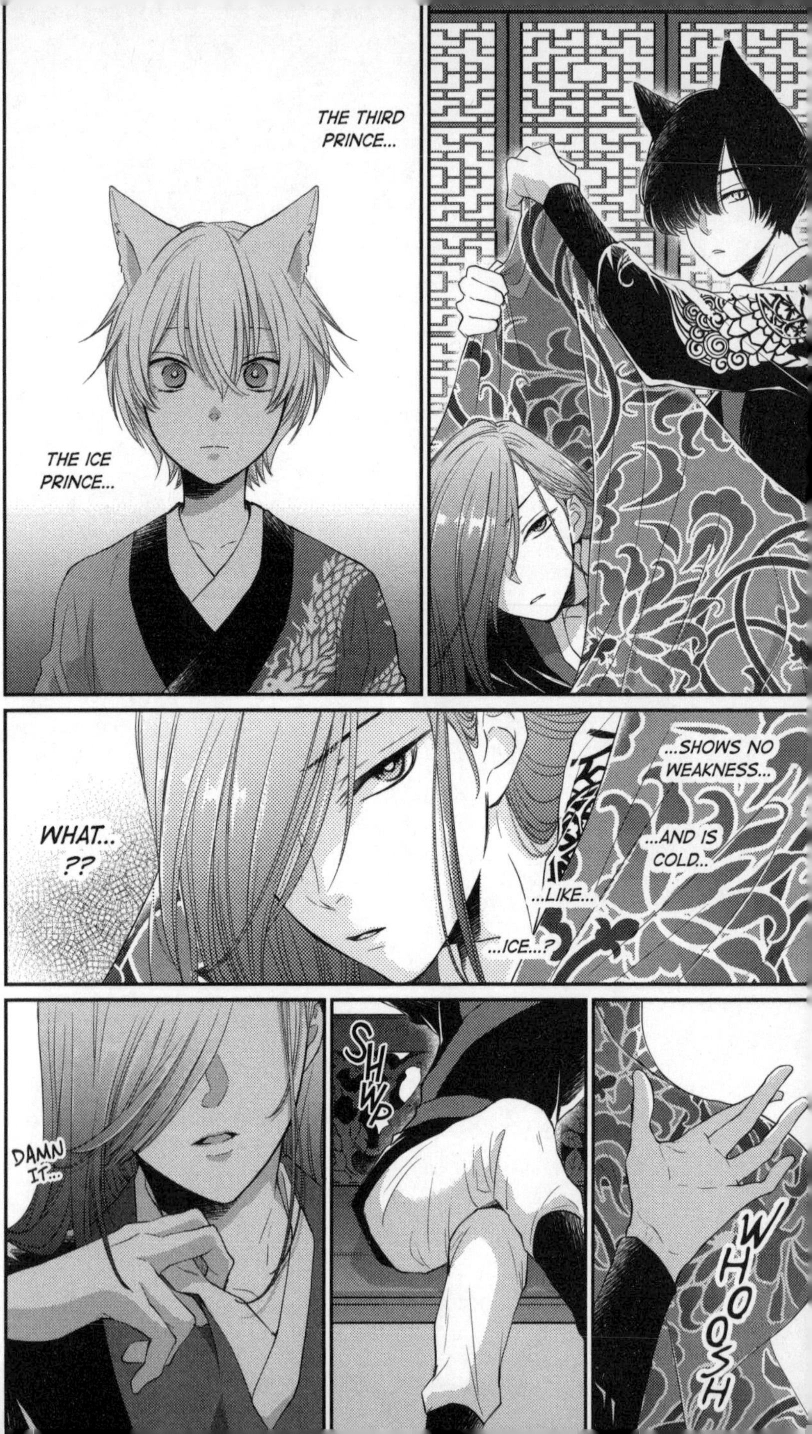
THE THIRD PRINCE...
THE ICE PRINCE...
...SHOWS NO WEAKNESS...
...AND IS COLD...
...LIKE...
...ICE...?
WHAT... ??
WHOOSH
SHWP
DAMN IT...

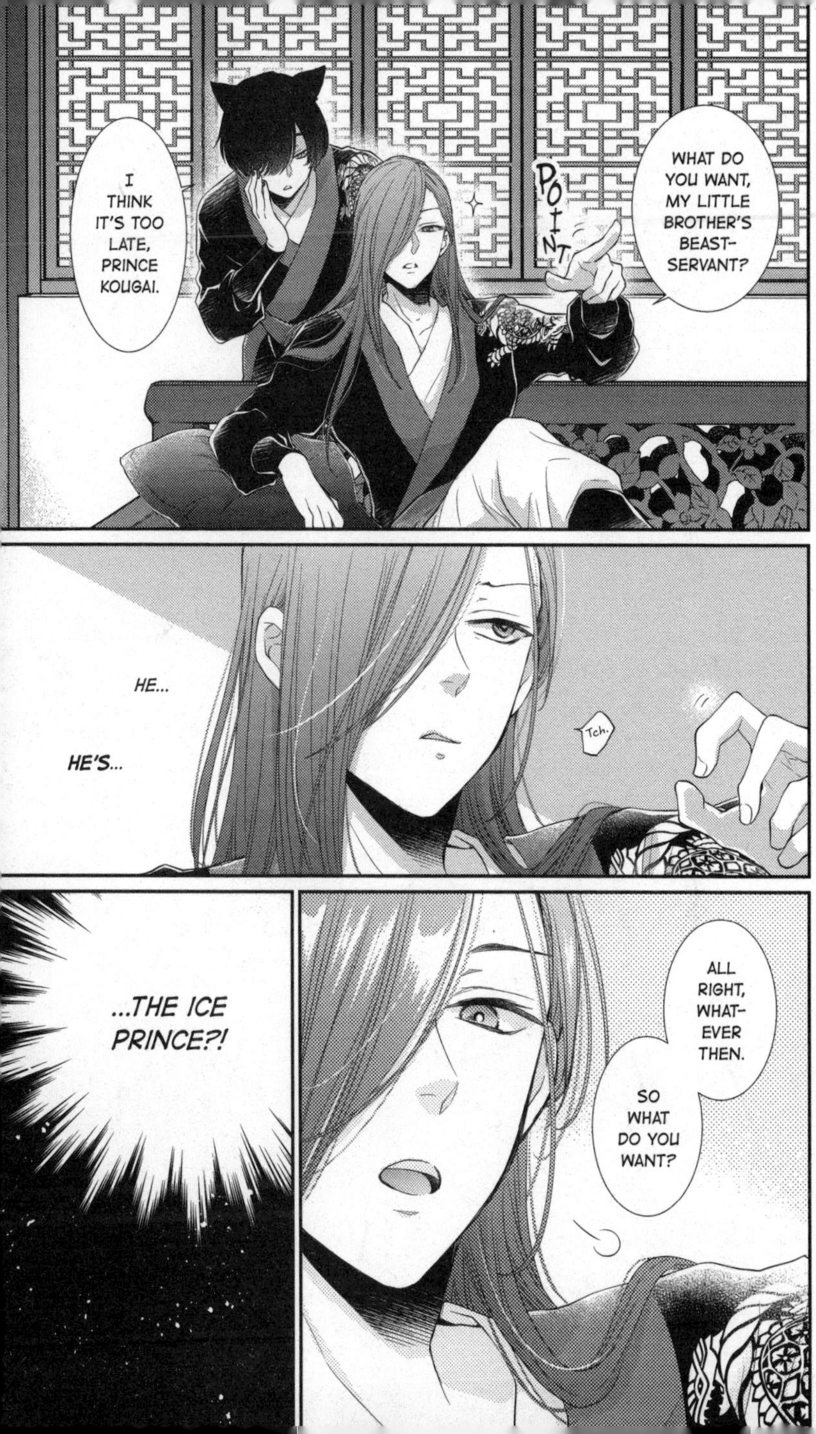
WHAT DO YOU WANT, MY LITTLE BROTHER'S BEAST-SERVANT?
POINT
I THINK IT'S TOO LATE, PRINCE KOUGAI.
Tch.
HE...
HE'S...
ALL RIGHT, WHATEVER THEN.
SO WHAT DO YOU WANT?
...THE ICE PRINCE?!

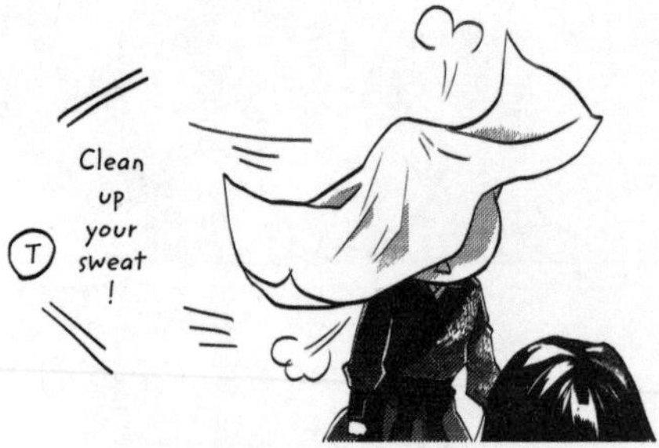
Clean up your sweat!
T

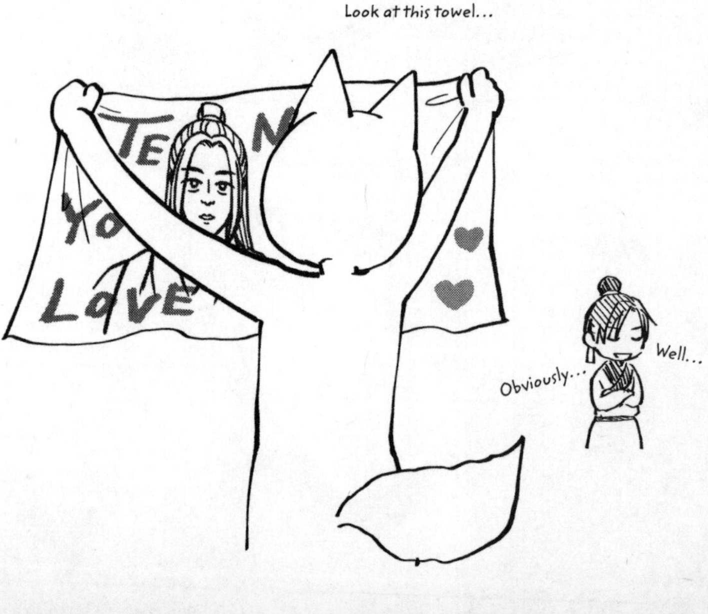
Look at this towel...
Well...
Obviously...

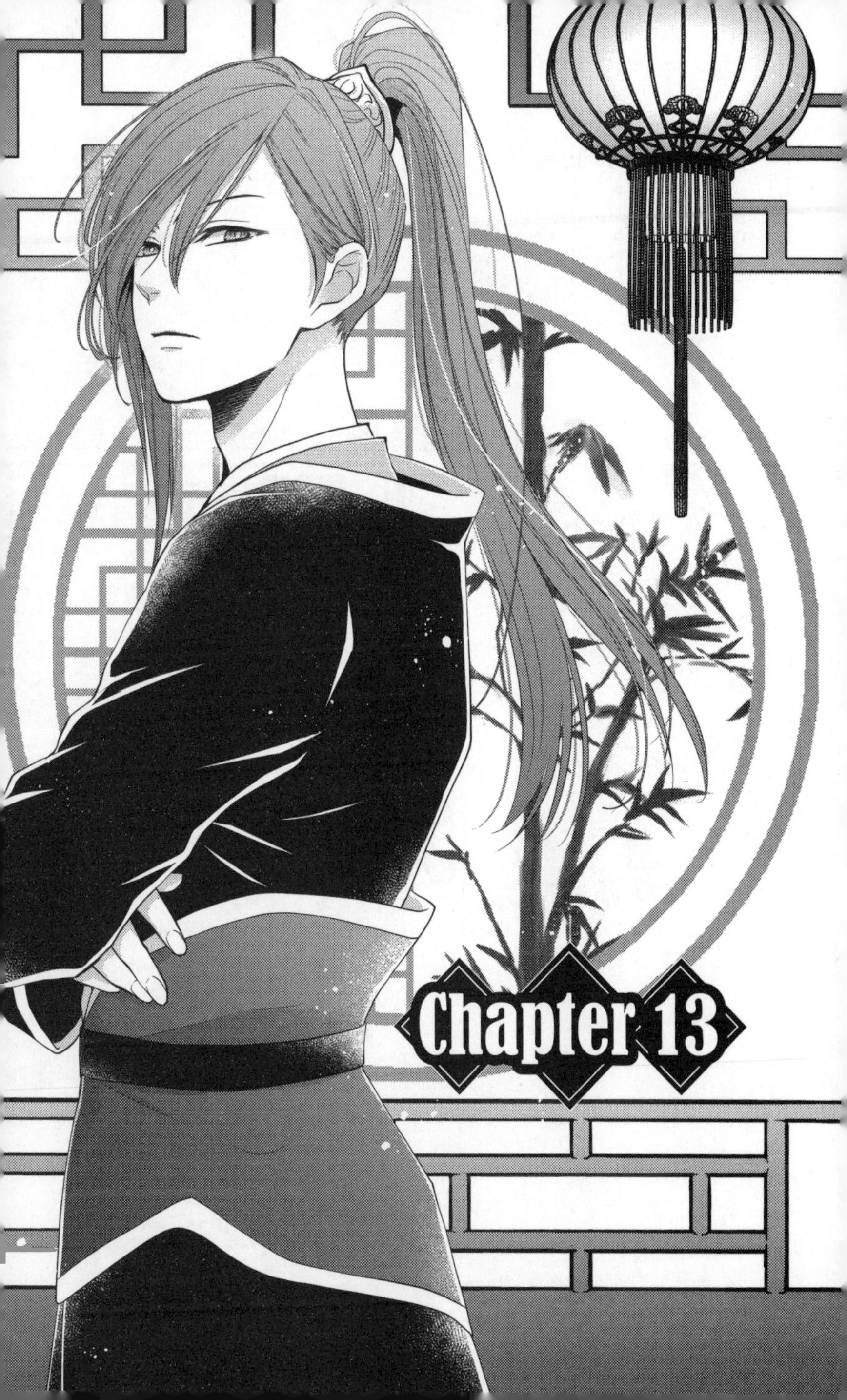
Chapter 13

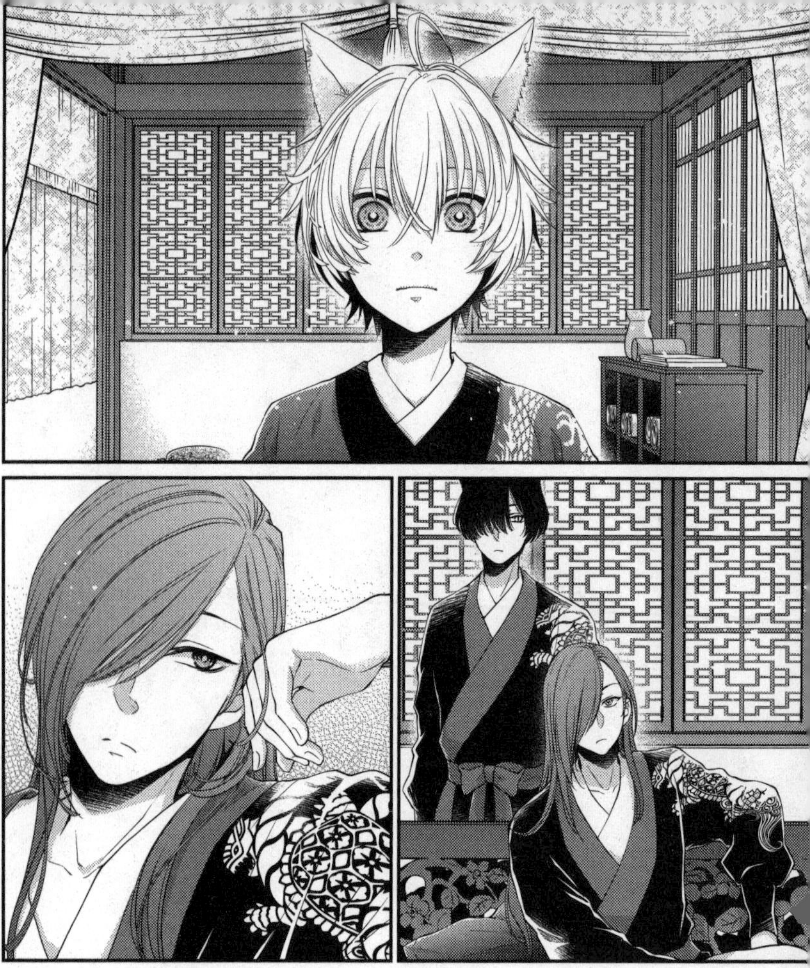

THE KING'S Beast

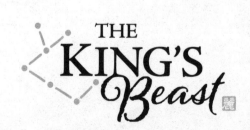

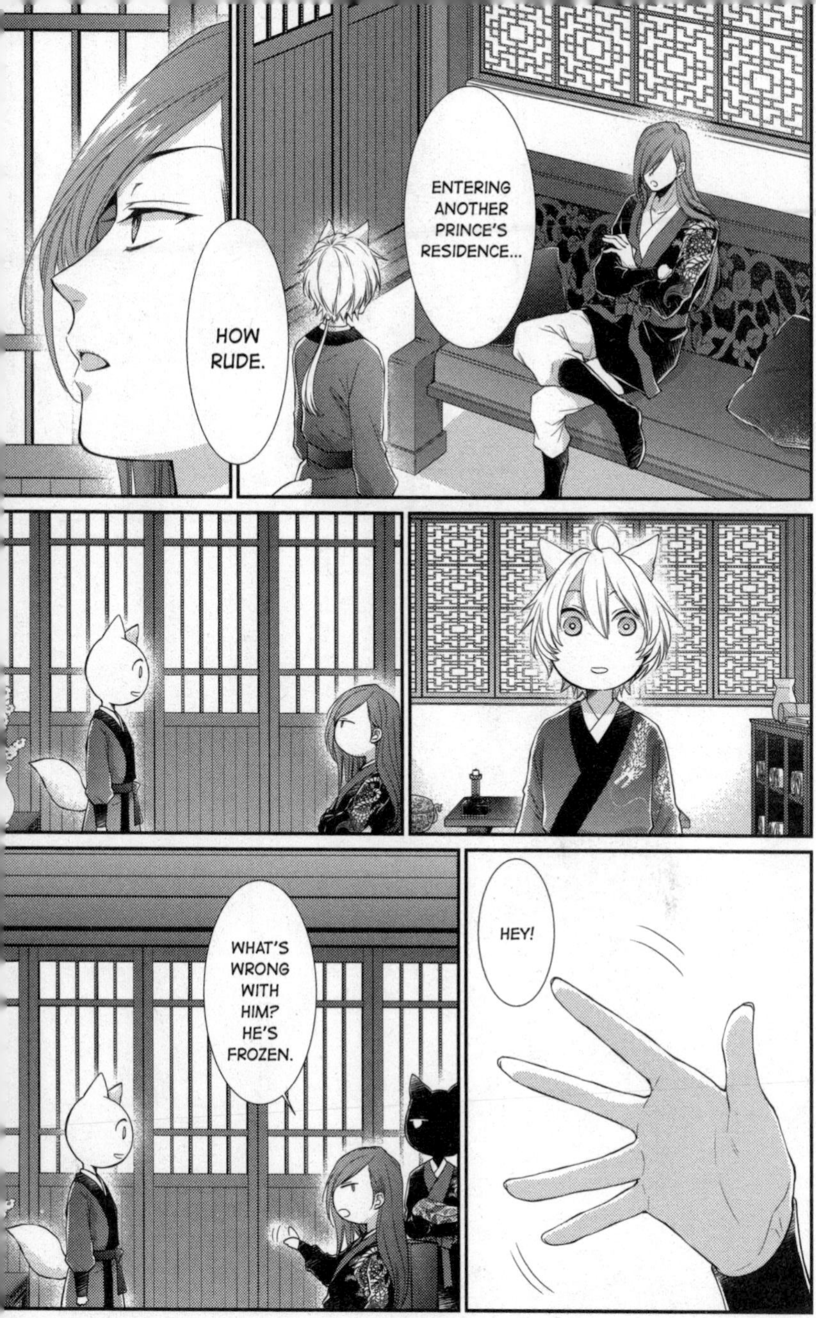
ENTERING ANOTHER PRINCE'S RESIDENCE...
HOW RUDE.
HEY!
WHAT'S WRONG WITH HIM? HE'S FROZEN.

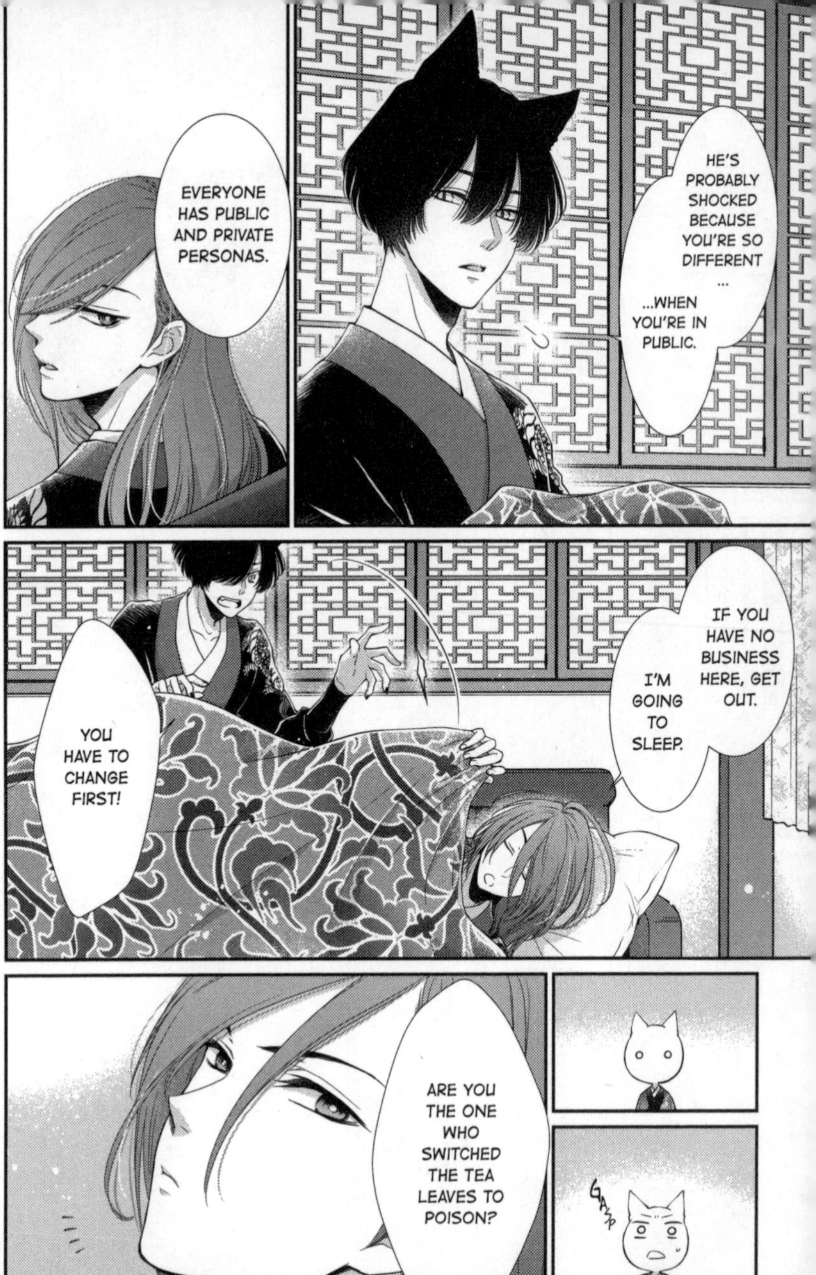
HE'S PROBABLY SHOCKED BECAUSE YOU'RE SO DIFFERENT ...
...WHEN YOU'RE IN PUBLIC.
EVERYONE HAS PUBLIC AND PRIVATE PERSONAS.
IF YOU HAVE NO BUSINESS HERE, GET OUT.
I'M GOING TO SLEEP.
YOU HAVE TO CHANGE FIRST!
GASP
ARE YOU THE ONE WHO SWITCHED THE TEA LEAVES TO POISON?

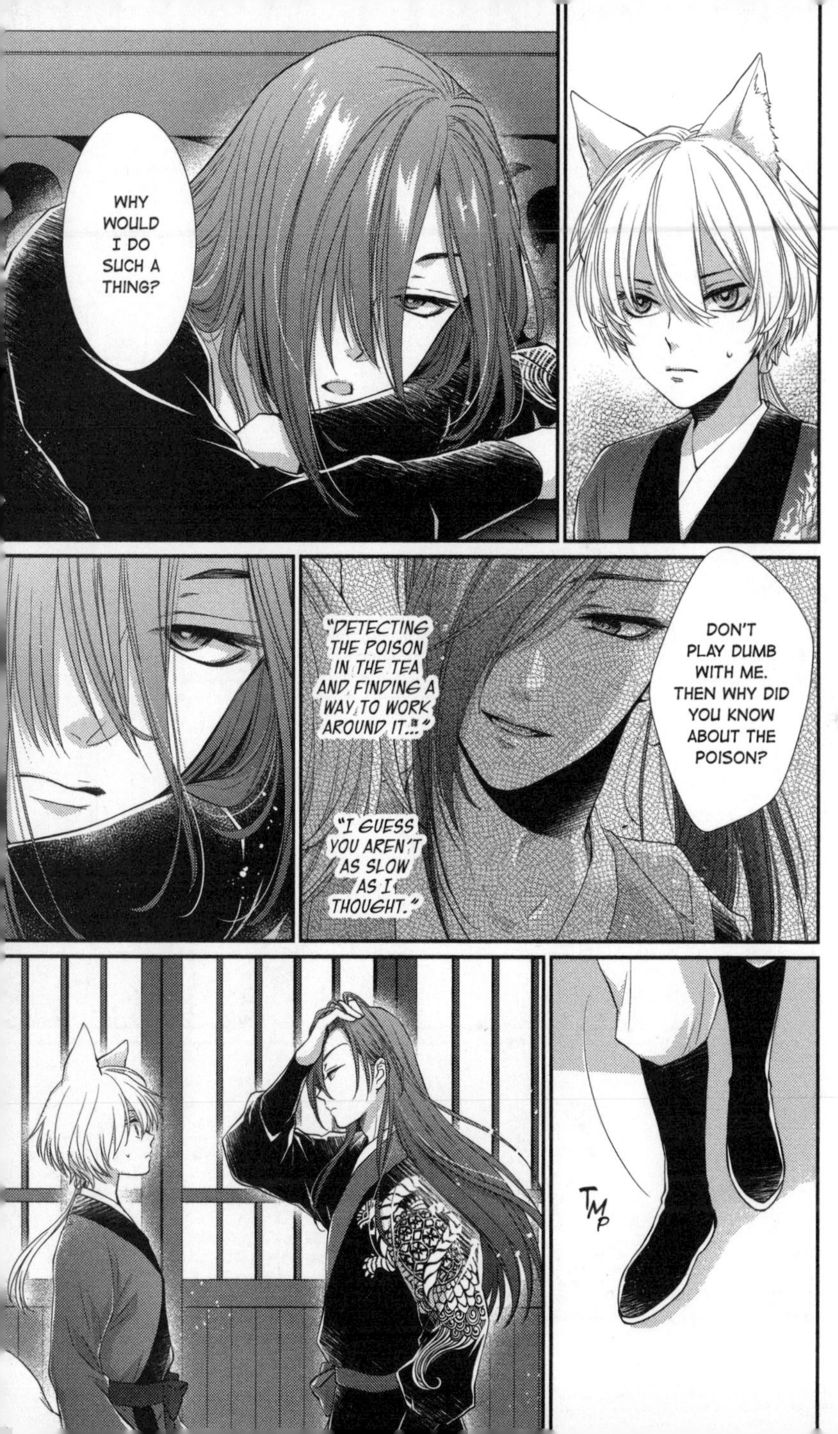
WHY WOULD I DO SUCH A THING?
DON'T PLAY DUMB WITH ME. THEN WHY DID YOU KNOW ABOUT THE POISON?
"DETECTING THE POISON IN THE TEA AND FINDING A WAY TO WORK AROUND IT..."
"I GUESS YOU AREN'T AS SLOW AS I THOUGHT."
TMP

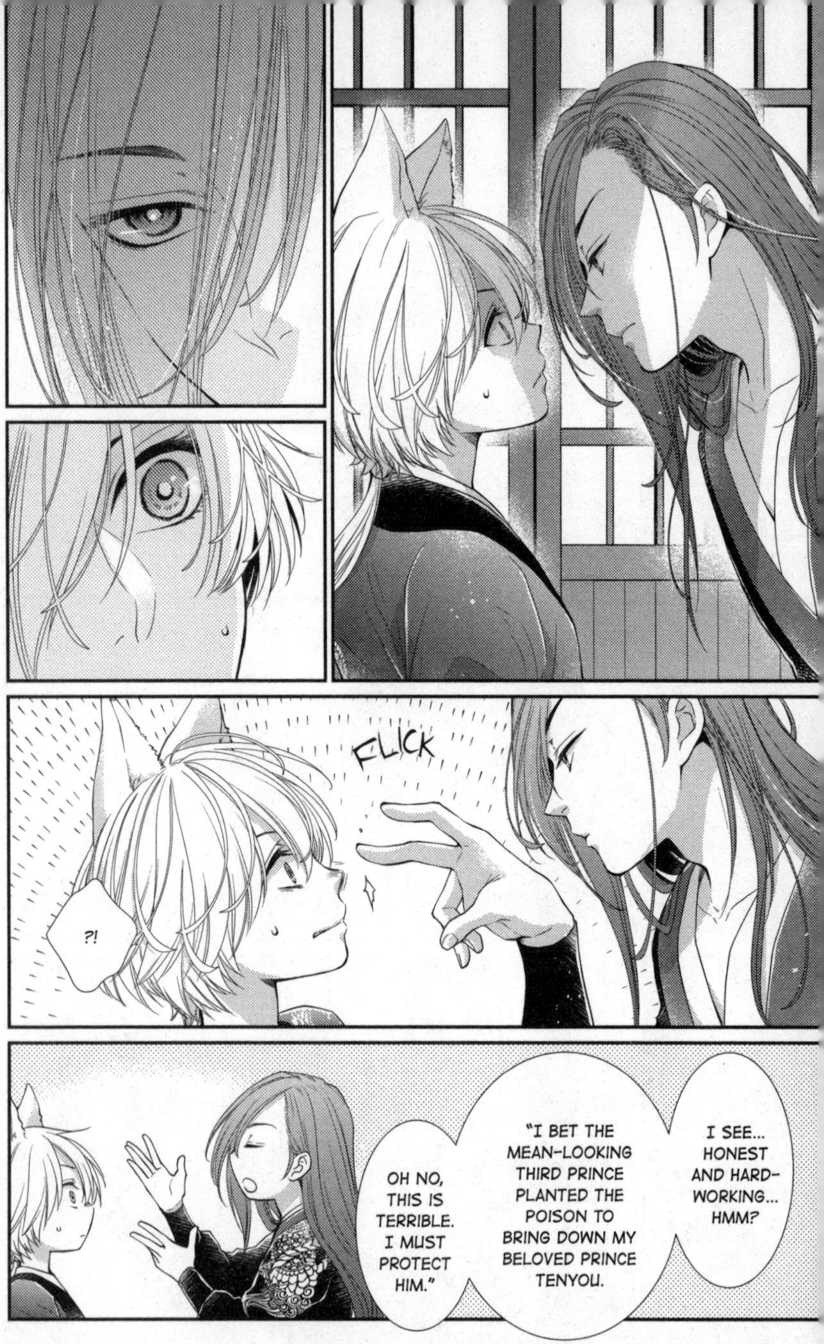
FLICK
?!
I SEE... HONEST AND HARD-WORKING... HMM?
"I BET THE MEAN-LOOKING THIRD PRINCE PLANTED THE POISON TO BRING DOWN MY BELOVED PRINCE TENYOU.
OH NO, THIS IS TERRIBLE. I MUST PROTECT HIM."

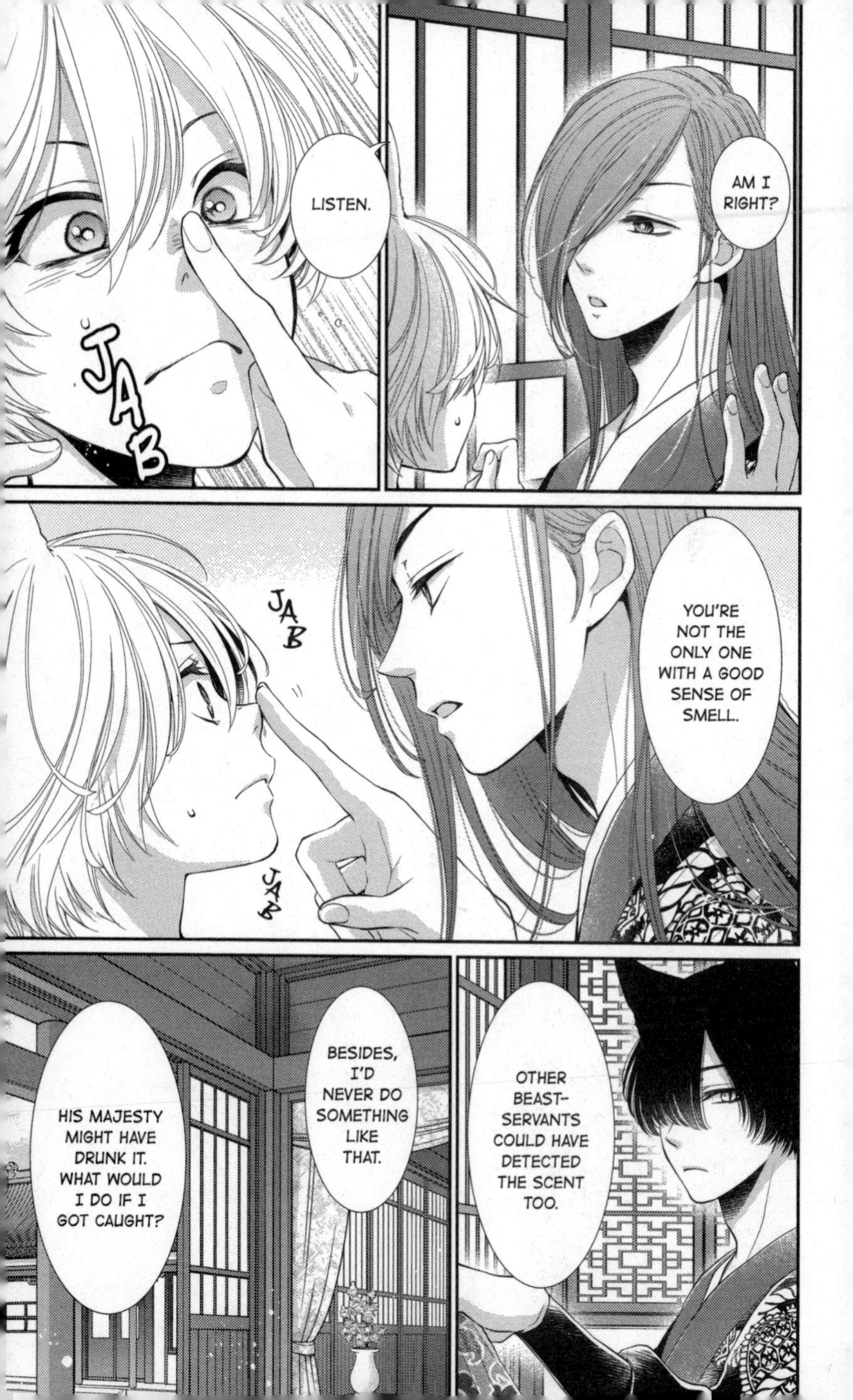
AM I RIGHT?
LISTEN.
JAB
YOU'RE NOT THE ONLY ONE WITH A GOOD SENSE OF SMELL.
JAB
JAB
OTHER BEAST-SERVANTS COULD HAVE DETECTED THE SCENT TOO.
BESIDES, I'D NEVER DO SOMETHING LIKE THAT.
HIS MAJESTY MIGHT HAVE DRUNK IT. WHAT WOULD I DO IF I GOT CAUGHT?

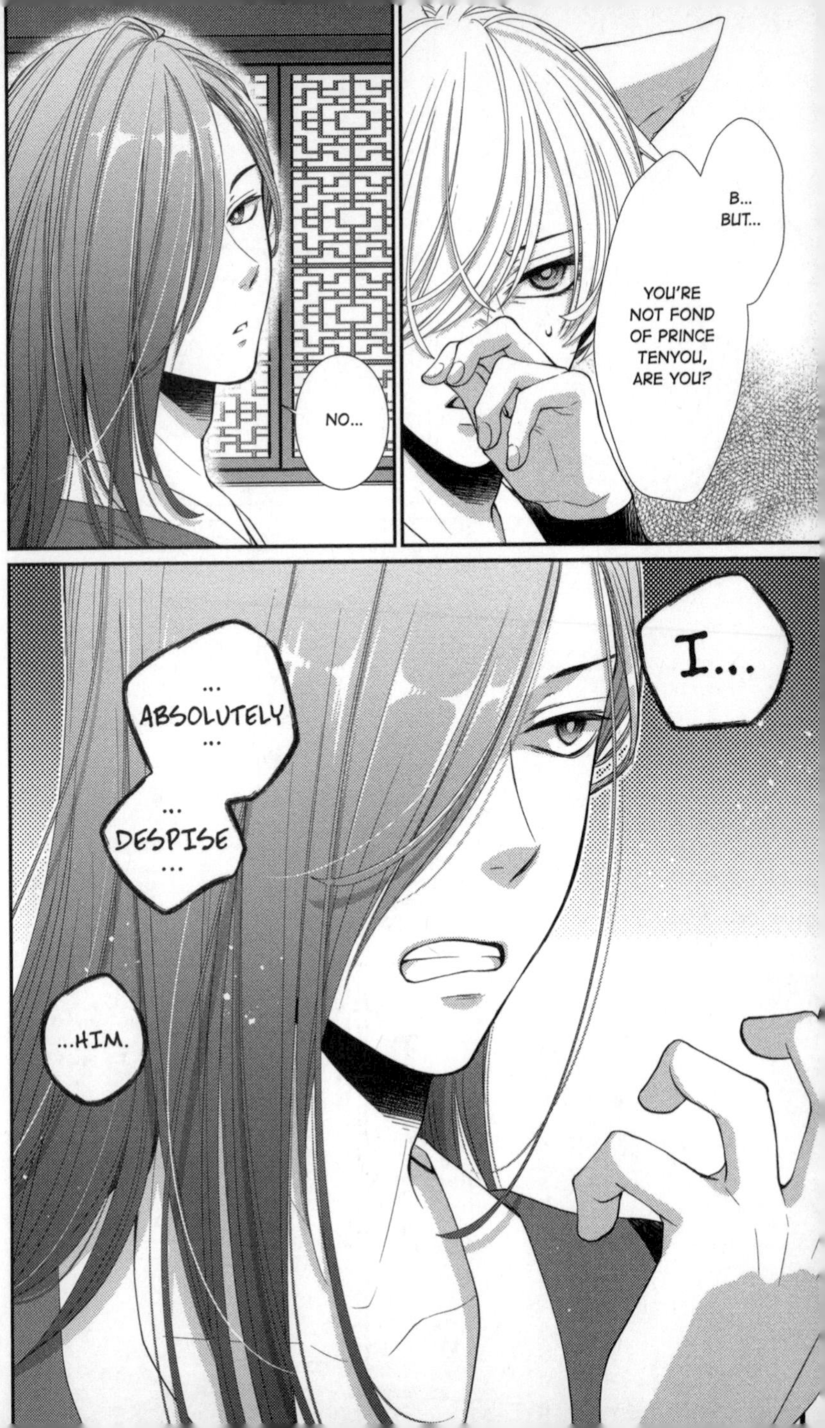
B... BUT...
YOU'RE NOT FOND OF PRINCE TENYOU, ARE YOU?
NO...
I...
...ABSOLUTELY...
...DESPISE...
...HIM.

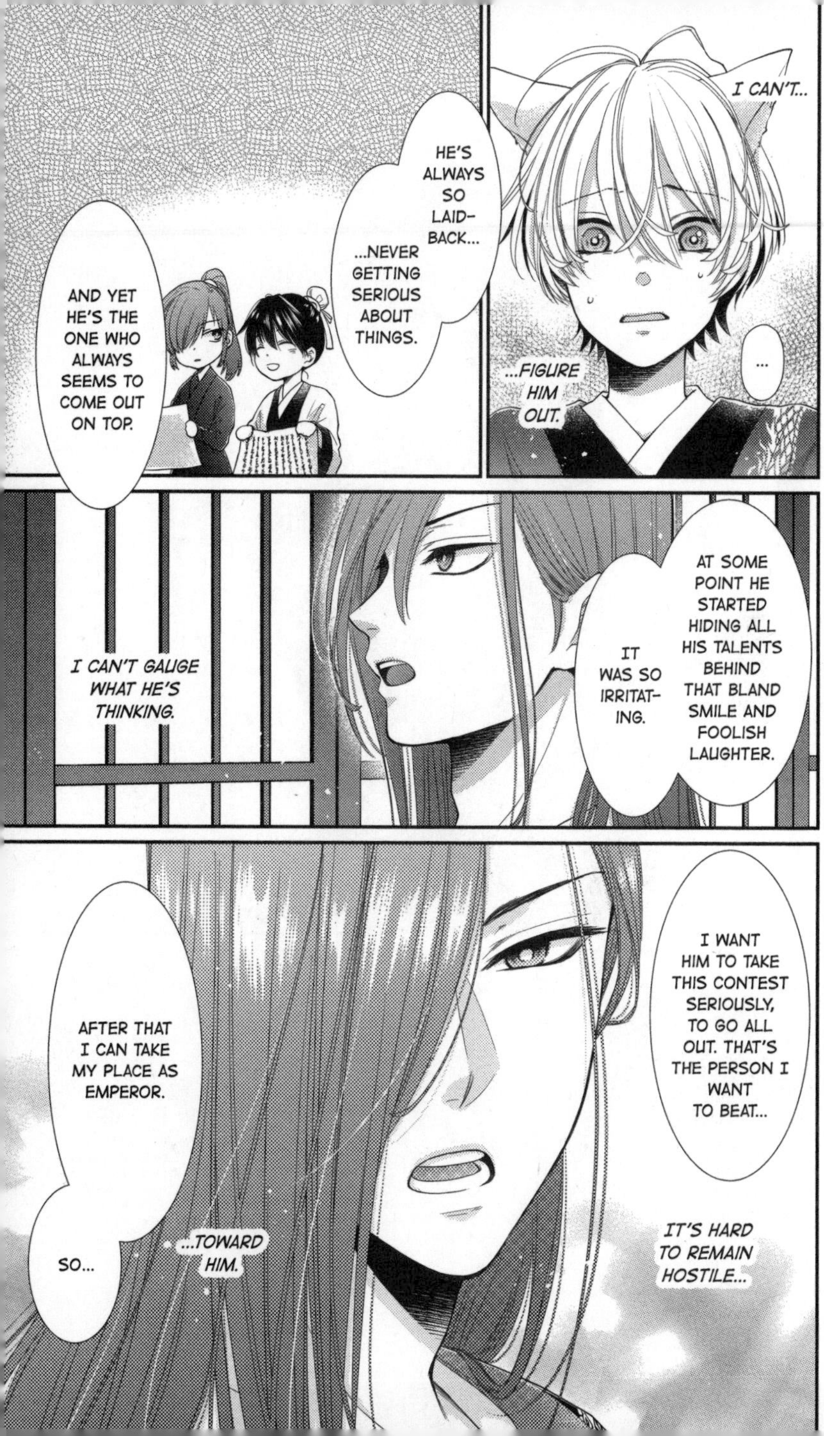
I CAN'T...
...
...FIGURE HIM OUT.
HE'S ALWAYS SO LAID-BACK...
...NEVER GETTING SERIOUS ABOUT THINGS.
AND YET HE'S THE ONE WHO ALWAYS SEEMS TO COME OUT ON TOP.
AT SOME POINT HE STARTED HIDING ALL HIS TALENTS BEHIND THAT BLAND SMILE AND FOOLISH LAUGHTER.
IT WAS SO IRRITAT-ING.
I CAN'T GAUGE WHAT HE'S THINKING.
I WANT HIM TO TAKE THIS CONTEST SERIOUSLY, TO GO ALL OUT. THAT'S THE PERSON I WANT TO BEAT...
AFTER THAT I CAN TAKE MY PLACE AS EMPEROR.
IT'S HARD TO REMAIN HOSTILE...
...TOWARD HIM.
SO...

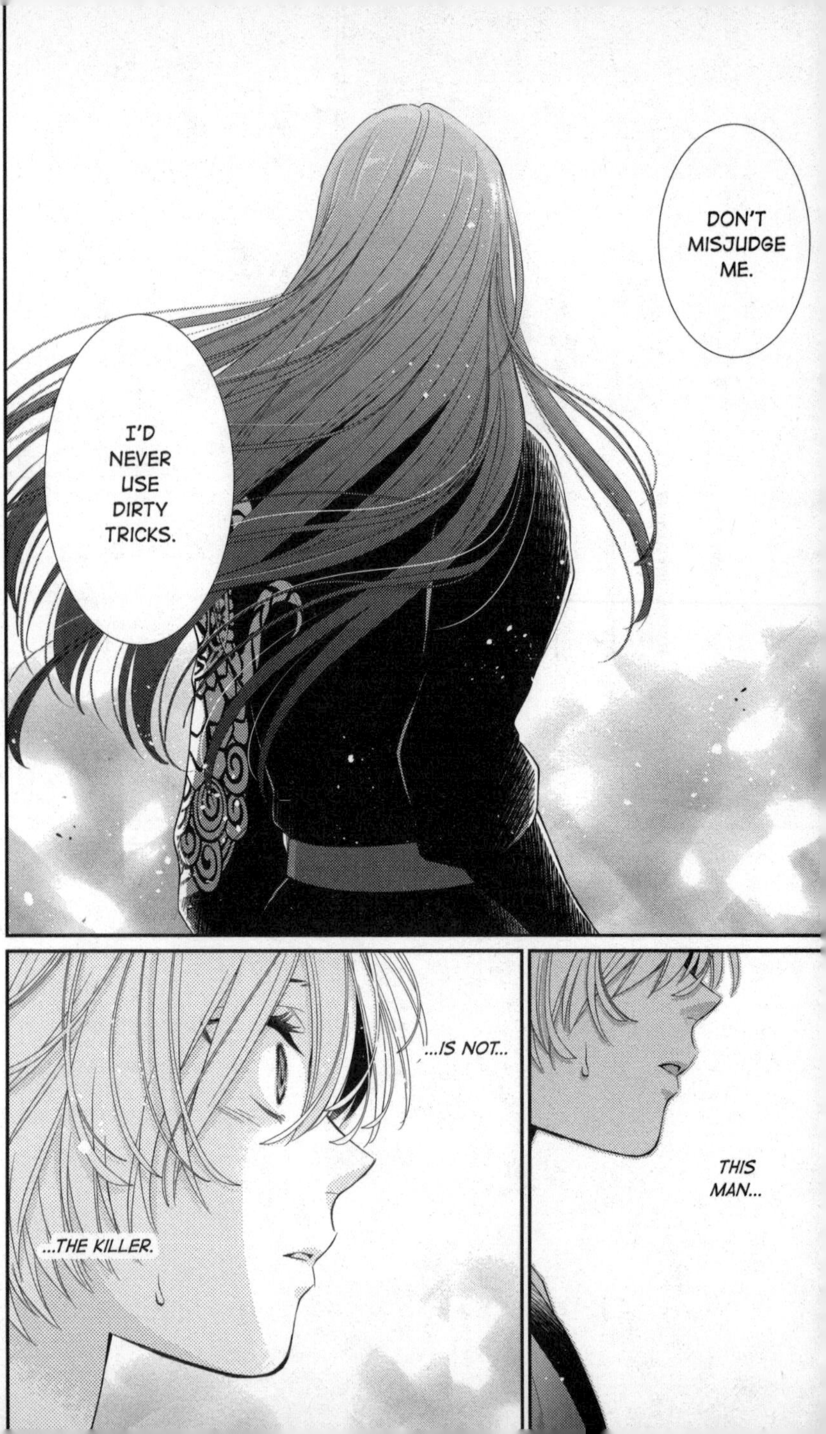
DON'T MISJUDGE ME.
I'D NEVER USE DIRTY TRICKS.
THIS MAN...
...IS NOT...
...THE KILLER.

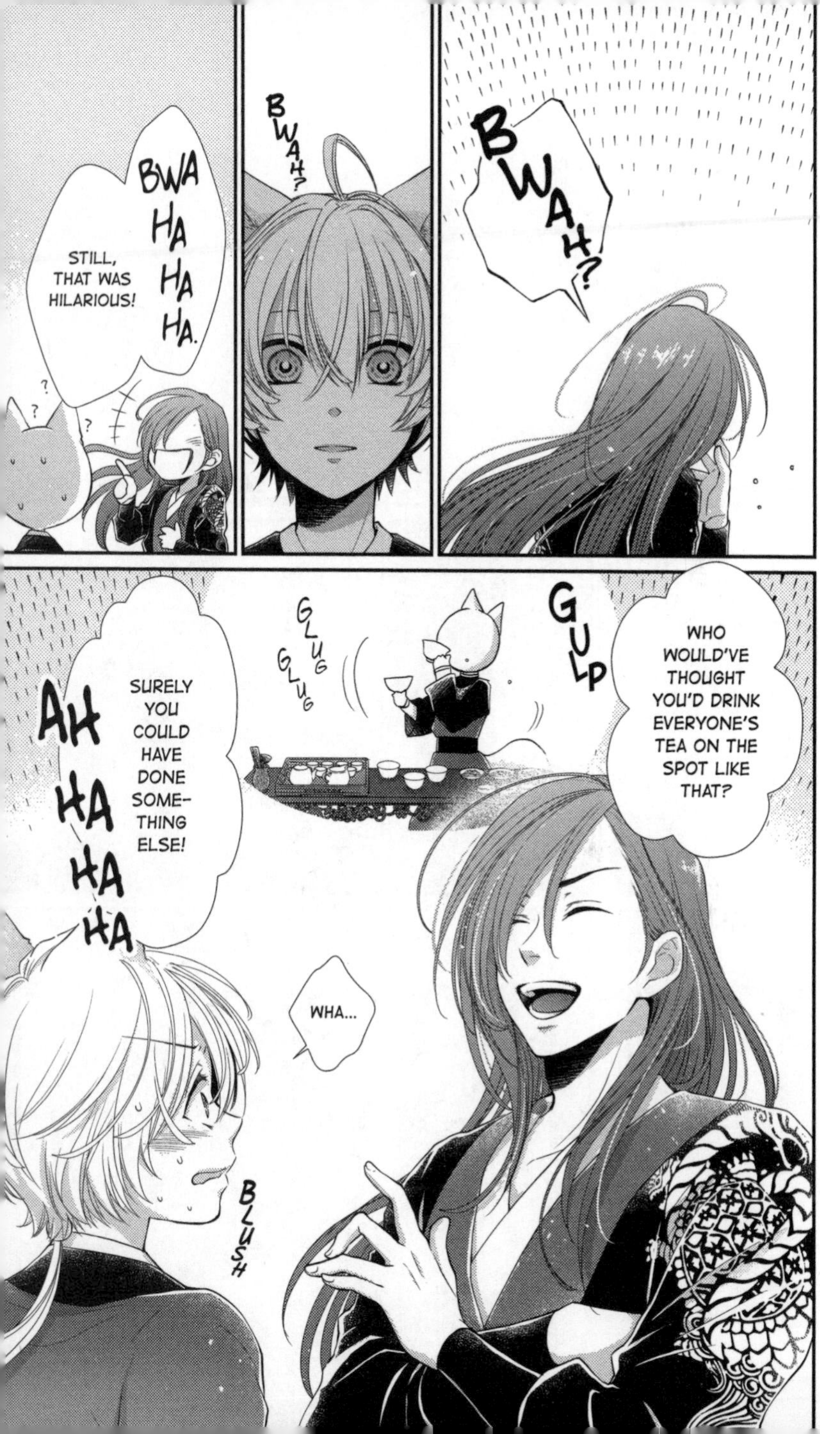
BWAH?
BWAH?
STILL, THAT WAS HILARIOUS!
BWA HA HA HA.
GULP
WHO WOULD'VE THOUGHT YOU'D DRINK EVERYONE'S TEA ON THE SPOT LIKE THAT?
GLUG GLUG
SURELY YOU COULD HAVE DONE SOME-THING ELSE!
AH HA HA HA HA
WHA...
BLUSH

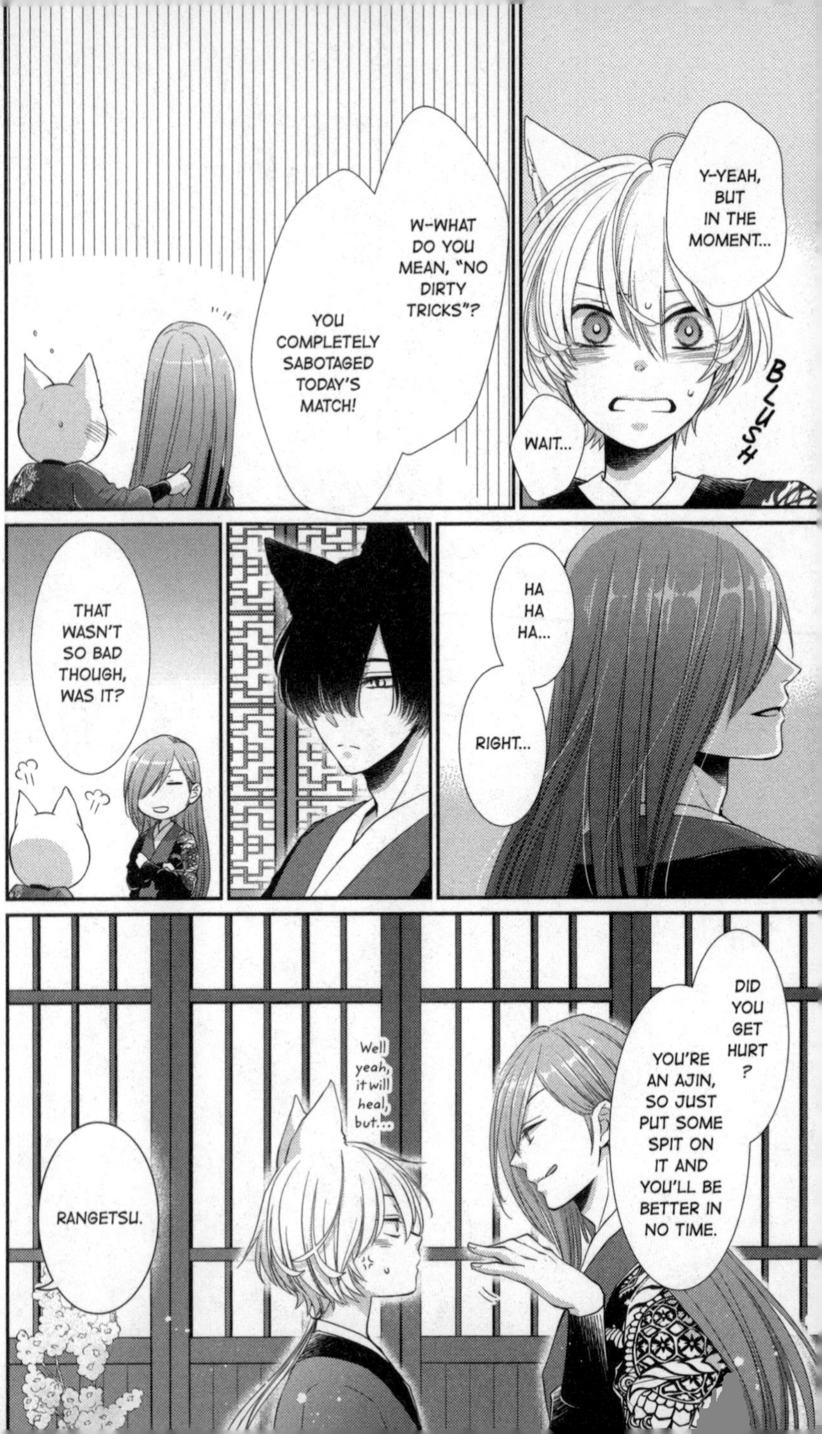
Y-YEAH, BUT IN THE MOMENT...
BLUSH
WAIT...
W-WHAT DO YOU MEAN, "NO DIRTY TRICKS"?
YOU COMPLETELY SABOTAGED TODAY'S MATCH!
HA HA HA...
RIGHT...
THAT WASN'T SO BAD THOUGH, WAS IT?
DID YOU GET HURT?
YOU'RE AN AJIN, SO JUST PUT SOME SPIT ON IT AND YOU'LL BE BETTER IN NO TIME.
Well yeah, it will heal, but...
RANGETSU.

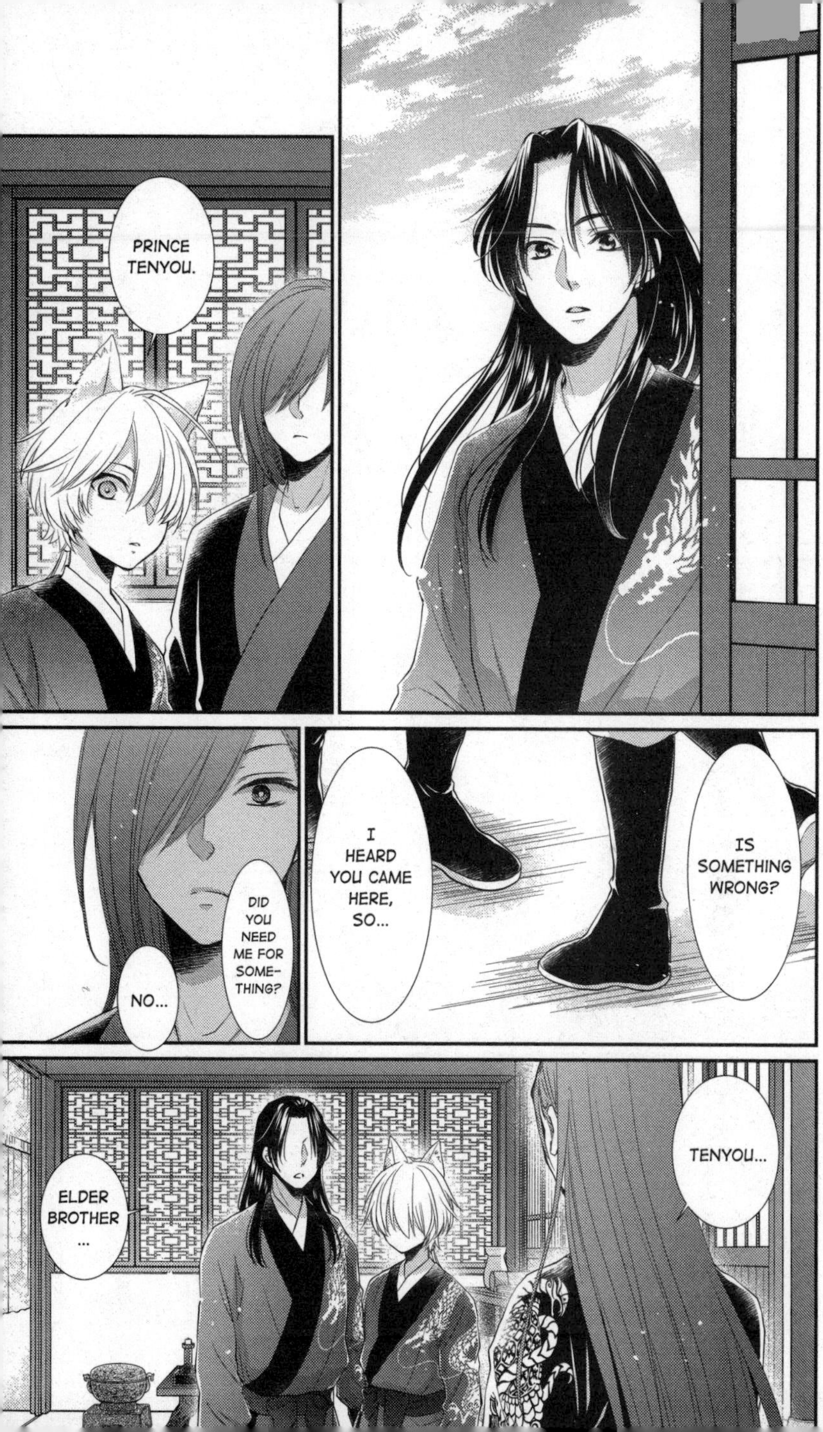
PRINCE TENYOU.
IS SOMETHING WRONG?
I HEARD YOU CAME HERE, SO...
DID YOU NEED ME FOR SOME-THING?
NO...
TENYOU...
ELDER BROTHER ...

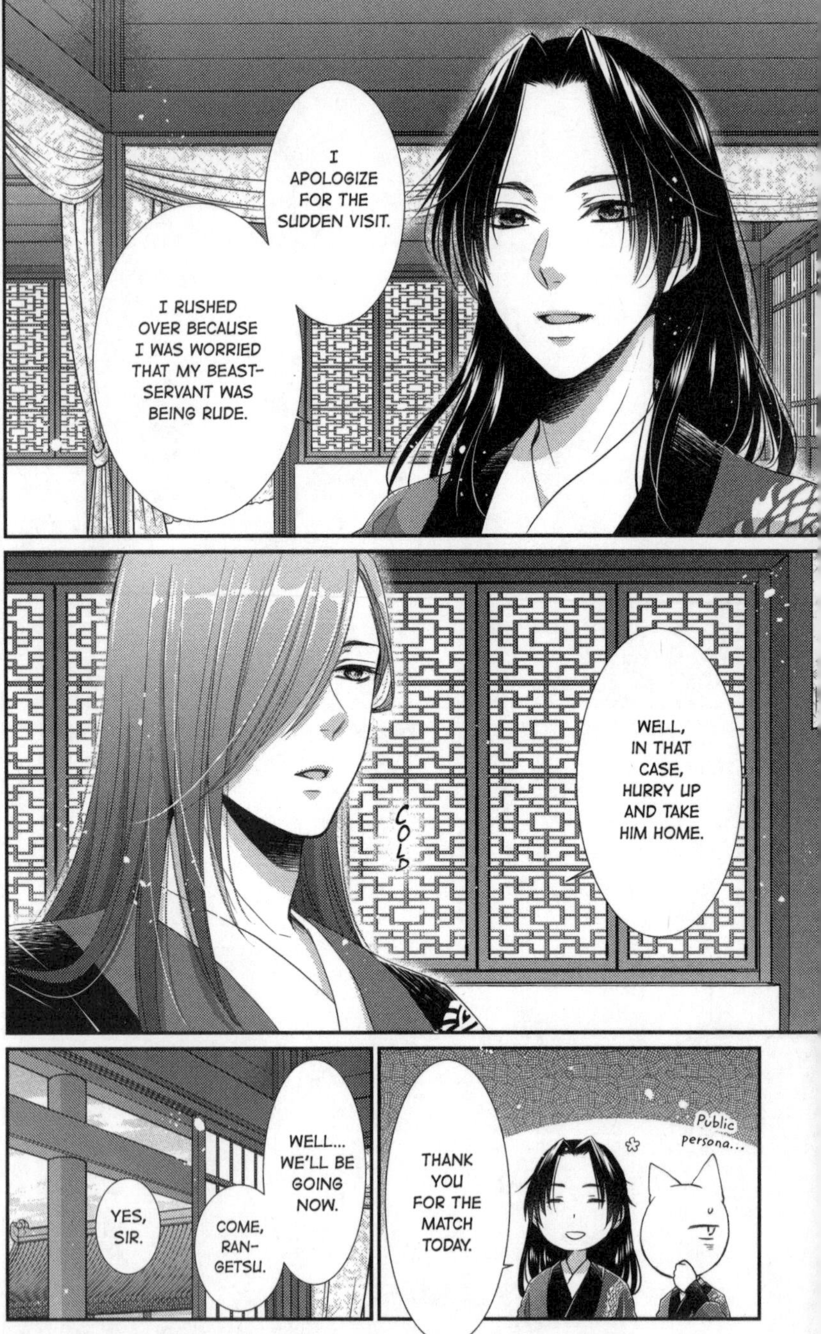
I APOLOGIZE FOR THE SUDDEN VISIT.
I RUSHED OVER BECAUSE I WAS WORRIED THAT MY BEAST-SERVANT WAS BEING RUDE.
WELL, IN THAT CASE, HURRY UP AND TAKE HIM HOME.
COLD
Public persona...
THANK YOU FOR THE MATCH TODAY.
WELL... WE'LL BE GOING NOW.
COME, RANGETSU.
YES, SIR.

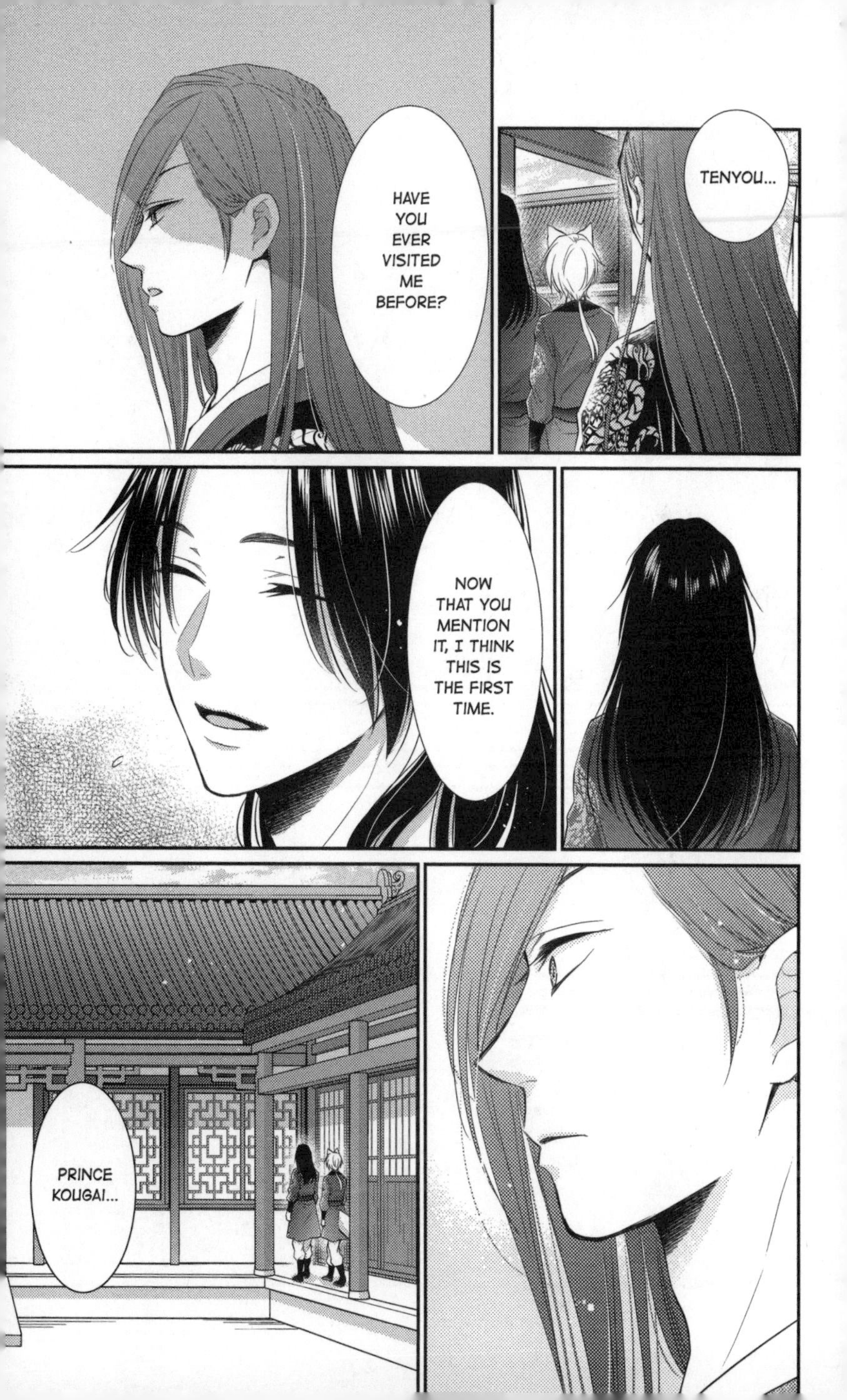
TENYOU...
HAVE YOU EVER VISITED ME BEFORE?
NOW THAT YOU MENTION IT, I THINK THIS IS THE FIRST TIME.
PRINCE KOUGAI...

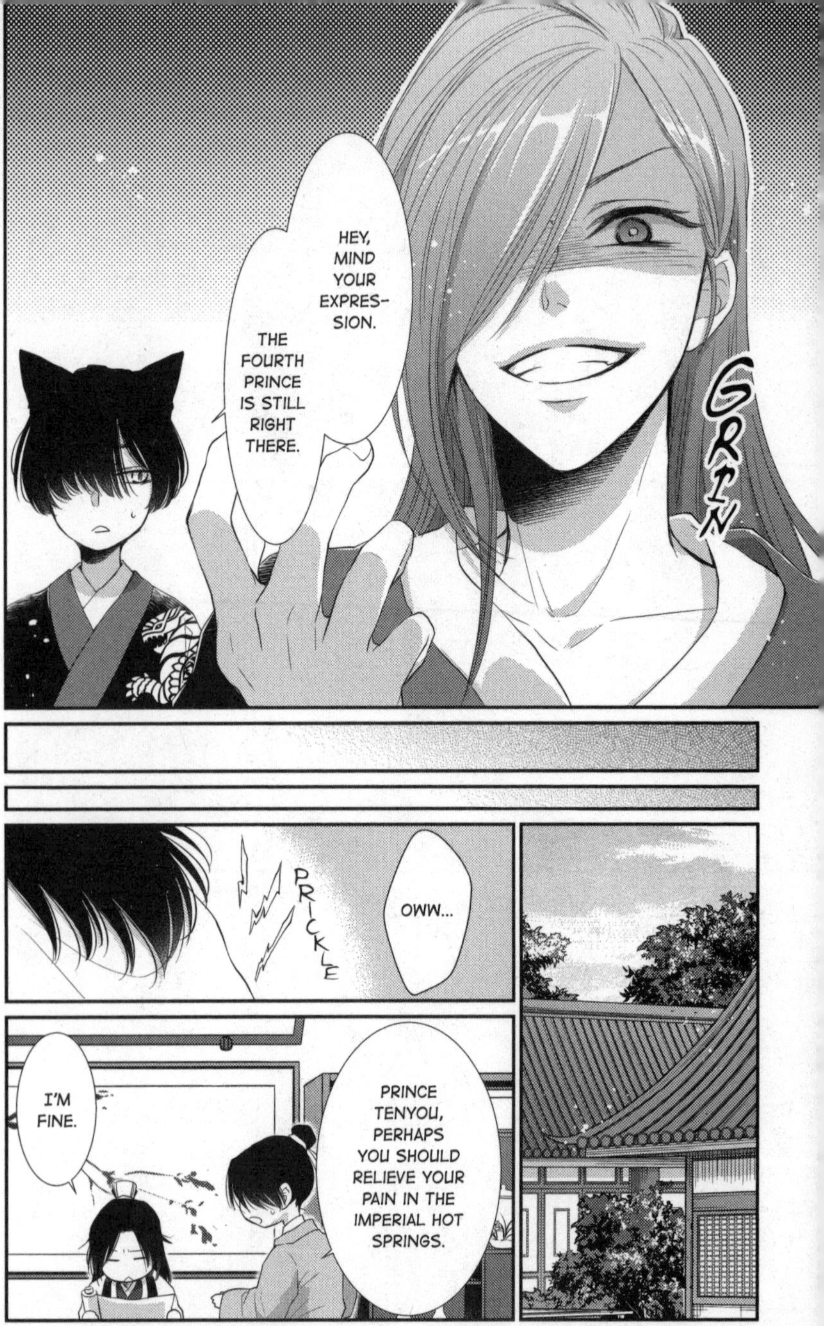
HEY, MIND YOUR EXPRESSION.
THE FOURTH PRINCE IS STILL RIGHT THERE.
GRIN
OWW...
PRICKLE
PRINCE TENYOU, PERHAPS YOU SHOULD RELIEVE YOUR PAIN IN THE IMPERIAL HOT SPRINGS.
I'M FINE.

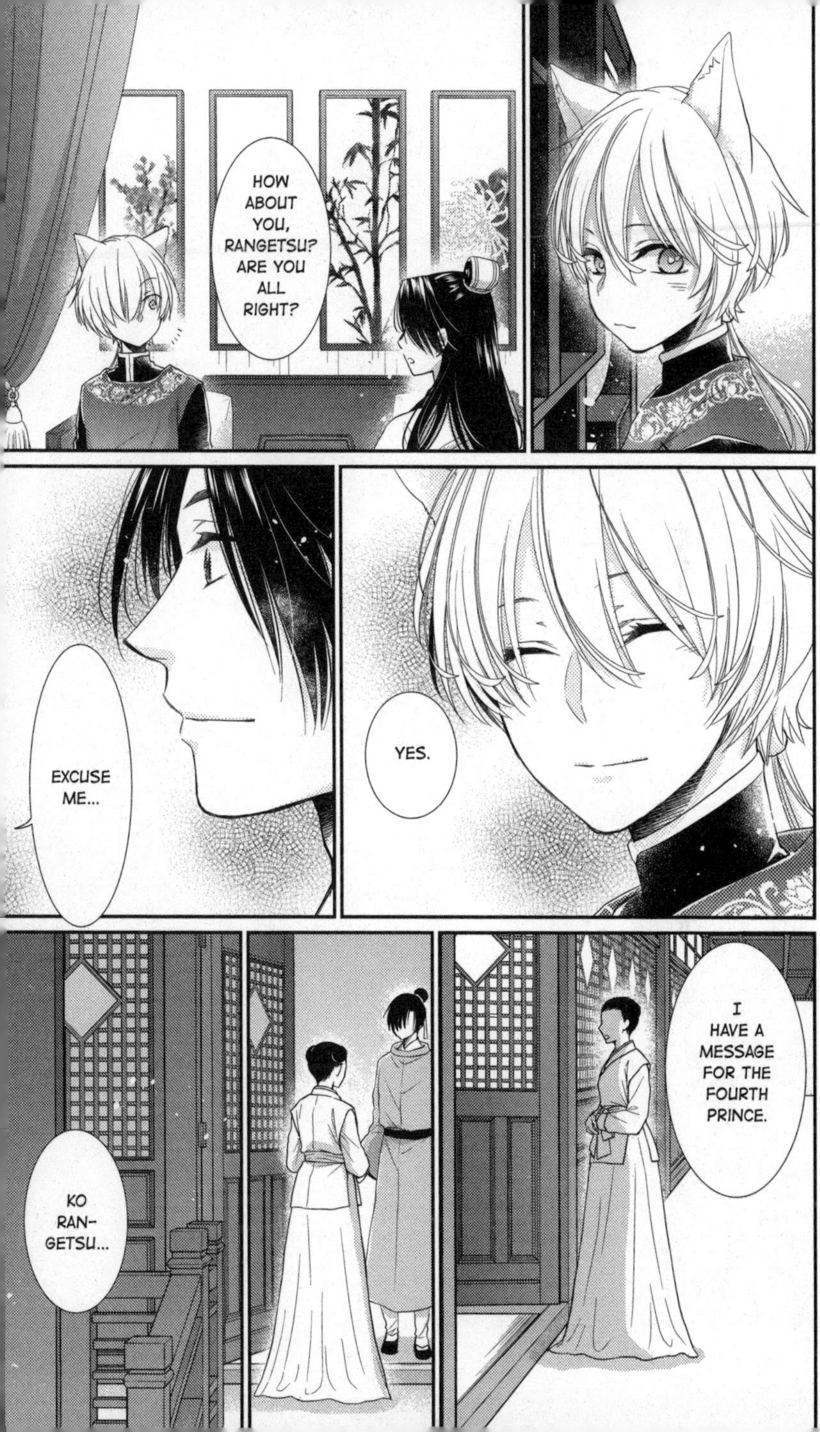
HOW ABOUT YOU, RANGETSU? ARE YOU ALL RIGHT?
YES.
EXCUSE ME...
I HAVE A MESSAGE FOR THE FOURTH PRINCE.
KO RANGETSU...

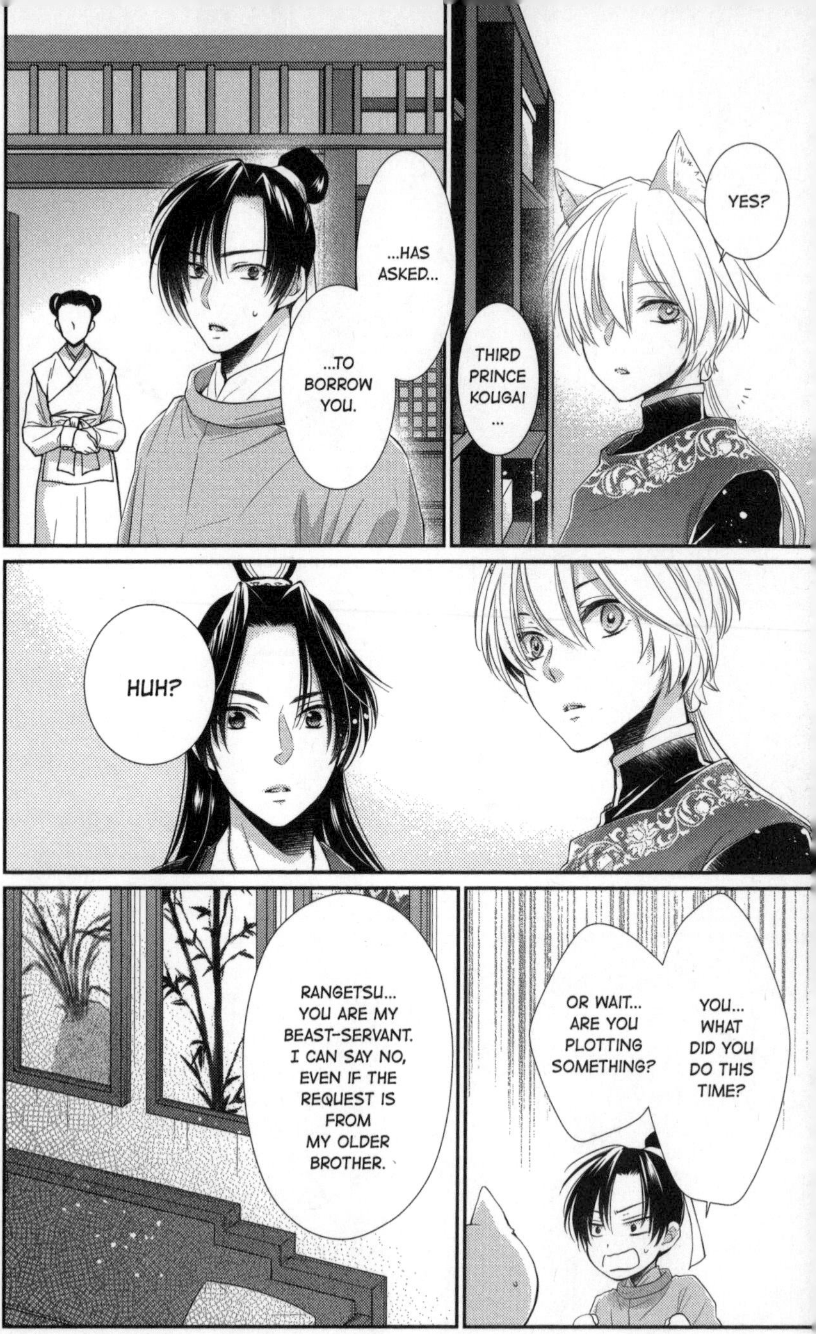
YES?
THIRD PRINCE KOUGAI ...
...HAS ASKED...
...TO BORROW YOU.
HUH?
YOU... WHAT DID YOU DO THIS TIME?
OR WAIT... ARE YOU PLOTTING SOMETHING?
RANGETSU... YOU ARE MY BEAST-SERVANT. I CAN SAY NO, EVEN IF THE REQUEST IS FROM MY OLDER BROTHER.

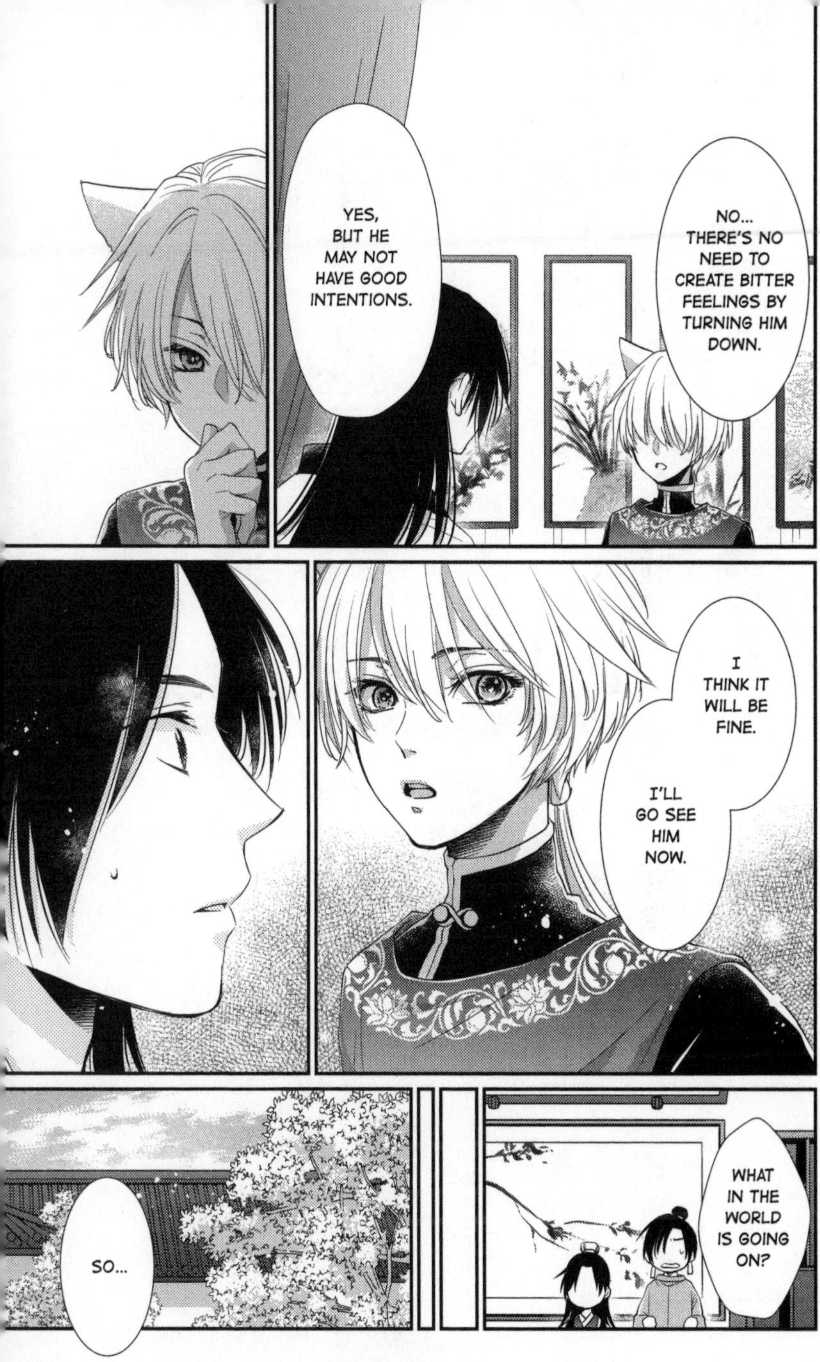
NO... THERE'S NO NEED TO CREATE BITTER FEELINGS BY TURNING HIM DOWN.
YES, BUT HE MAY NOT HAVE GOOD INTENTIONS.
I THINK IT WILL BE FINE.
I'LL GO SEE HIM NOW.
WHAT IN THE WORLD IS GOING ON?
SO...

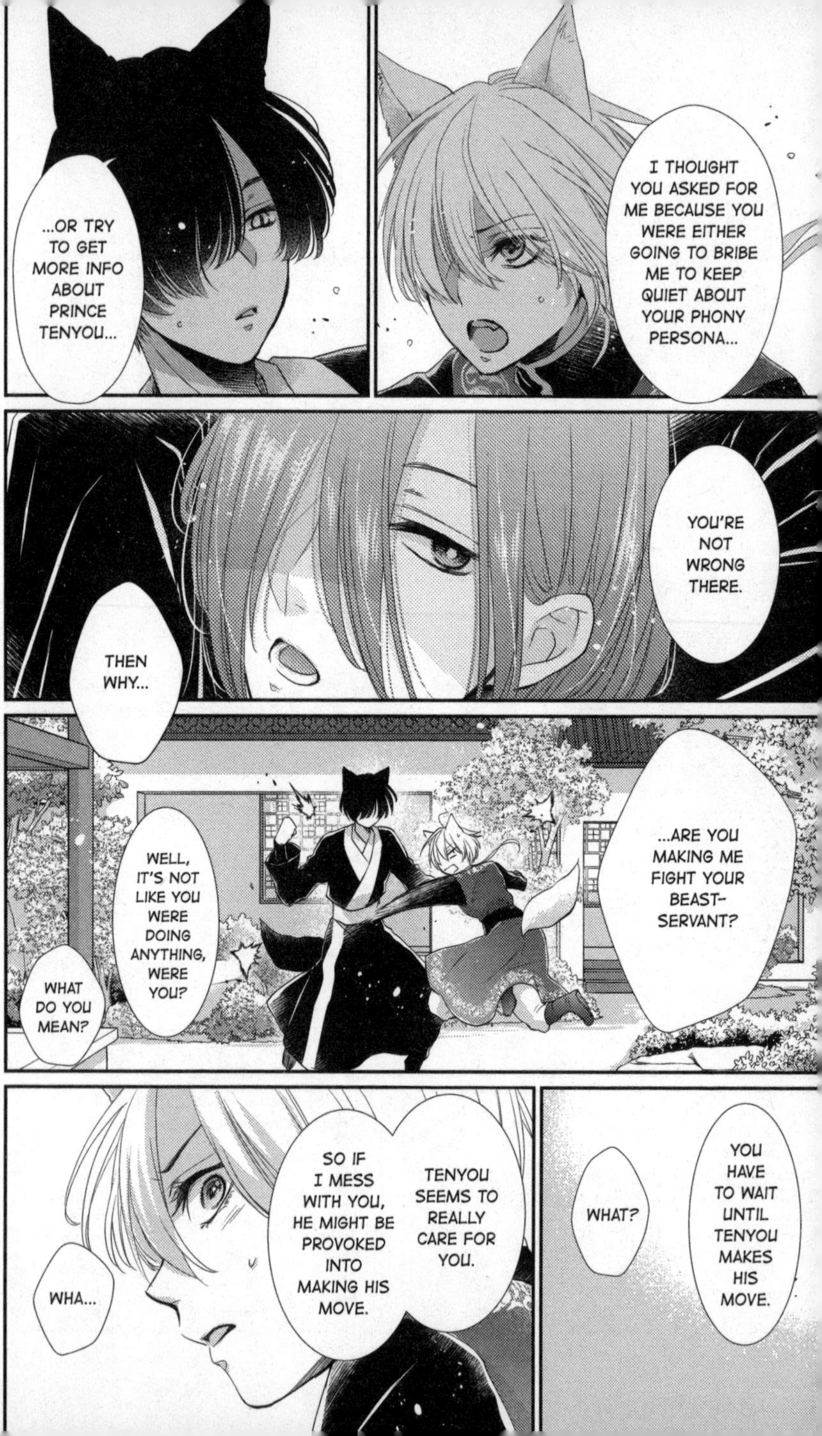
I THOUGHT YOU ASKED FOR ME BECAUSE YOU WERE EITHER GOING TO BRIBE ME TO KEEP QUIET ABOUT YOUR PHONY PERSONA...
...OR TRY TO GET MORE INFO ABOUT PRINCE TENYOU...
YOU'RE NOT WRONG THERE.
THEN WHY...
...ARE YOU MAKING ME FIGHT YOUR BEAST-SERVANT?
WELL, IT'S NOT LIKE YOU WERE DOING ANYTHING, WERE YOU?
WHAT DO YOU MEAN?
YOU HAVE TO WAIT UNTIL TENYOU MAKES HIS MOVE.
WHAT?
TENYOU SEEMS TO REALLY CARE FOR YOU.
SO IF I MESS WITH YOU, HE MIGHT BE PROVOKED INTO MAKING HIS MOVE.
WHA...

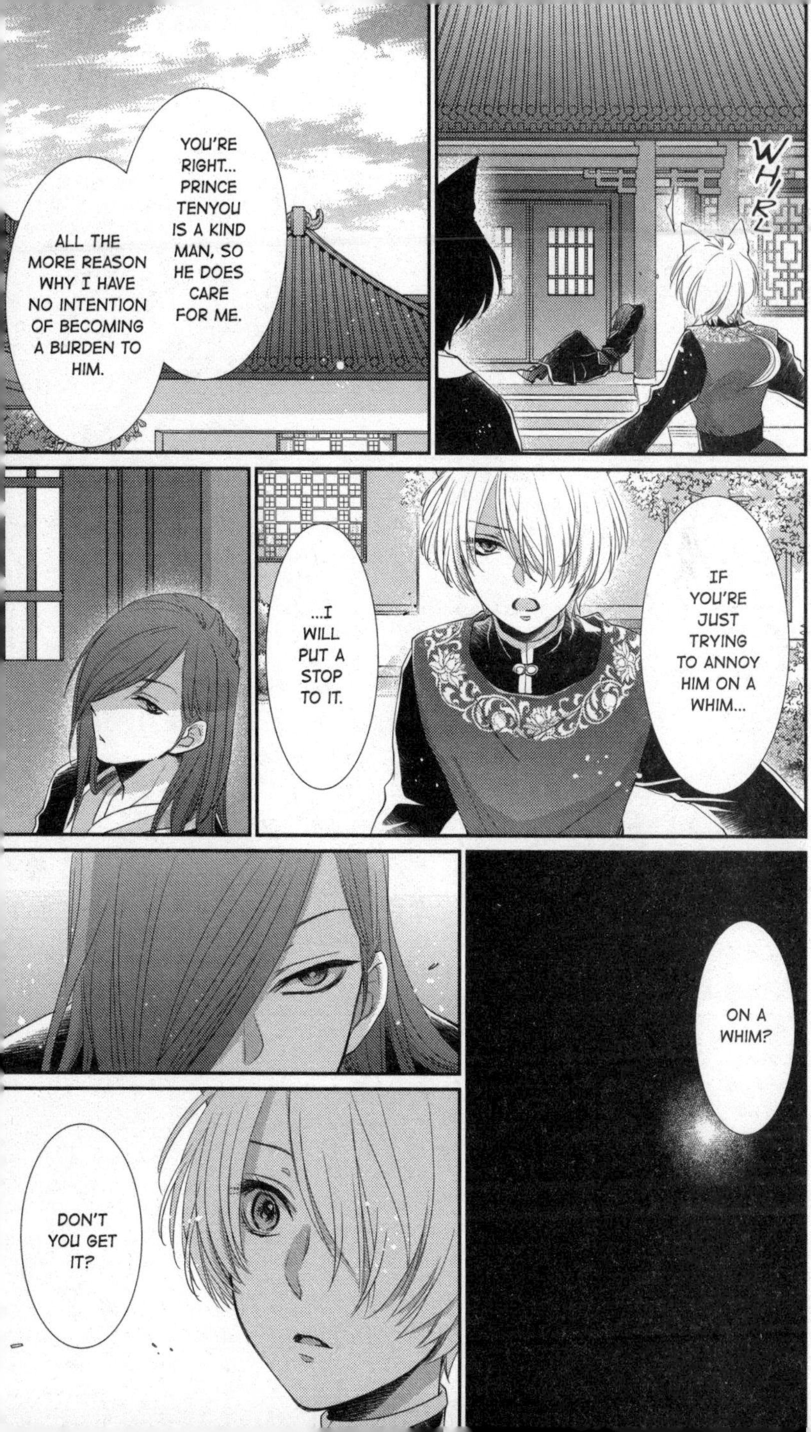
WHIRL
YOU'RE RIGHT... PRINCE TENYOU IS A KIND MAN, SO HE DOES CARE FOR ME.
ALL THE MORE REASON WHY I HAVE NO INTENTION OF BECOMING A BURDEN TO HIM.
IF YOU'RE JUST TRYING TO ANNOY HIM ON A WHIM...
...I WILL PUT A STOP TO IT.
ON A WHIM?
DON'T YOU GET IT?

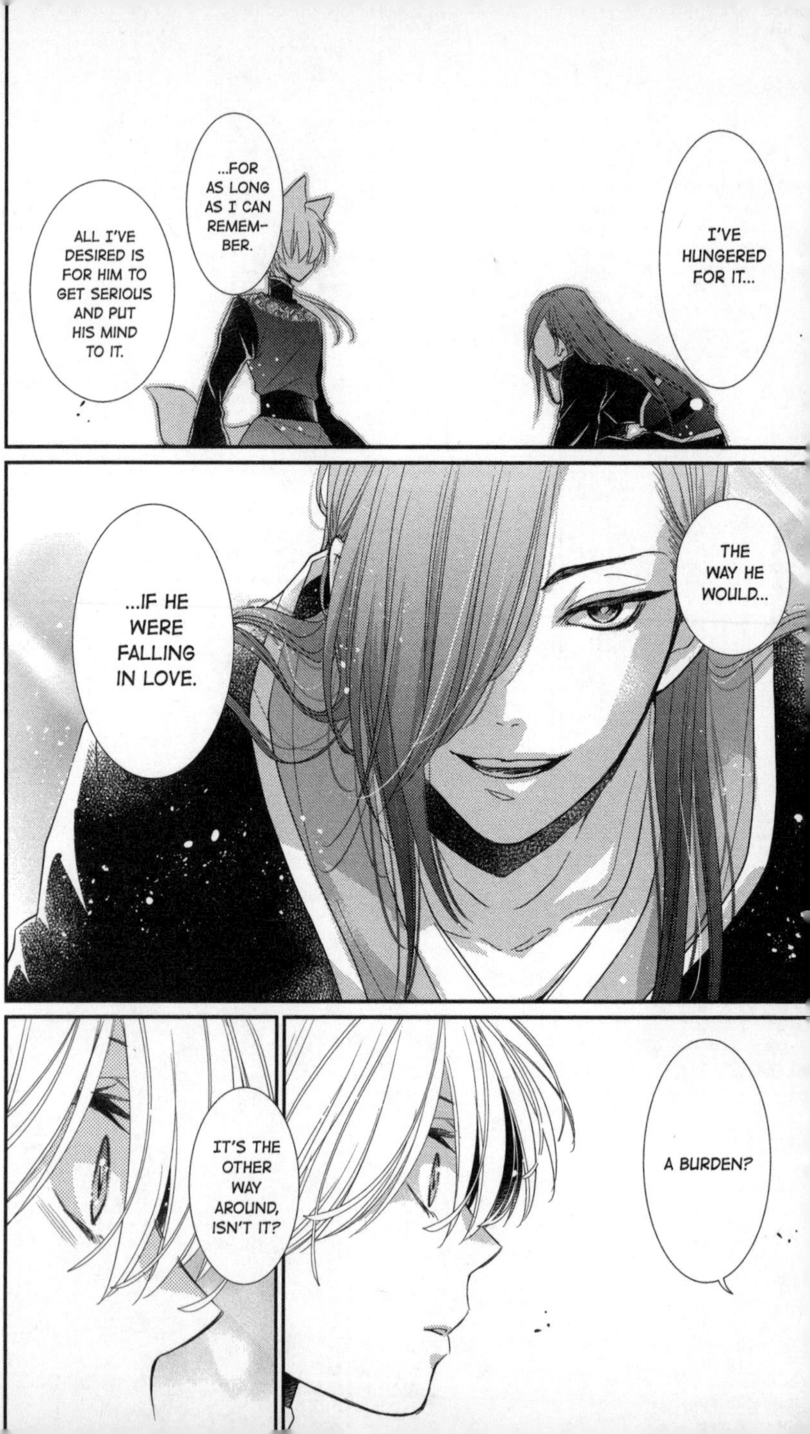

I'VE HUNGERED FOR IT...
...FOR AS LONG AS I CAN REMEMBER.
ALL I'VE DESIRED IS FOR HIM TO GET SERIOUS AND PUT HIS MIND TO IT.
THE WAY HE WOULD...
...IF HE WERE FALLING IN LOVE.
A BURDEN?
IT'S THE OTHER WAY AROUND, ISN'T IT?

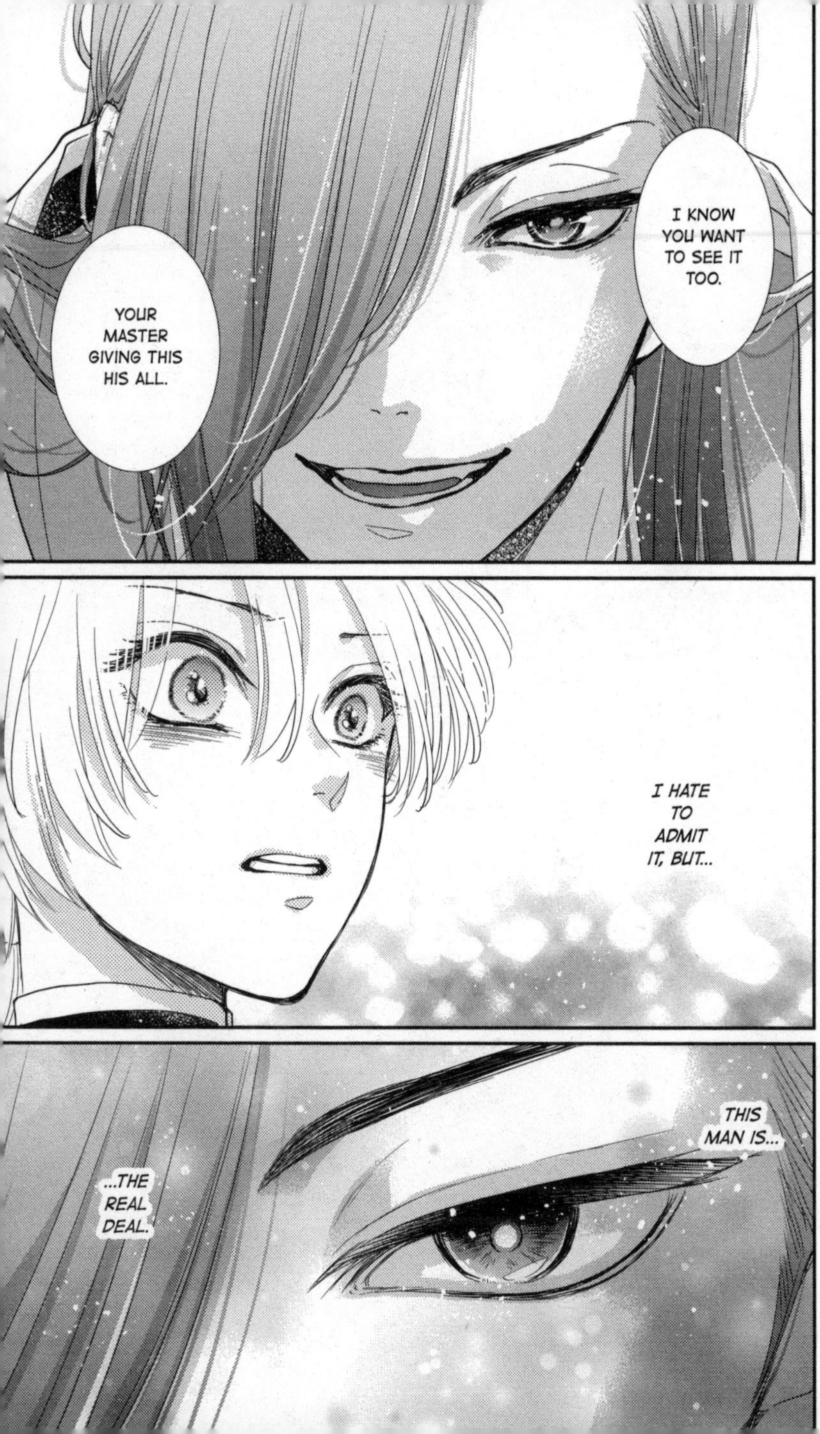
I KNOW YOU WANT TO SEE IT TOO.
YOUR MASTER GIVING THIS HIS ALL.
I HATE TO ADMIT IT, BUT...
THIS MAN IS...
...THE REAL DEAL.

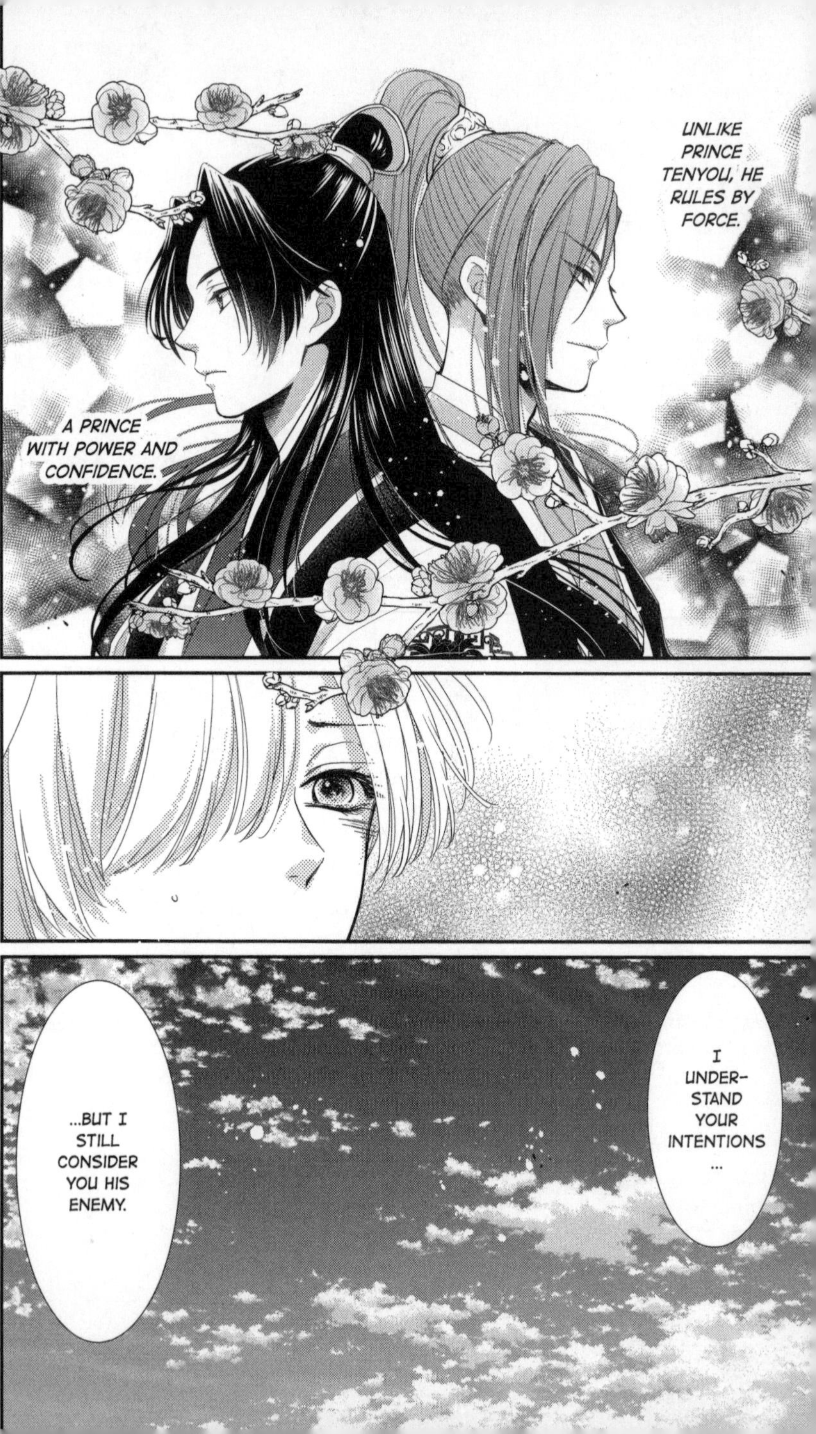
UNLIKE PRINCE TENYOU, HE RULES BY FORCE.
A PRINCE WITH POWER AND CONFIDENCE.
I UNDER-STAND YOUR INTENTIONS ...
...BUT I STILL CONSIDER YOU HIS ENEMY.

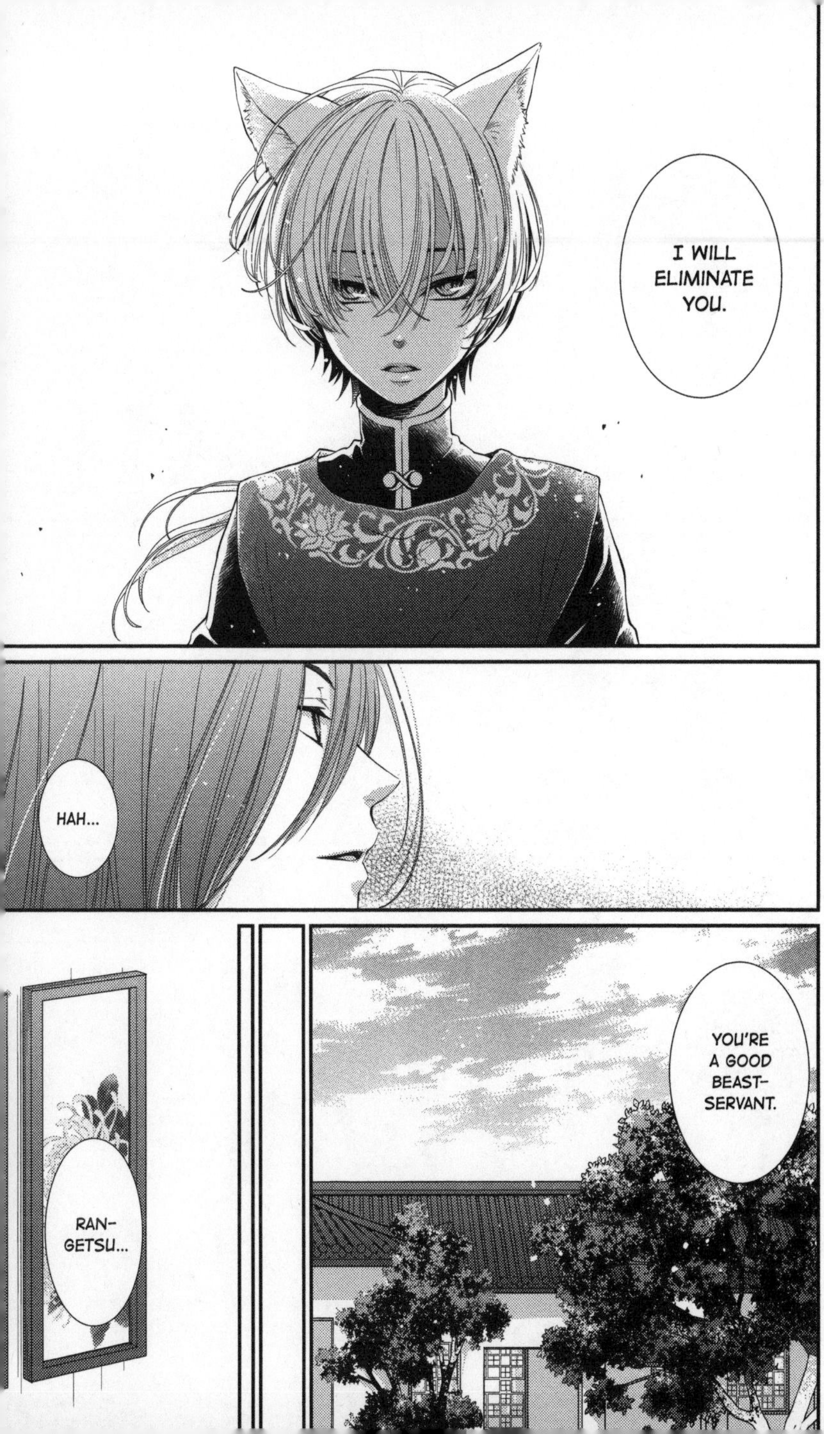
I WILL ELIMINATE YOU.
HAH...
YOU'RE A GOOD BEAST-SERVANT.
RAN-GETSU...

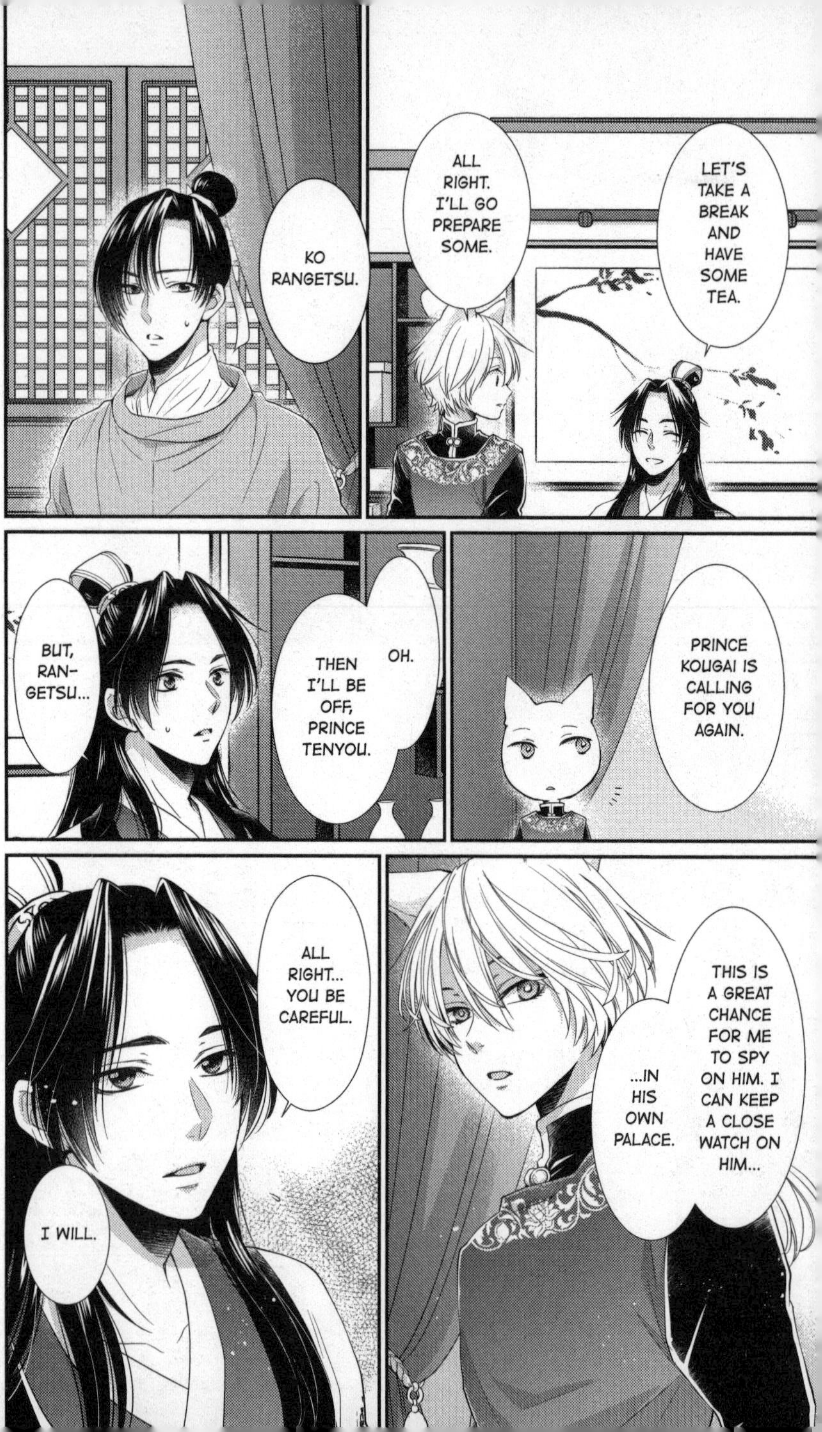
LET'S TAKE A BREAK AND HAVE SOME TEA.
ALL RIGHT. I'LL GO PREPARE SOME.
KO RANGETSU.
PRINCE KOUGAI IS CALLING FOR YOU AGAIN.
OH.
THEN I'LL BE OFF, PRINCE TENYOU.
BUT, RAN-GETSU...
THIS IS A GREAT CHANCE FOR ME TO SPY ON HIM. I CAN KEEP A CLOSE WATCH ON HIM...
...IN HIS OWN PALACE.
ALL RIGHT... YOU BE CAREFUL.
I WILL.

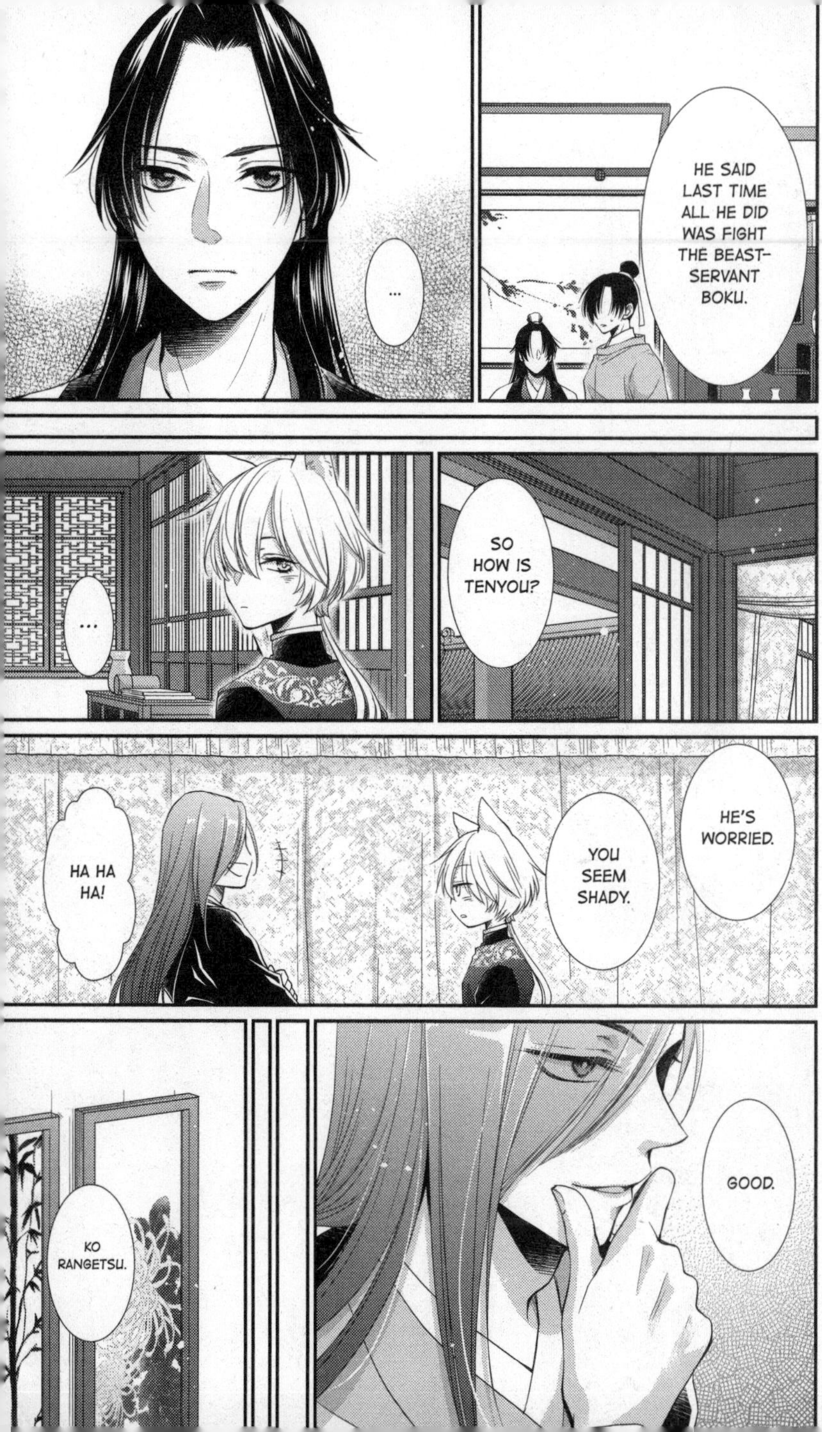
HE SAID LAST TIME ALL HE DID WAS FIGHT THE BEAST-SERVANT BOKU.
...
SO HOW IS TENYOU?
...
HE'S WORRIED.
YOU SEEM SHADY.
HA HA HA!
GOOD.
KO RANGETSU.

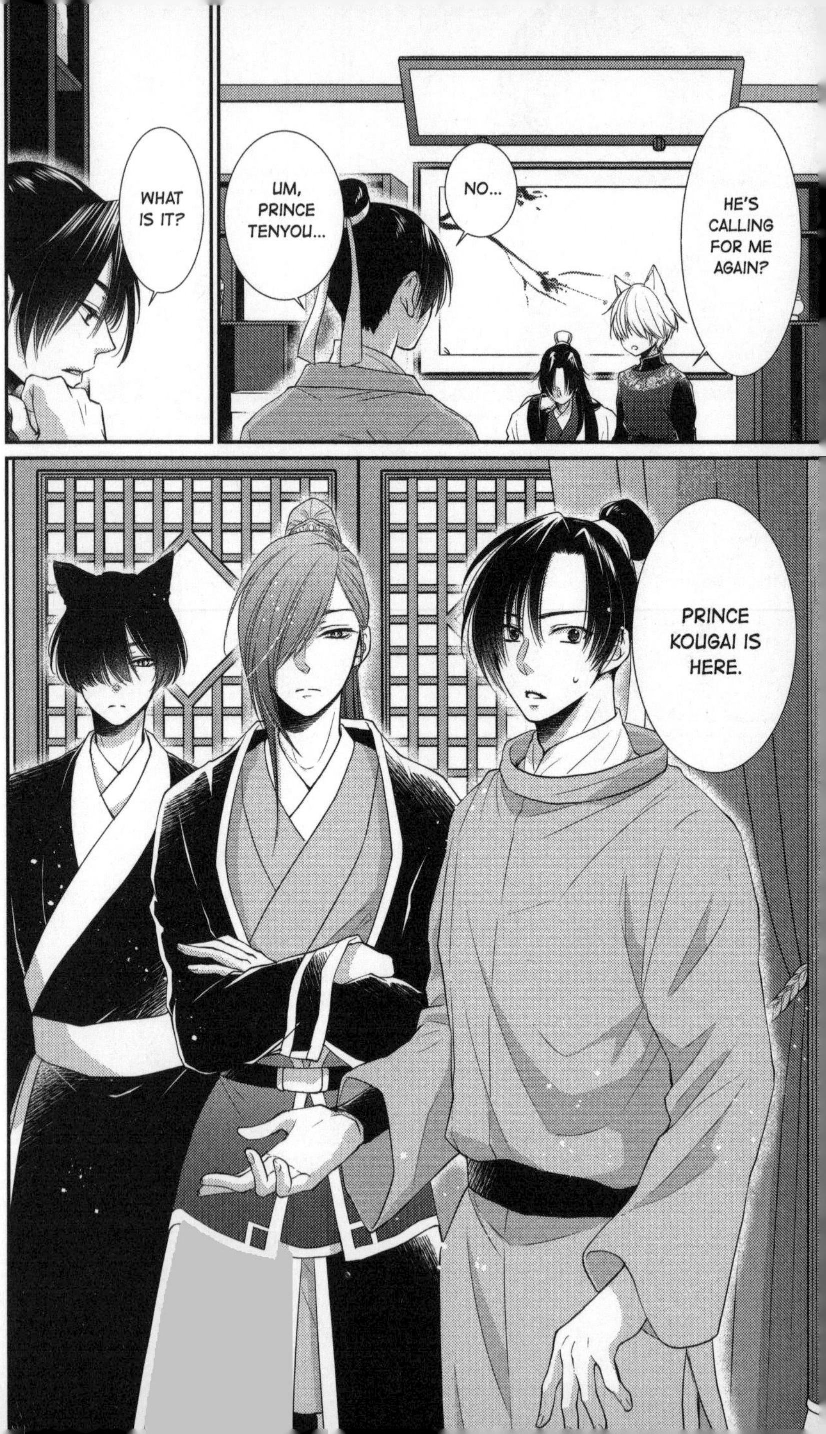
HE'S CALLING FOR ME AGAIN?
NO...
UM, PRINCE TENYOU...
WHAT IS IT?
PRINCE KOUGAI IS HERE.

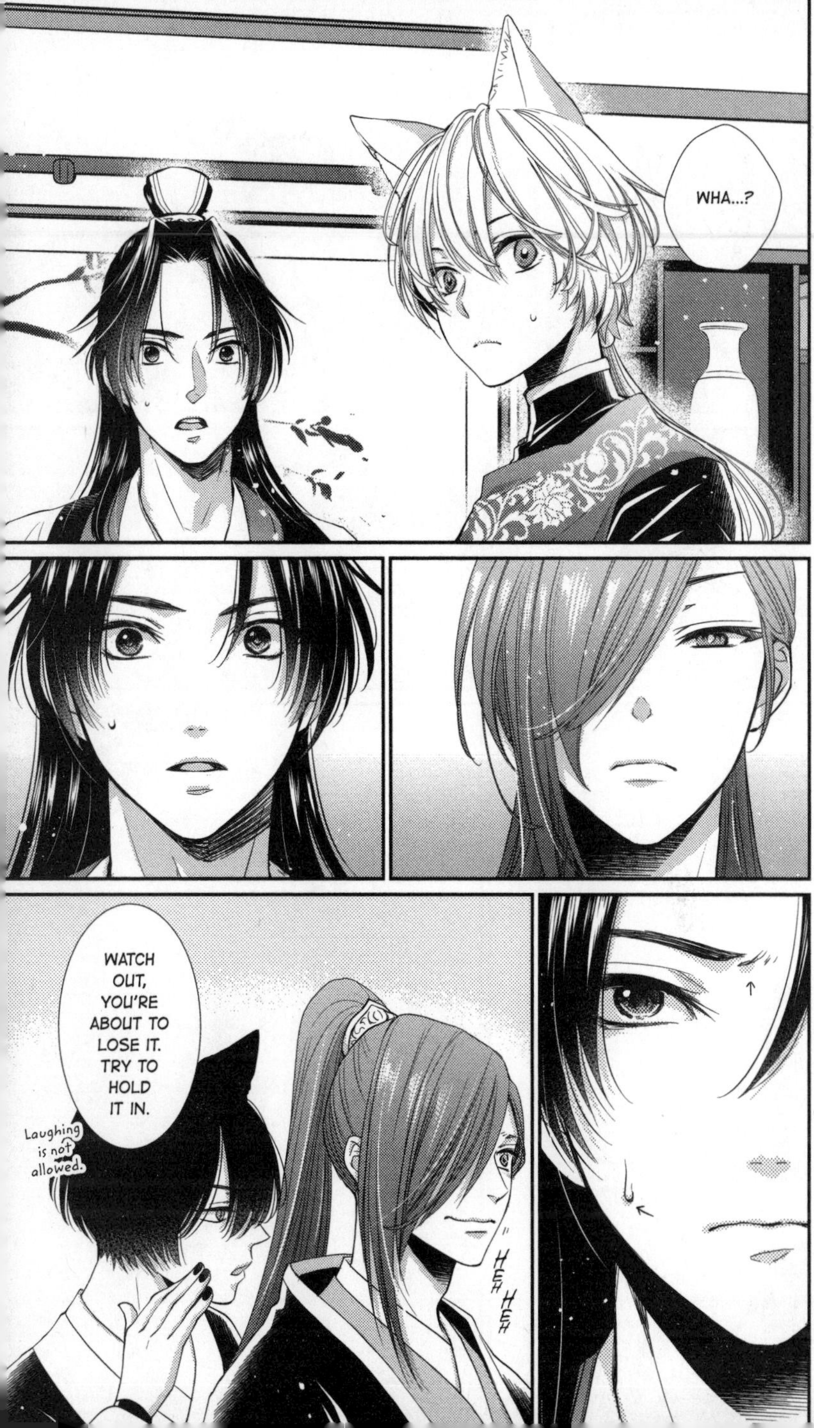
WHA...?
WATCH OUT, YOU'RE ABOUT TO LOSE IT. TRY TO HOLD IT IN.
HEH HEH
Laughing is not allowed.

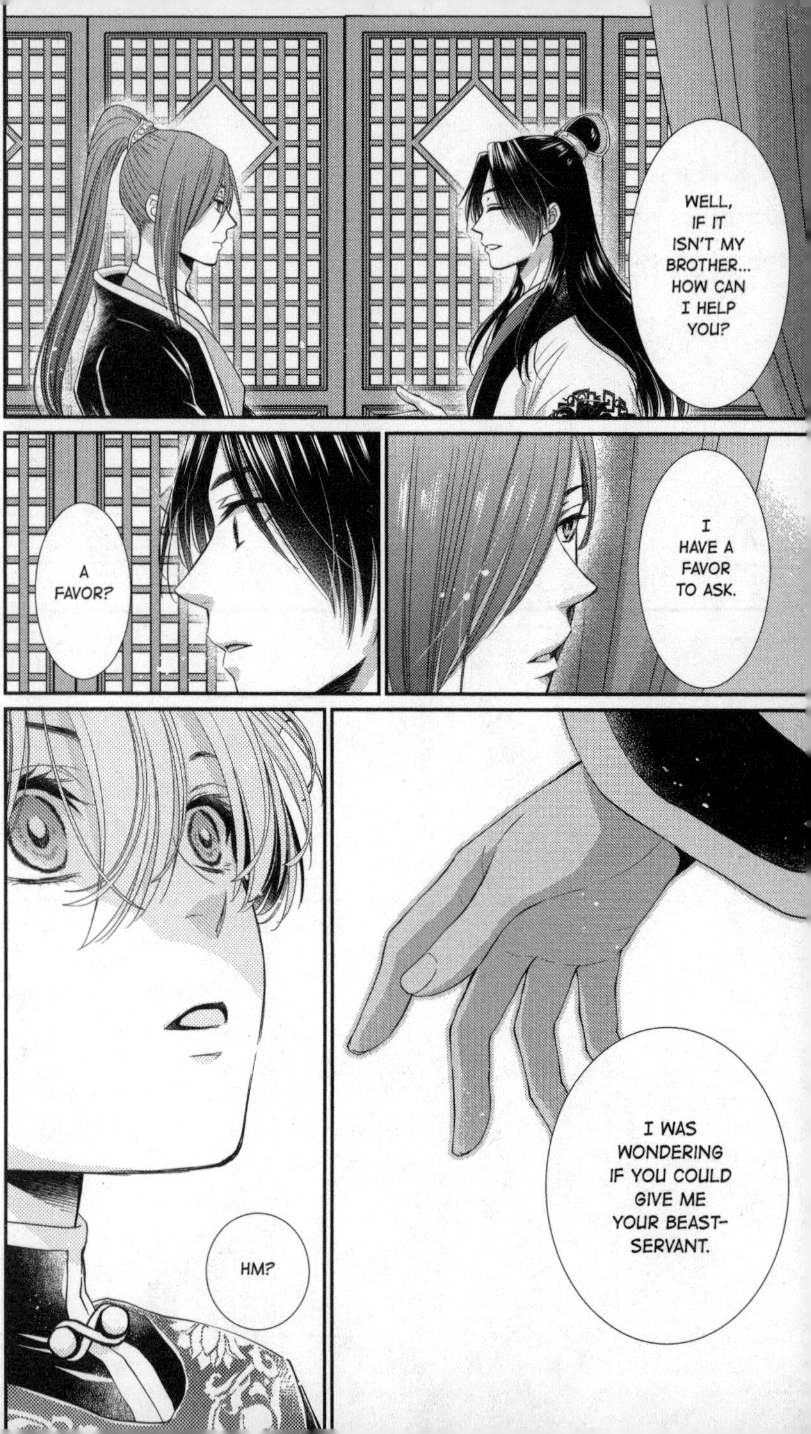
WELL, IF IT ISN'T MY BROTHER... HOW CAN I HELP YOU?
I HAVE A FAVOR TO ASK.
A FAVOR?
I WAS WONDERING IF YOU COULD GIVE ME YOUR BEAST-SERVANT.
HM?

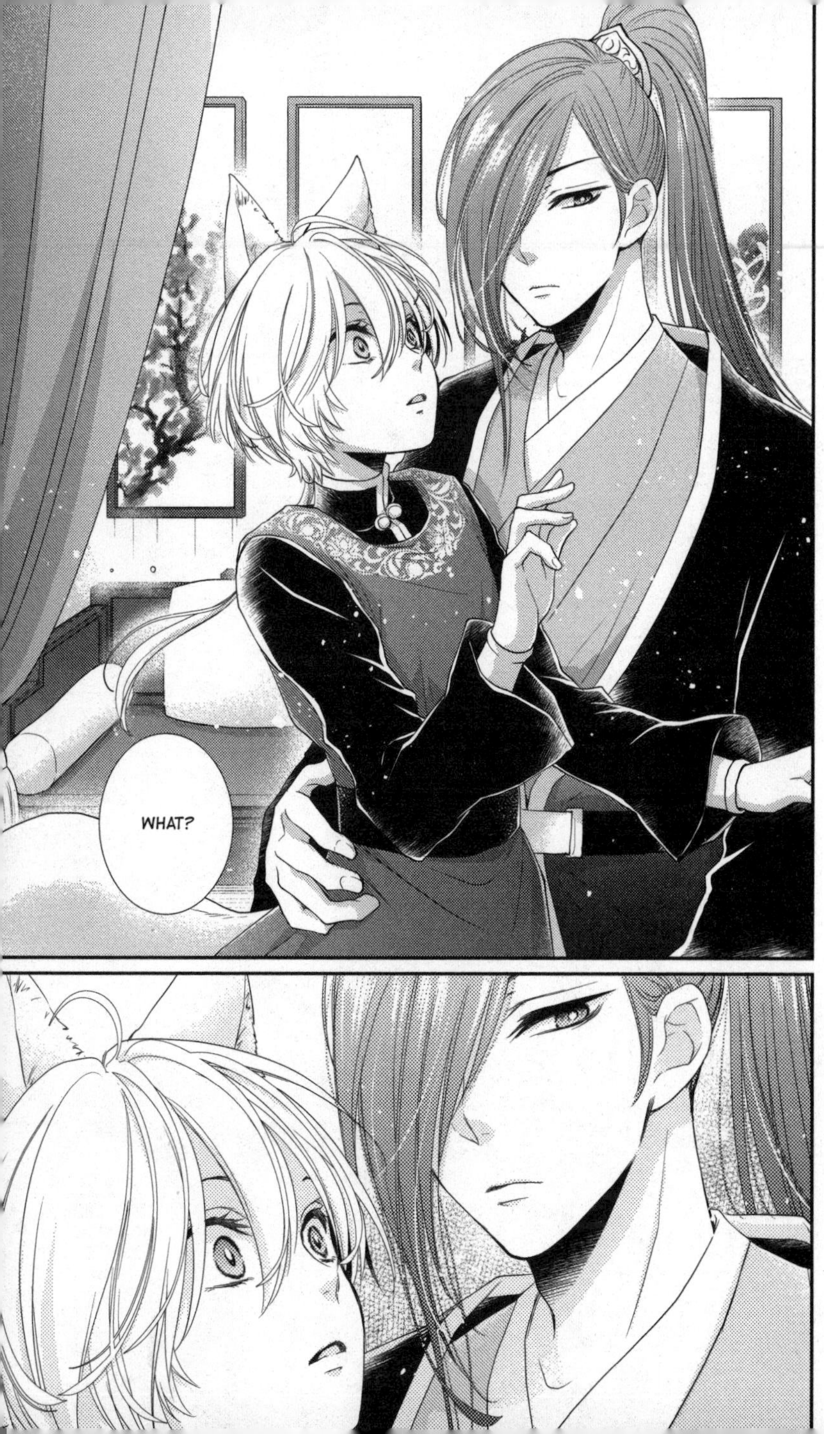
WHAT?

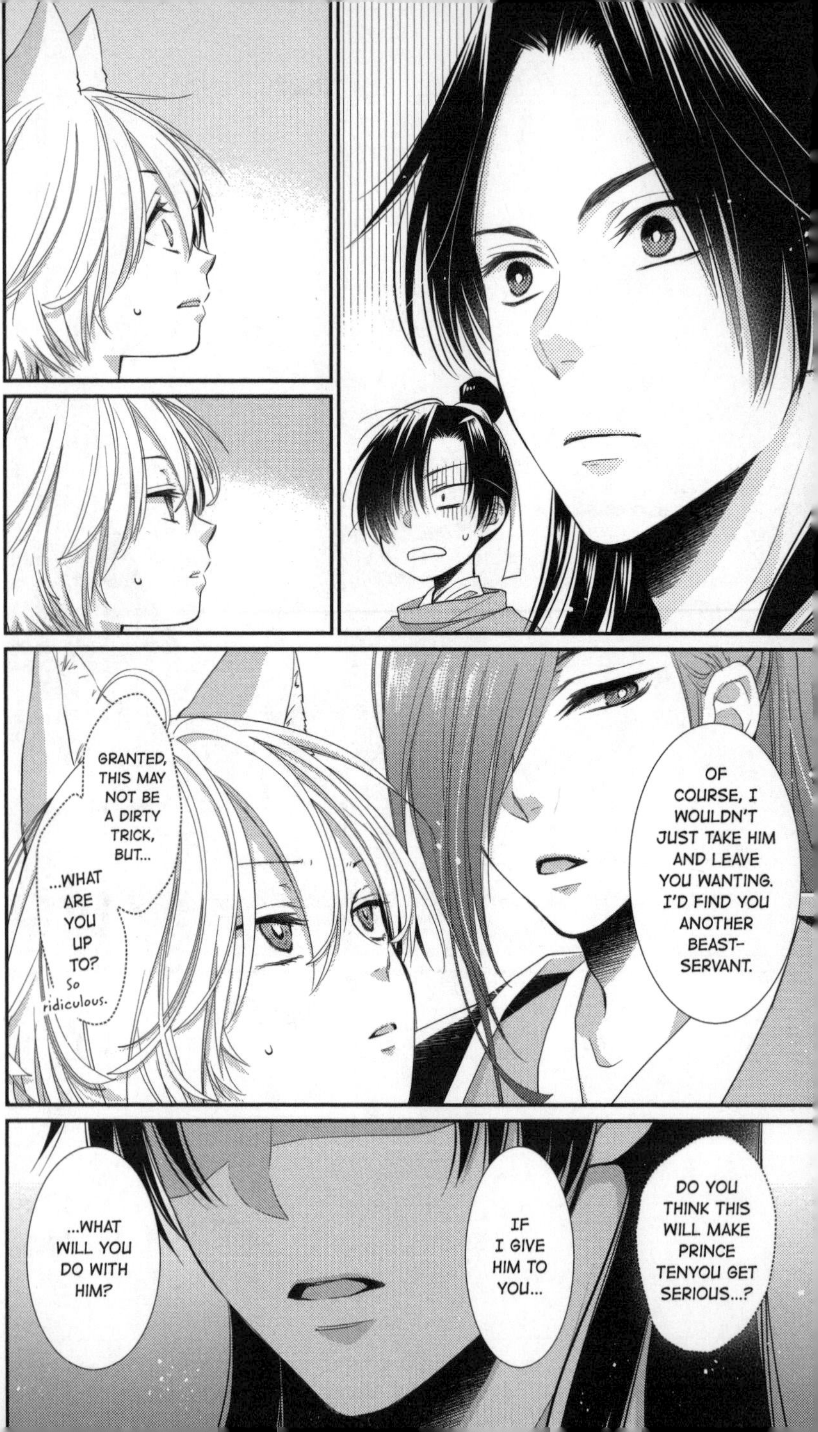
OF COURSE, I WOULDN'T JUST TAKE HIM AND LEAVE YOU WANTING. I'D FIND YOU ANOTHER BEAST-SERVANT.
GRANTED, THIS MAY NOT BE A DIRTY TRICK, BUT...
...WHAT ARE YOU UP TO?
So ridiculous.
DO YOU THINK THIS WILL MAKE PRINCE TENYOU GET SERIOUS...?
IF I GIVE HIM TO YOU...
...WHAT WILL YOU DO WITH HIM?

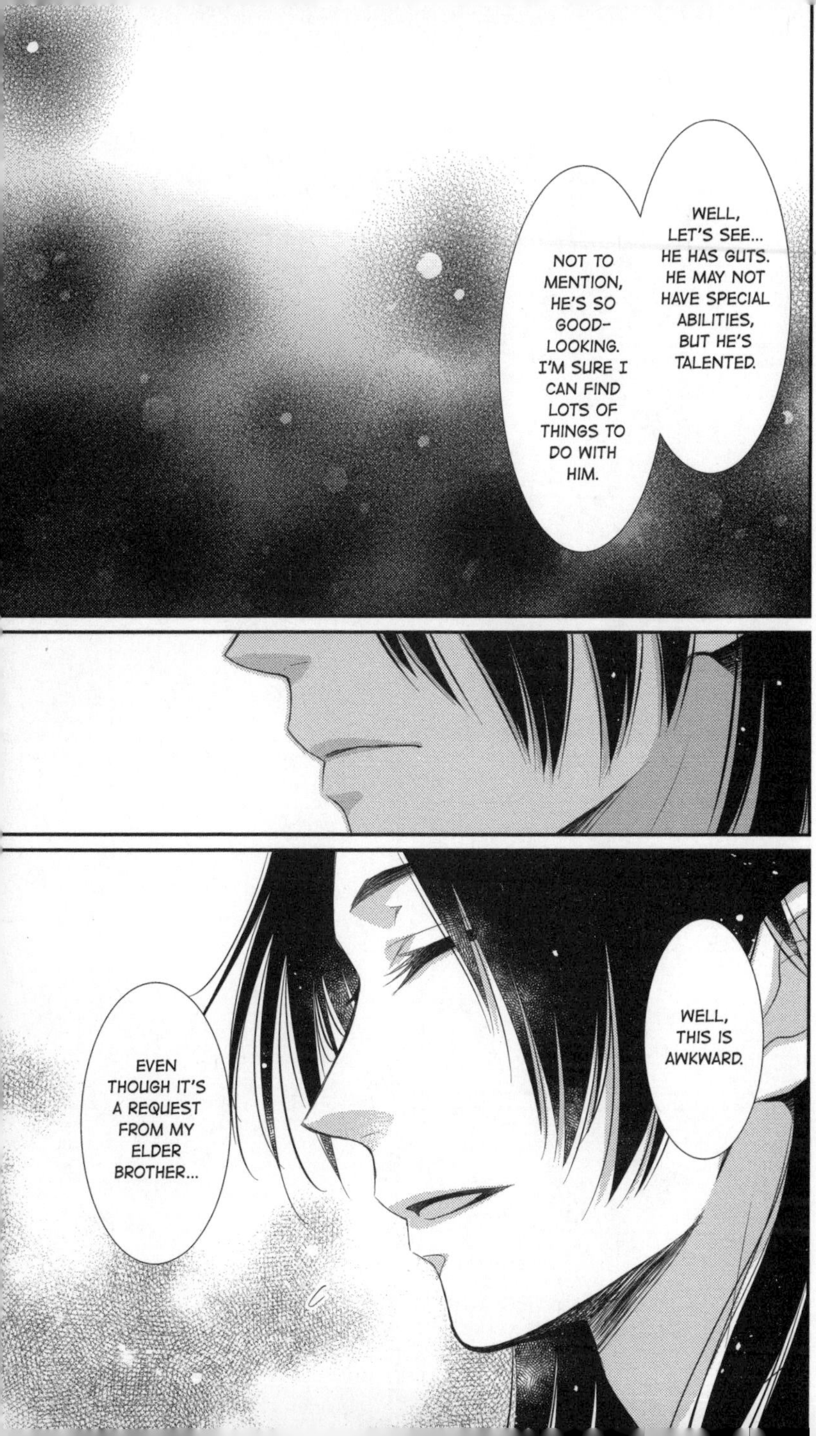
WELL, LET'S SEE... HE HAS GUTS. HE MAY NOT HAVE SPECIAL ABILITIES, BUT HE'S TALENTED.
NOT TO MENTION, HE'S SO GOOD-LOOKING. I'M SURE I CAN FIND LOTS OF THINGS TO DO WITH HIM.
WELL, THIS IS AWKWARD.
EVEN THOUGH IT'S A REQUEST FROM MY ELDER BROTHER...

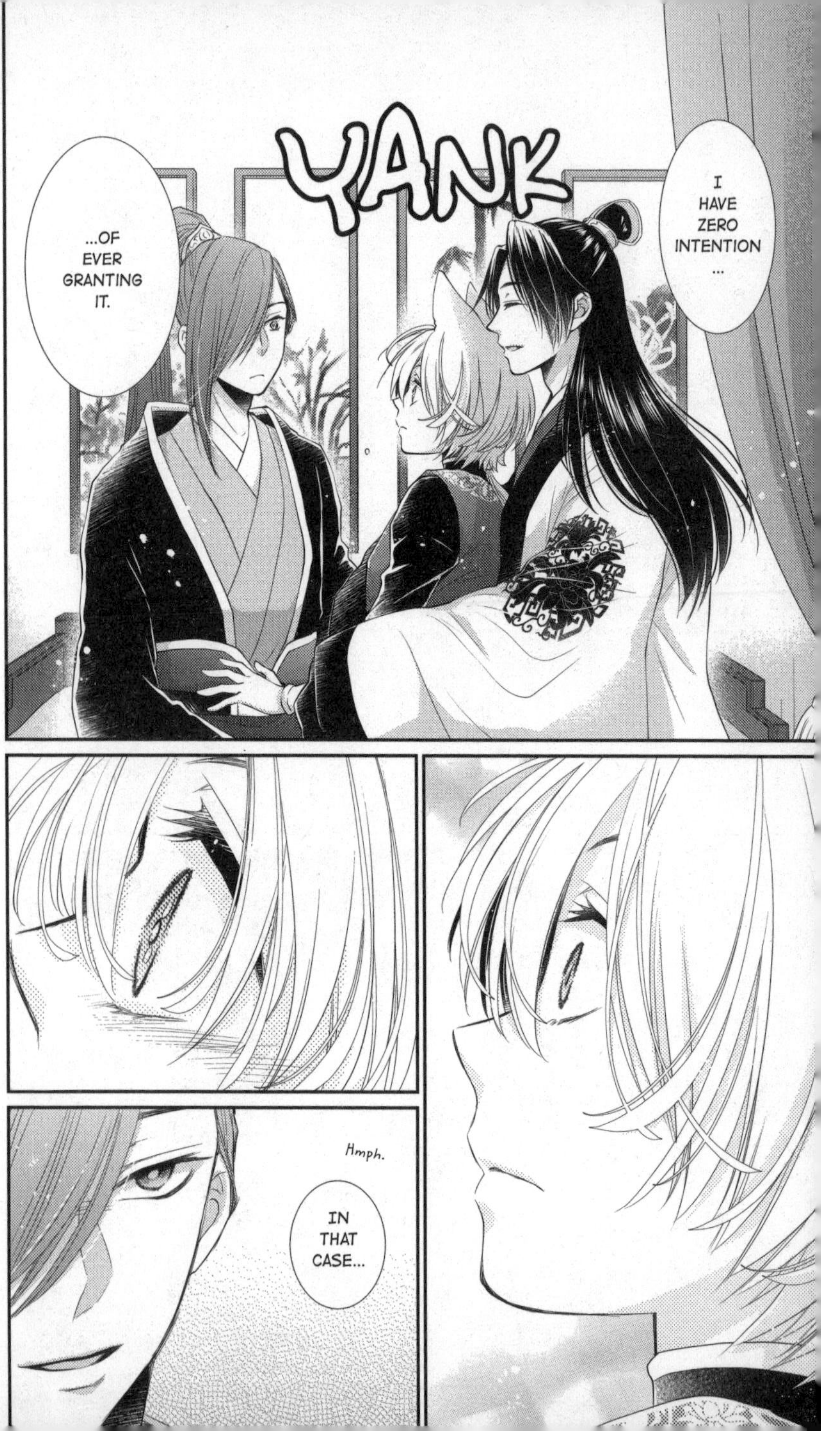
I HAVE ZERO INTENTION ...
YANK
...OF EVER GRANTING IT.
Hmph.
IN THAT CASE...

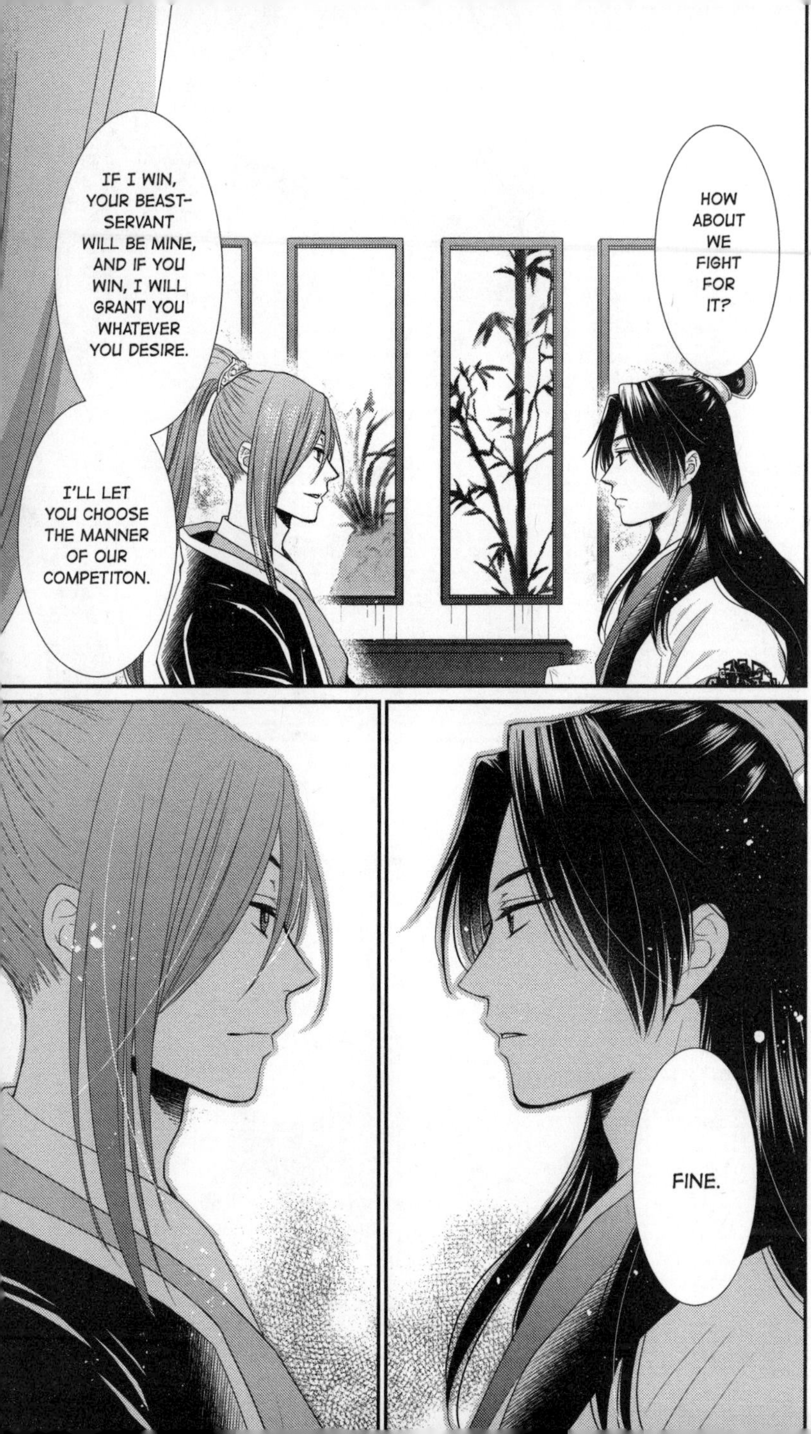
HOW ABOUT WE FIGHT FOR IT?
IF I WIN, YOUR BEAST-SERVANT WILL BE MINE, AND IF YOU WIN, I WILL GRANT YOU WHATEVER YOU DESIRE.
I'LL LET YOU CHOOSE THE MANNER OF OUR COMPETITON.
FINE.

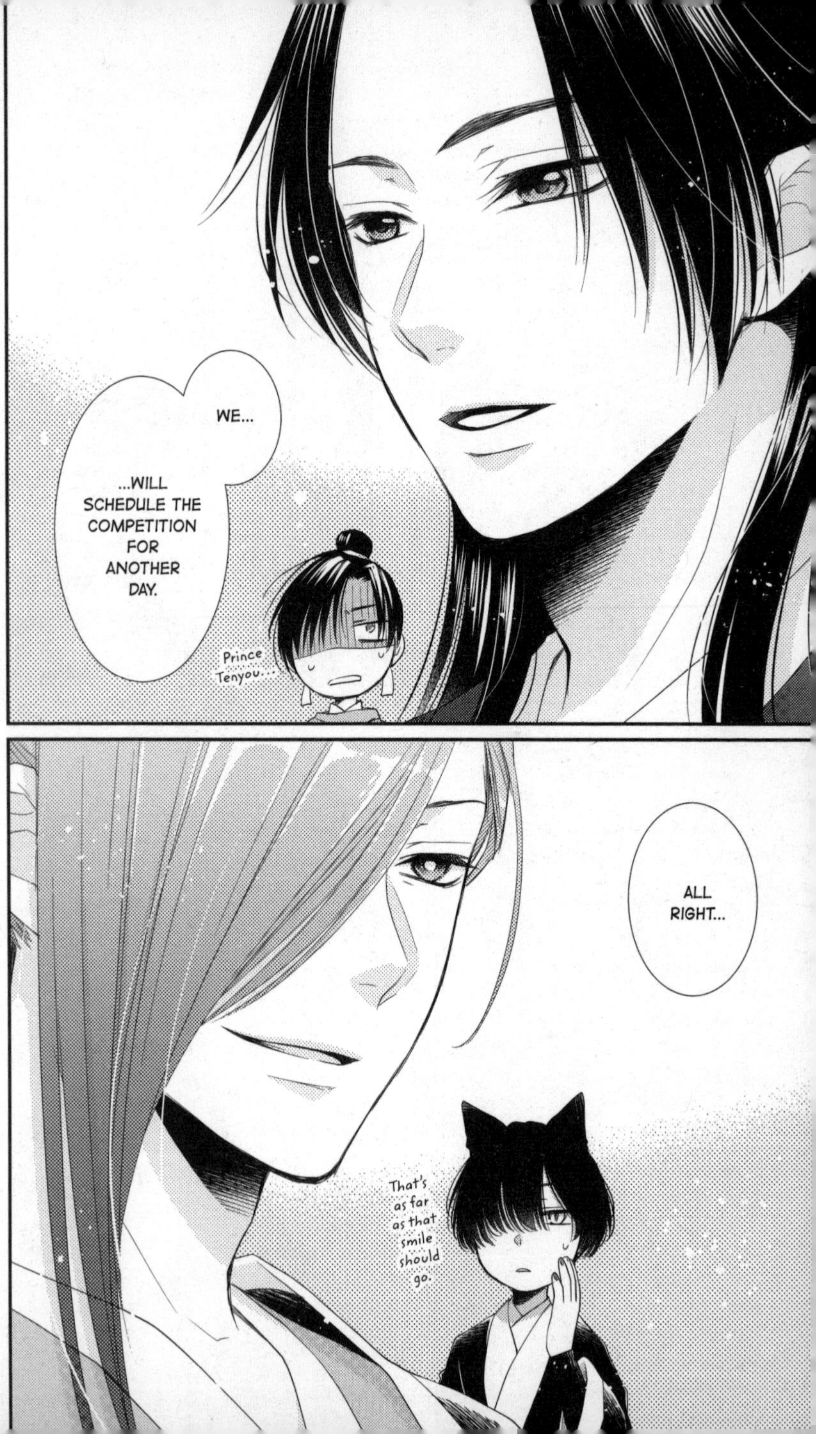
WE...
...WILL SCHEDULE THE COMPETITION FOR ANOTHER DAY.
Prince Tenyou...
ALL RIGHT...
That's as far as that smile should go.

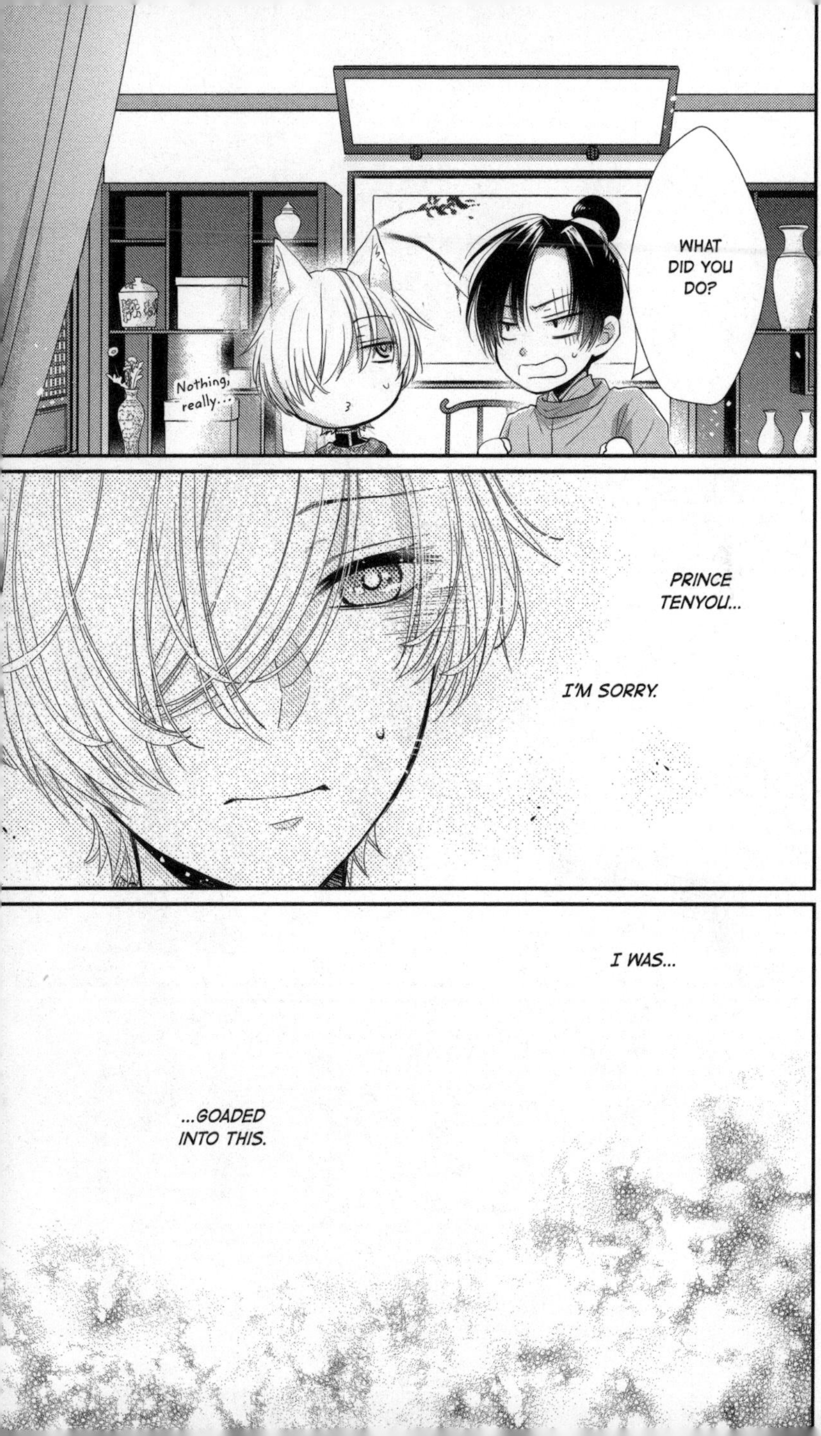
WHAT DID YOU DO?
Nothing, really...
PRINCE TENYOU...
I'M SORRY.
I WAS...
...GOADED INTO THIS.

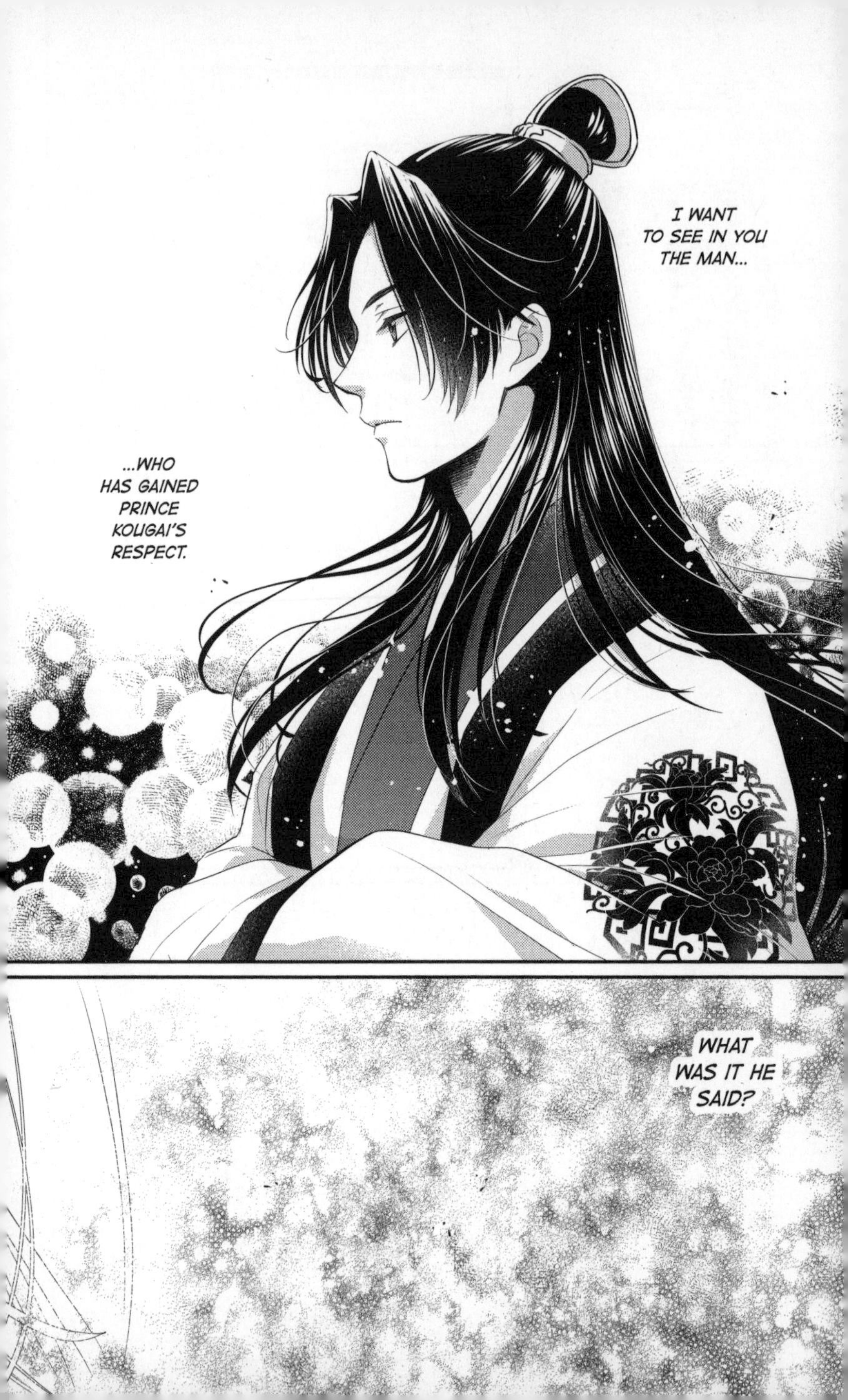
I WANT TO SEE IN YOU THE MAN...
...WHO HAS GAINED PRINCE KOUGAI'S RESPECT.
WHAT WAS IT HE SAID?

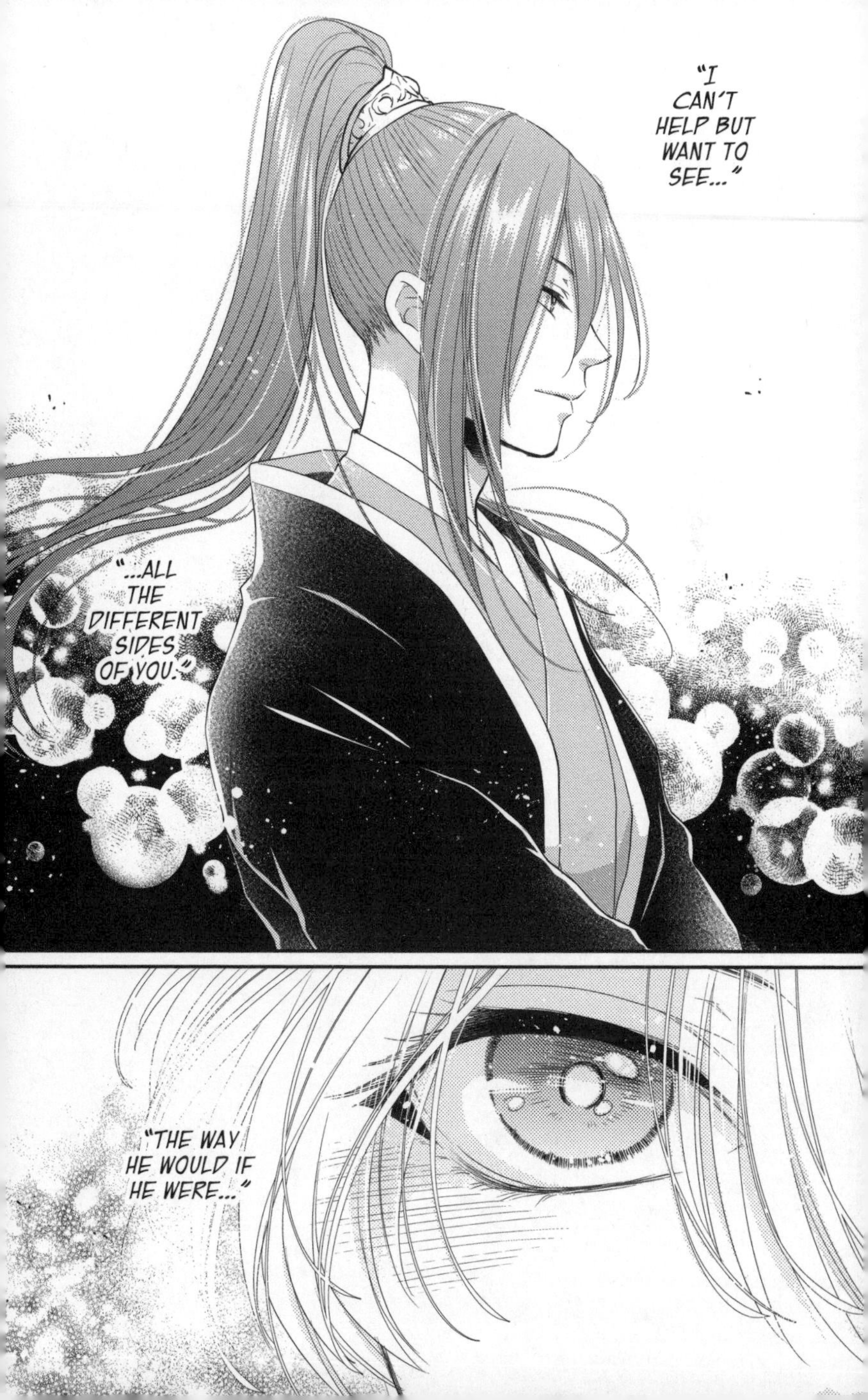
"I CAN'T HELP BUT WANT TO SEE..."
"...ALL THE DIFFERENT SIDES OF YOU."
"THE WAY HE WOULD IF HE WERE..."

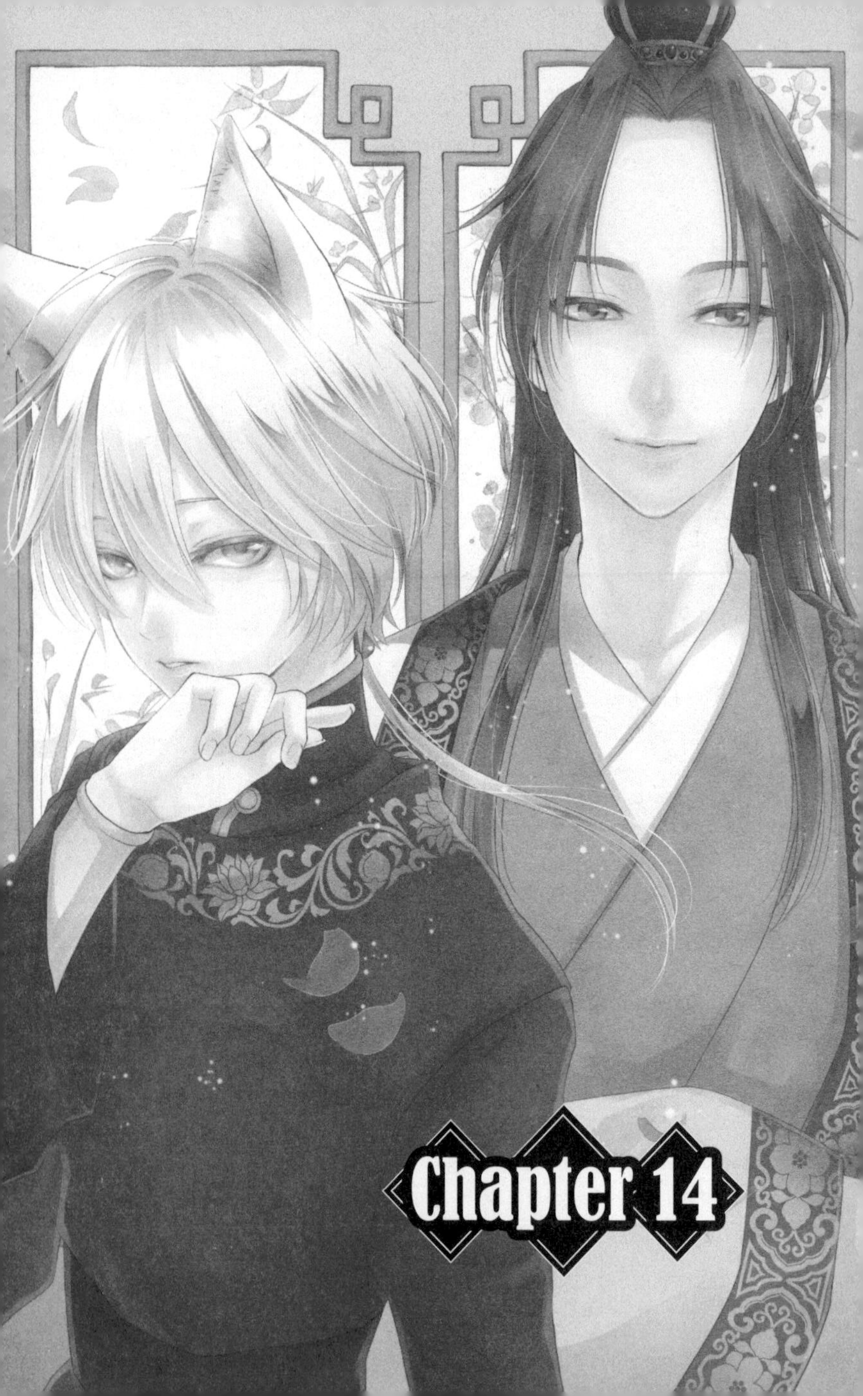
Chapter 14

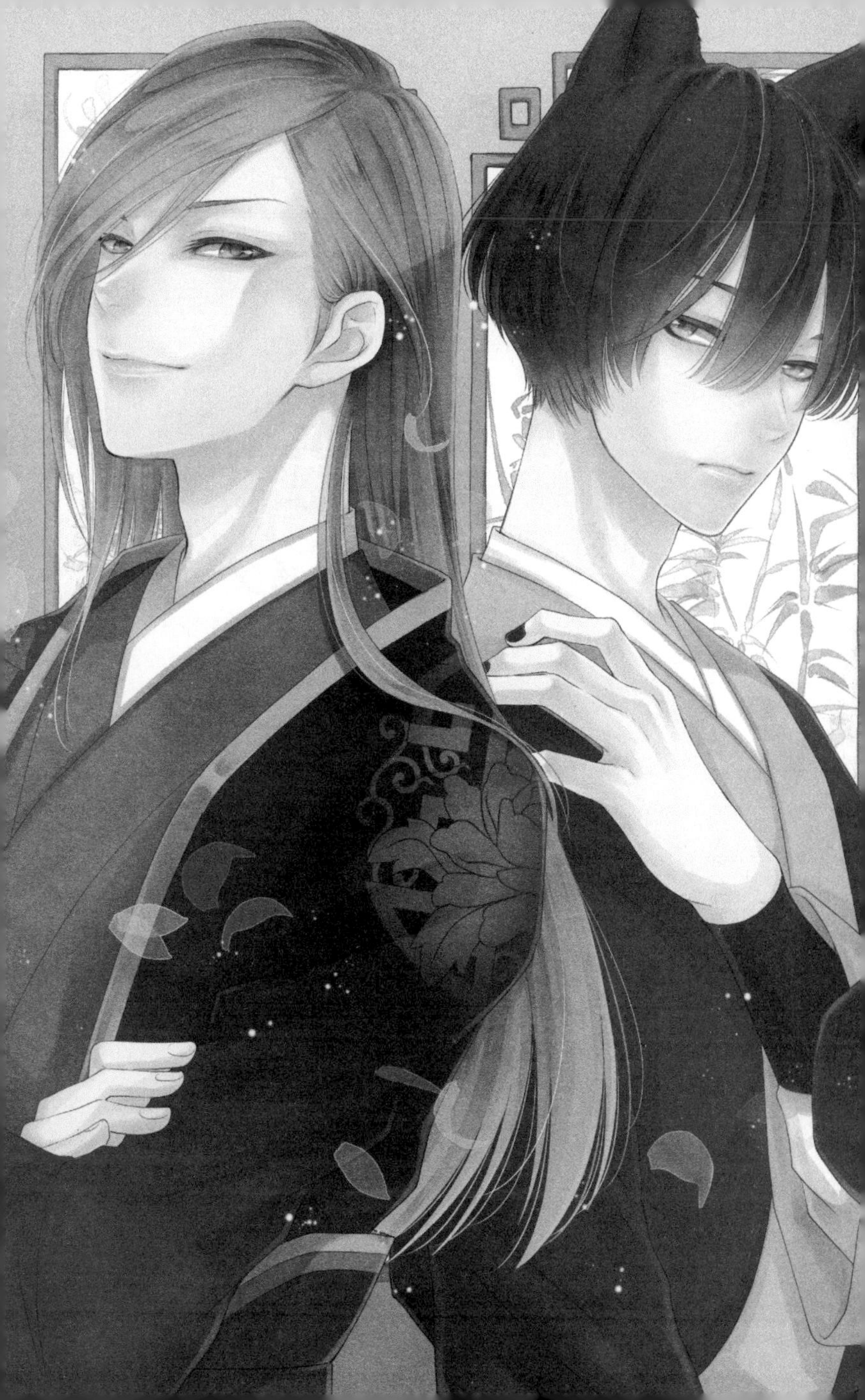

THE
KING'S
Beast

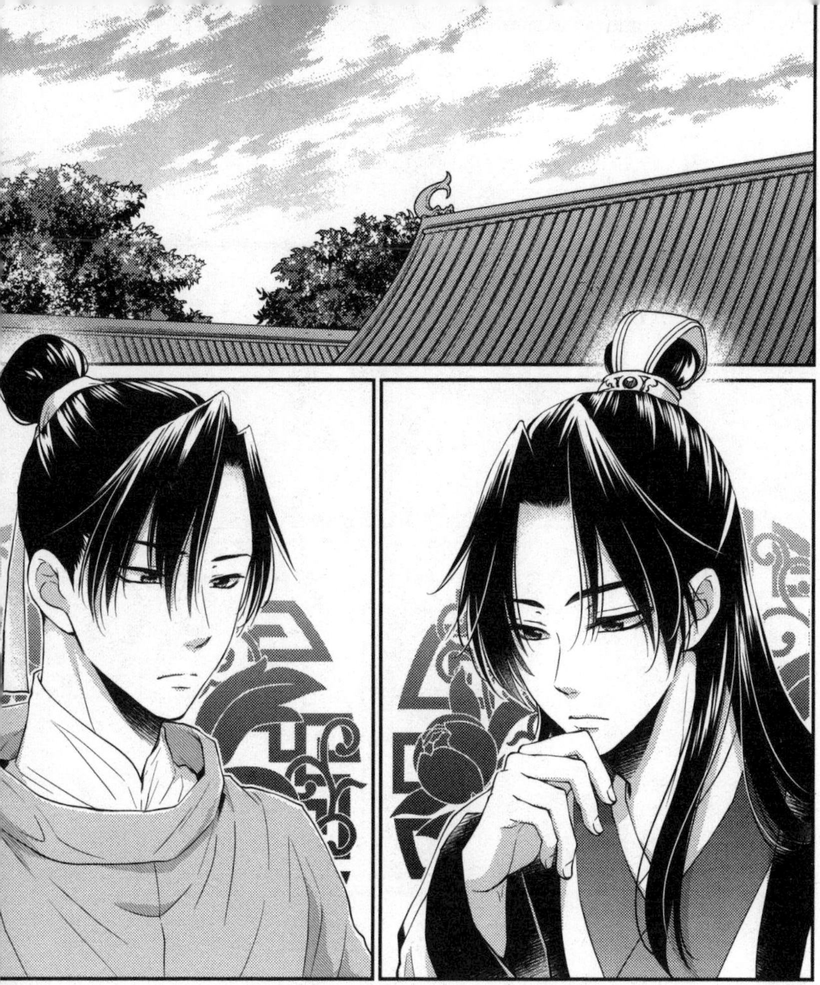

THE KING'S Beast

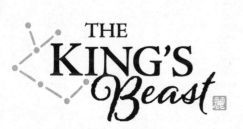

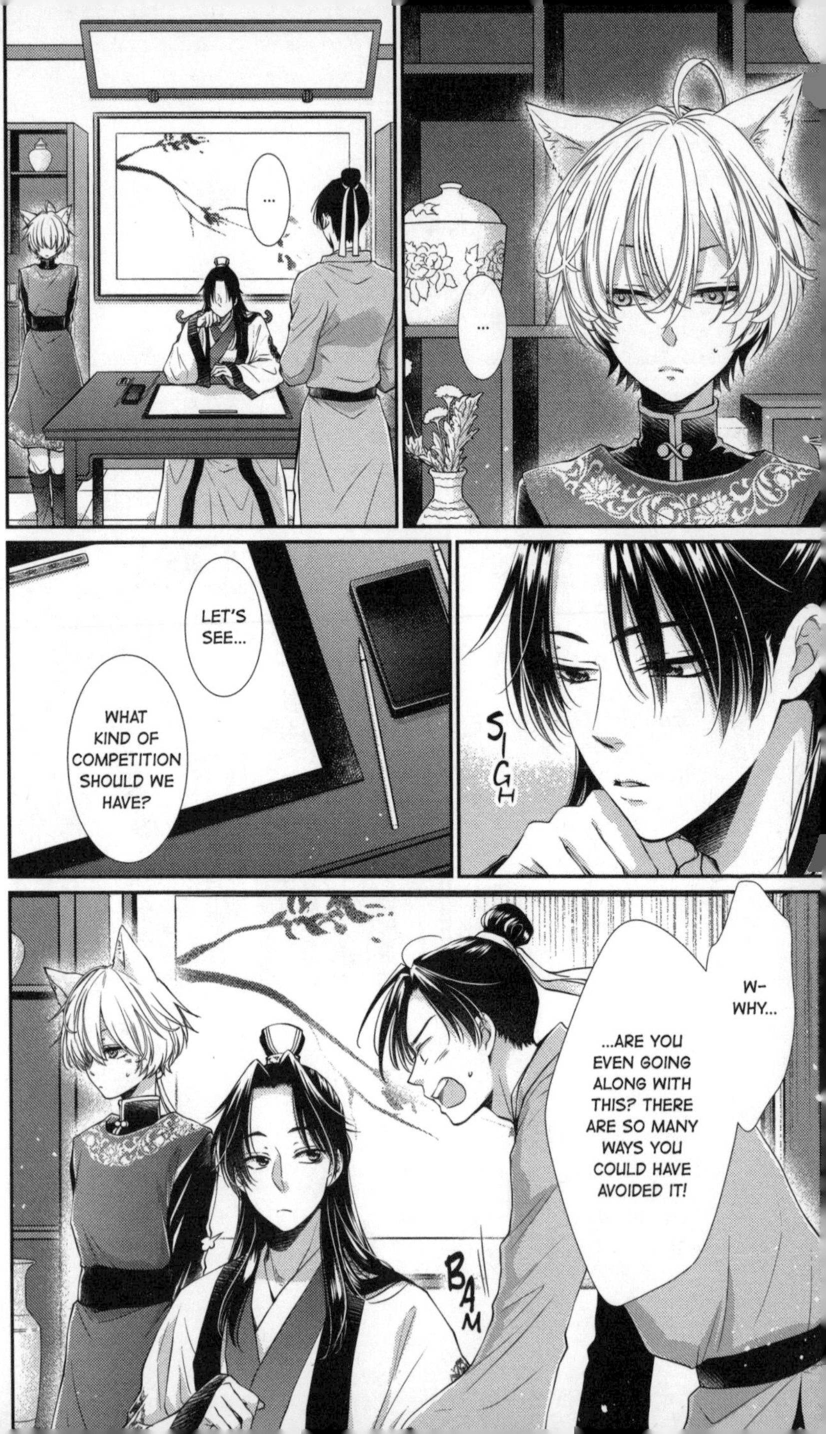
...
...
SIGH
LET'S SEE...
WHAT KIND OF COMPETITION SHOULD WE HAVE?
W-WHY...
...ARE YOU EVEN GOING ALONG WITH THIS? THERE ARE SO MANY WAYS YOU COULD HAVE AVOIDED IT!
BAM

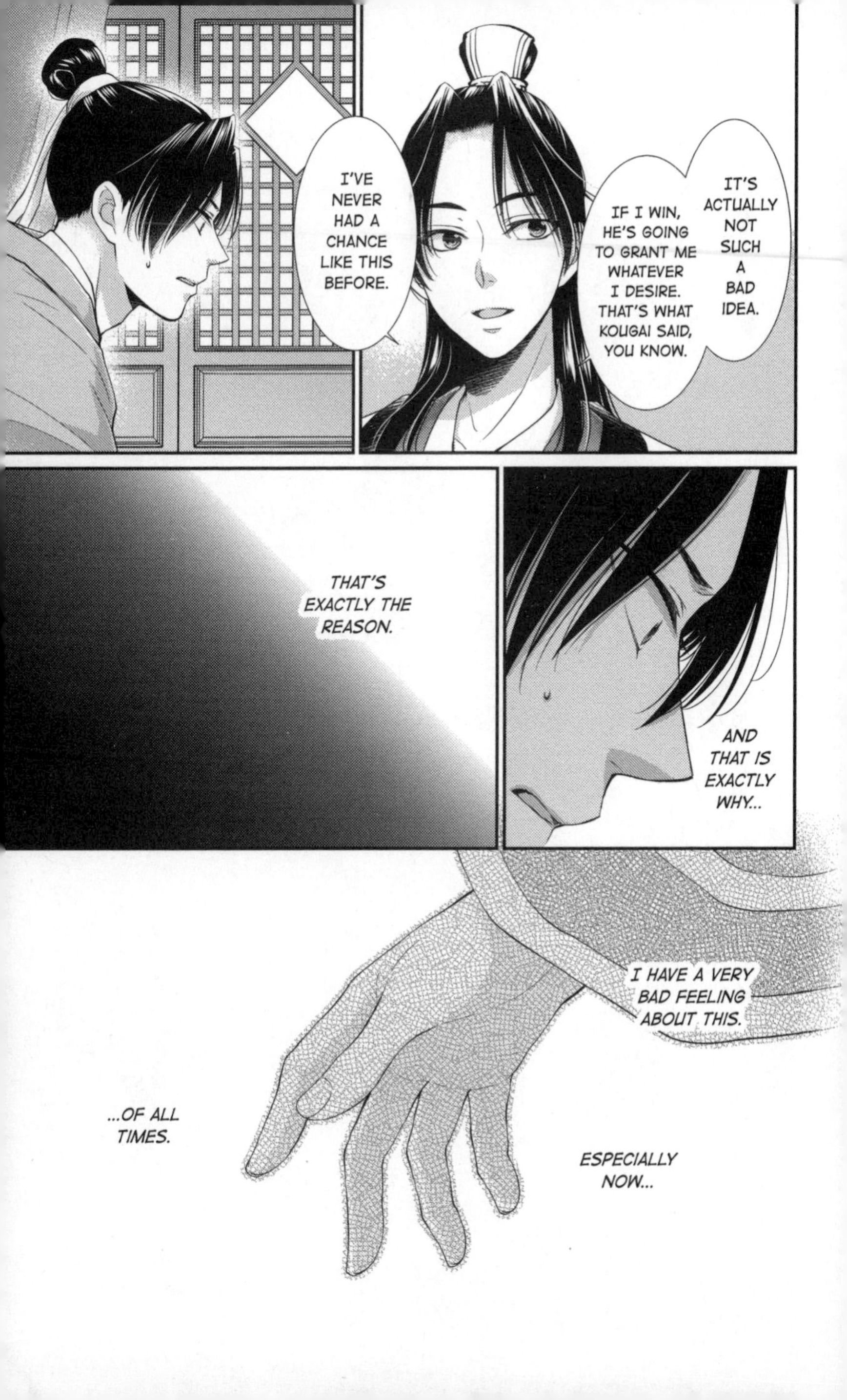
IT'S ACTUALLY NOT SUCH A BAD IDEA.
IF I WIN, HE'S GOING TO GRANT ME WHATEVER I DESIRE. THAT'S WHAT KOUGAI SAID, YOU KNOW.
I'VE NEVER HAD A CHANCE LIKE THIS BEFORE.
AND THAT IS EXACTLY WHY...
THAT'S EXACTLY THE REASON.
I HAVE A VERY BAD FEELING ABOUT THIS.
ESPECIALLY NOW...
...OF ALL TIMES.

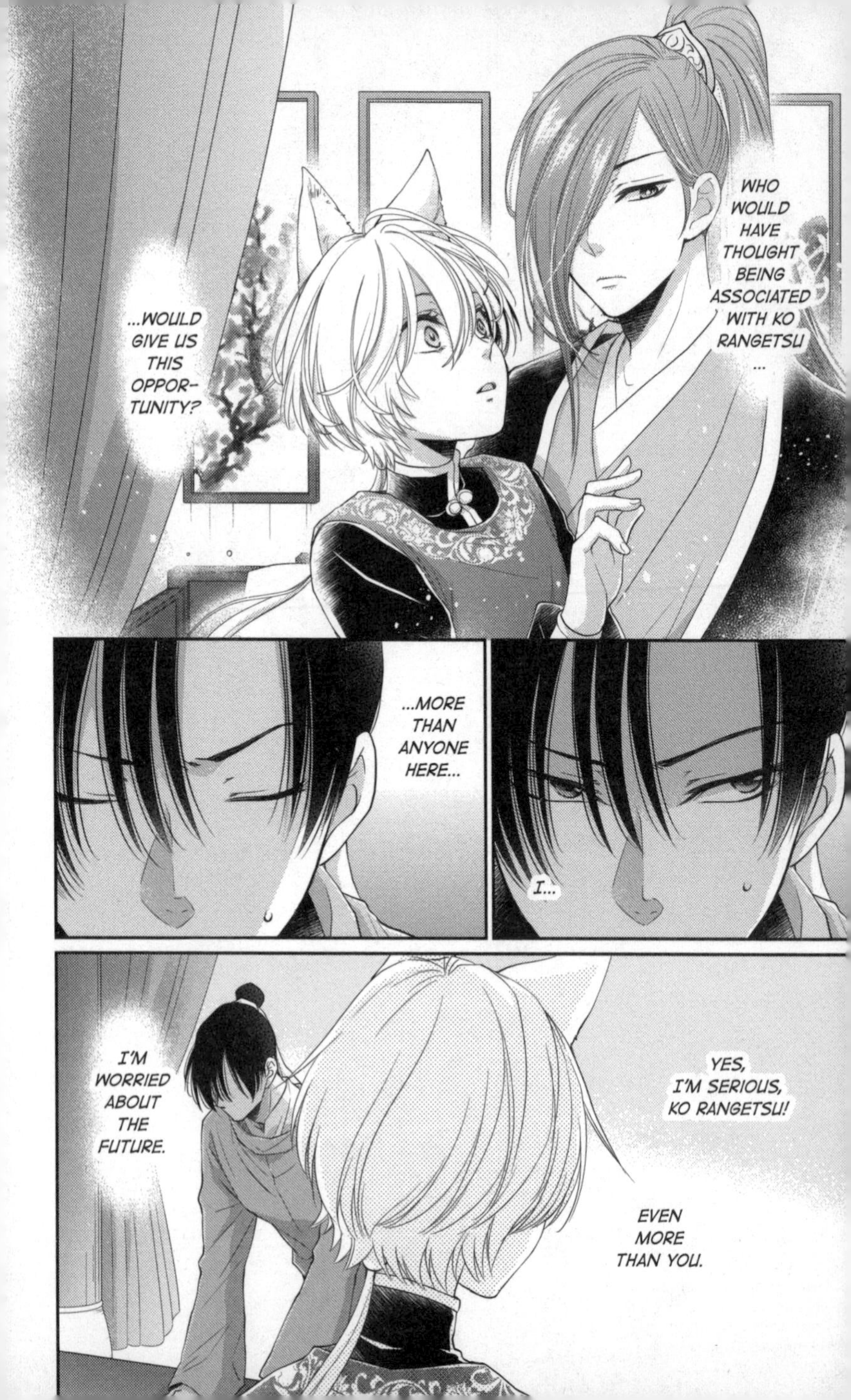
WHO WOULD HAVE THOUGHT BEING ASSOCIATED WITH KO RANGETSU ...
...WOULD GIVE US THIS OPPOR-TUNITY?
I...
...MORE THAN ANYONE HERE...
YES, I'M SERIOUS, KO RANGETSU!
I'M WORRIED ABOUT THE FUTURE.
EVEN MORE THAN YOU.

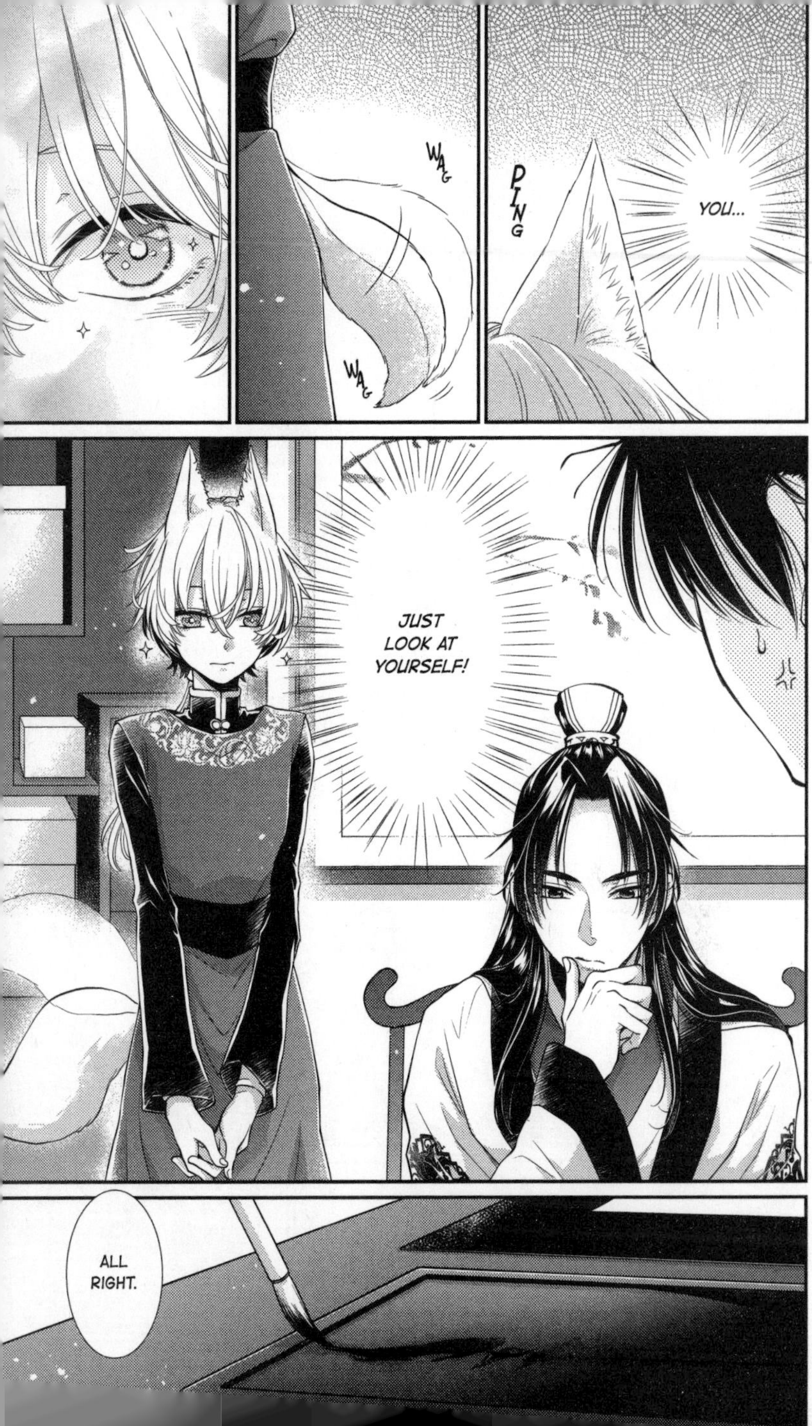
YOU...
PING
WAG
WAG
JUST LOOK AT YOURSELF!
ALL RIGHT.

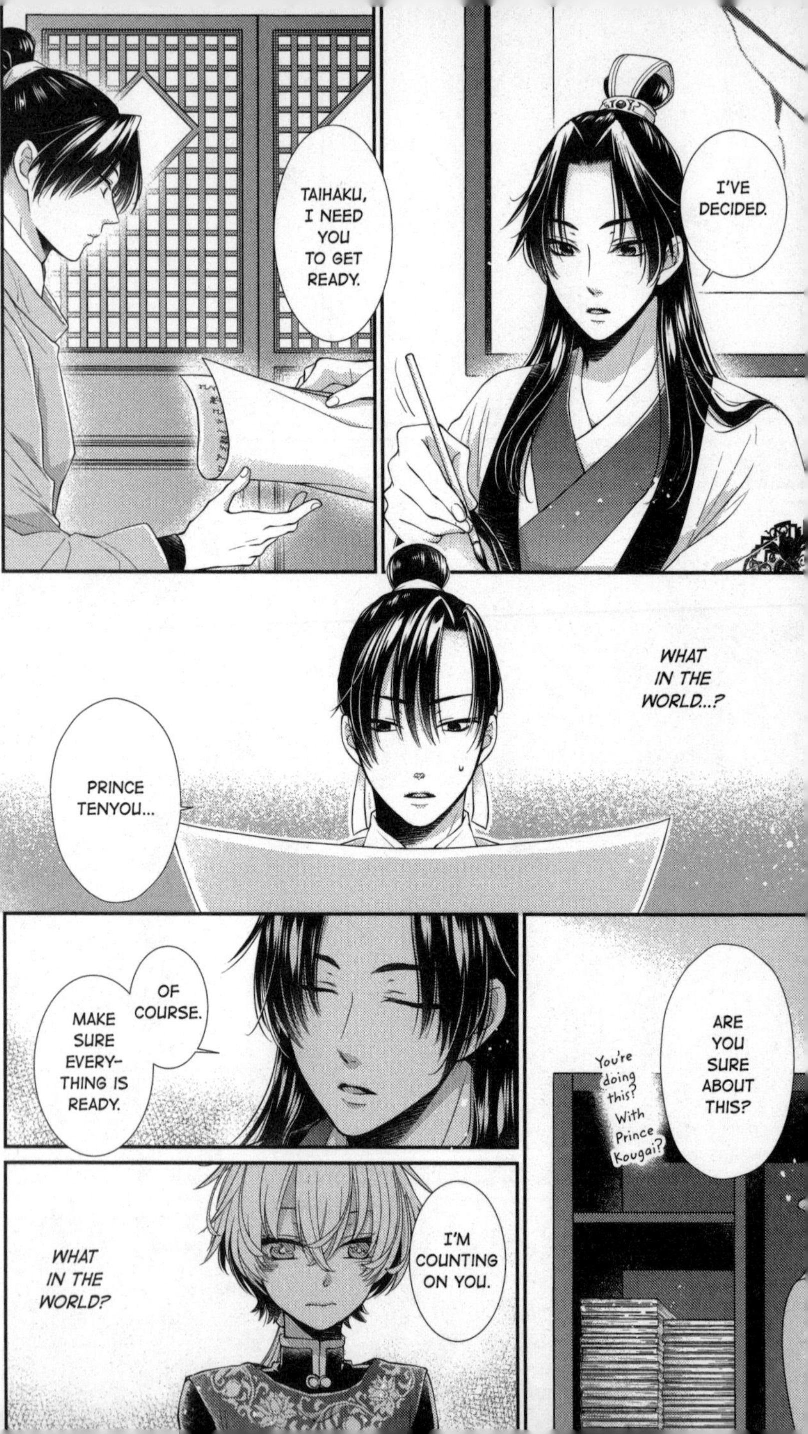
I'VE DECIDED.
TAIHAKU, I NEED YOU TO GET READY.
WHAT IN THE WORLD...?
PRINCE TENYOU...
ARE YOU SURE ABOUT THIS?
You're doing this? With Prince Kougai?
OF COURSE.
MAKE SURE EVERY-THING IS READY.
I'M COUNTING ON YOU.
WHAT IN THE WORLD?

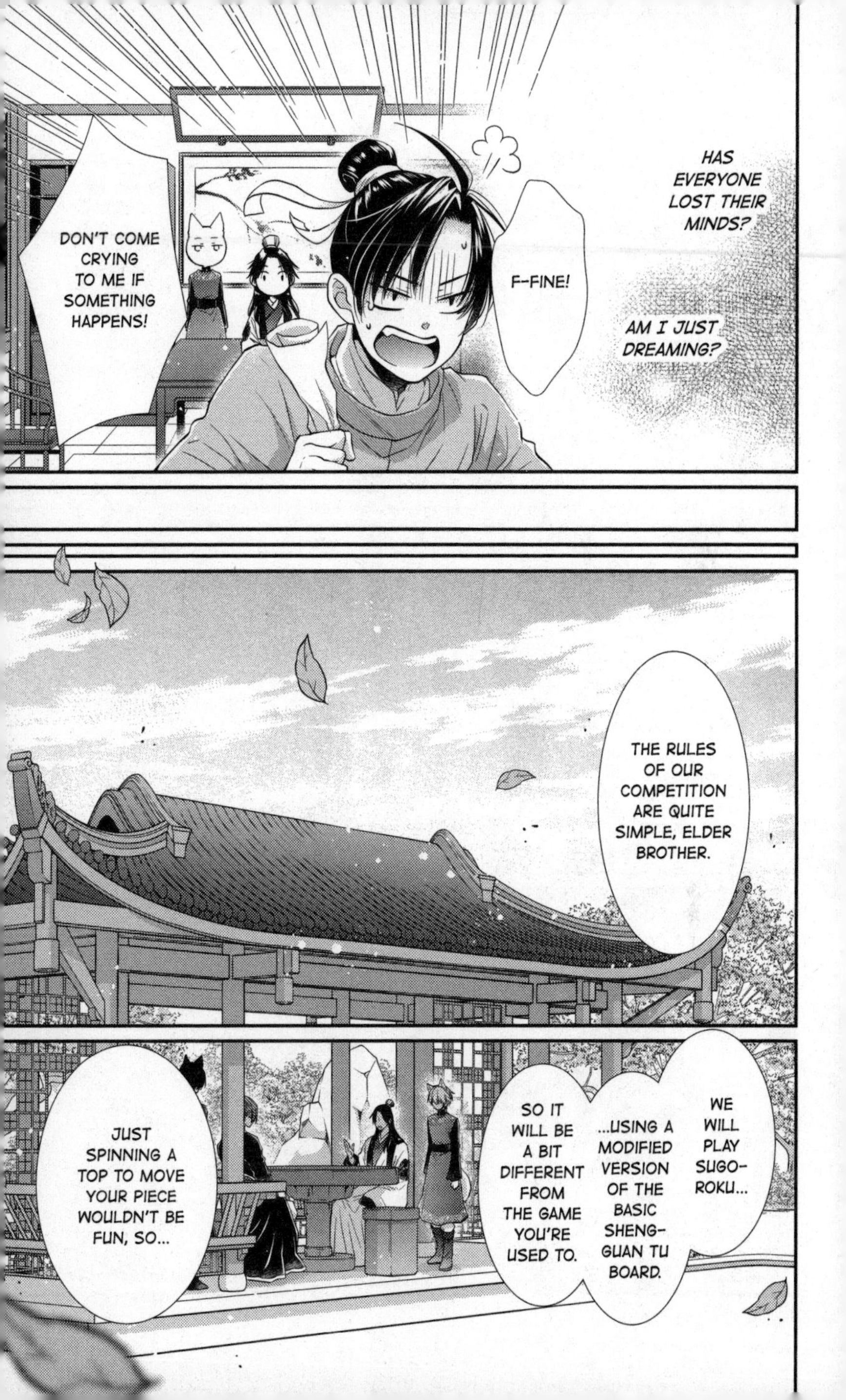
HAS EVERYONE LOST THEIR MINDS?
AM I JUST DREAMING?
F-FINE!
DON'T COME CRYING TO ME IF SOMETHING HAPPENS!
THE RULES OF OUR COMPETITION ARE QUITE SIMPLE, ELDER BROTHER.
WE WILL PLAY SUGO-ROKU...
...USING A MODIFIED VERSION OF THE BASIC SHENG-GUAN TU BOARD.
SO IT WILL BE A BIT DIFFERENT FROM THE GAME YOU'RE USED TO.
JUST SPINNING A TOP TO MOVE YOUR PIECE WOULDN'T BE FUN, SO...

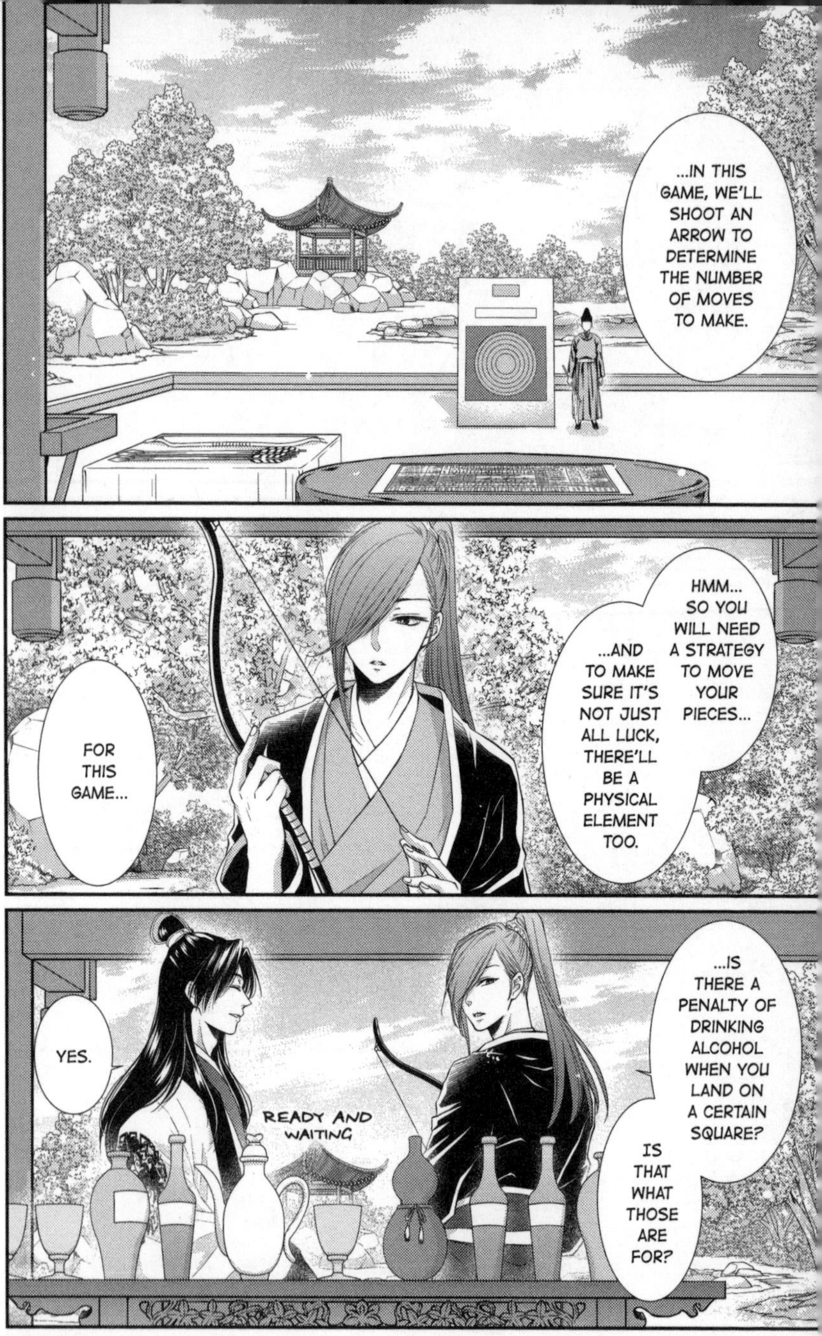
...IN THIS GAME, WE'LL SHOOT AN ARROW TO DETERMINE THE NUMBER OF MOVES TO MAKE.
HMM... SO YOU WILL NEED A STRATEGY TO MOVE YOUR PIECES...
...AND TO MAKE SURE IT'S NOT JUST ALL LUCK, THERE'LL BE A PHYSICAL ELEMENT TOO.
FOR THIS GAME...
...IS THERE A PENALTY OF DRINKING ALCOHOL WHEN YOU LAND ON A CERTAIN SQUARE?
IS THAT WHAT THOSE ARE FOR?
READY AND WAITING
YES.

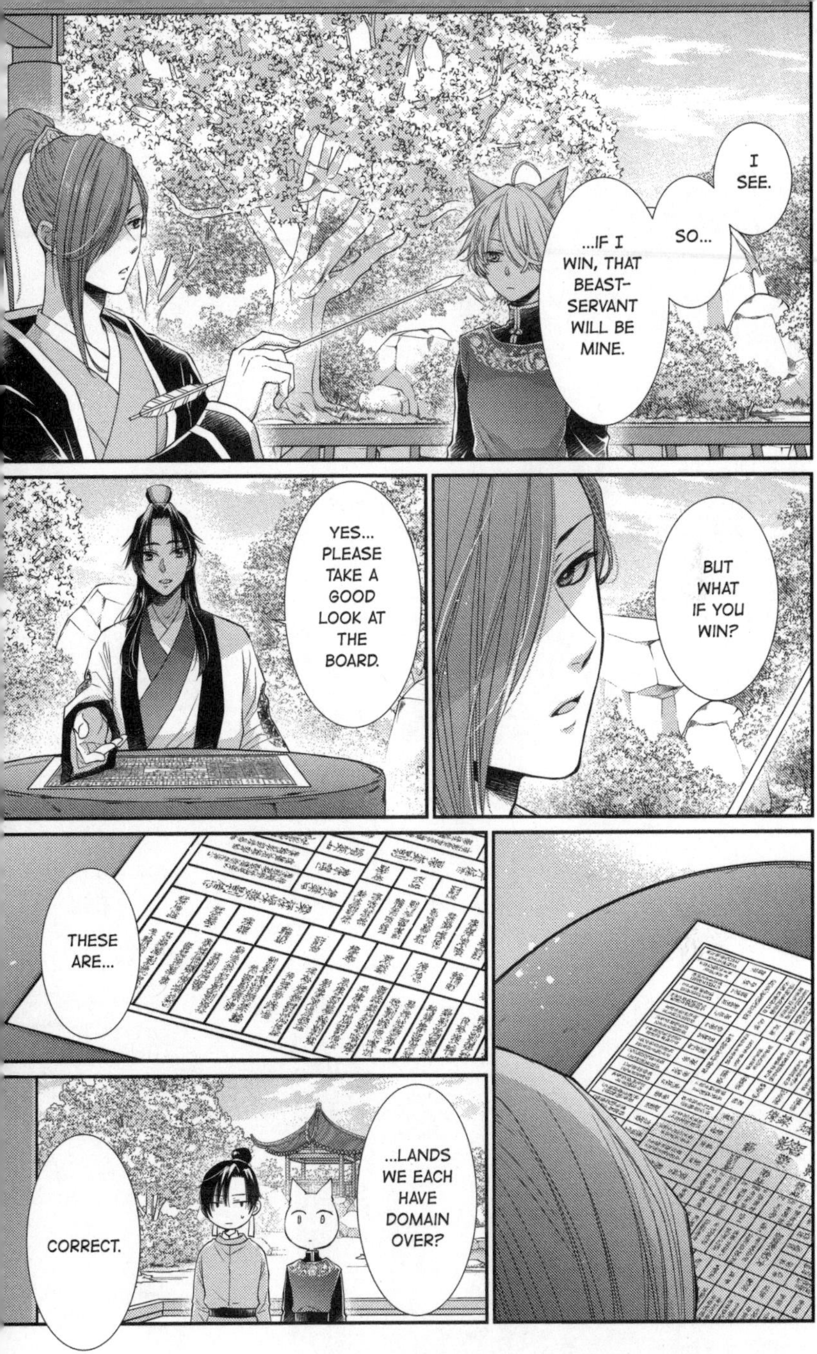
I SEE.
SO...
...IF I WIN, THAT BEAST-SERVANT WILL BE MINE.
BUT WHAT IF YOU WIN?
YES... PLEASE TAKE A GOOD LOOK AT THE BOARD.
THESE ARE...
...LANDS WE EACH HAVE DOMAIN OVER?
CORRECT.

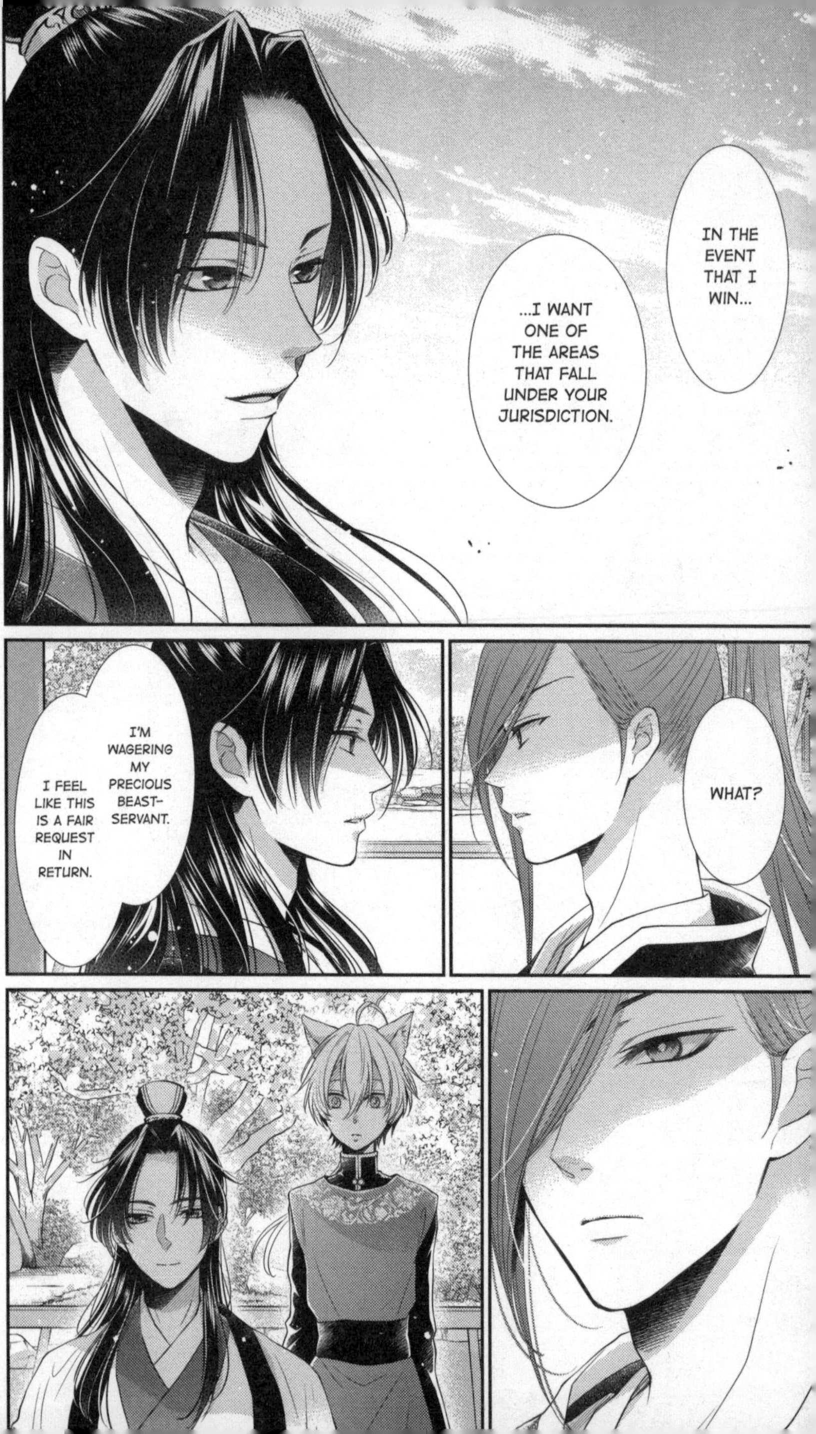
IN THE EVENT THAT I WIN...
...I WANT ONE OF THE AREAS THAT FALL UNDER YOUR JURISDICTION.
WHAT?
I'M WAGERING MY PRECIOUS BEAST-SERVANT.
I FEEL LIKE THIS IS A FAIR REQUEST IN RETURN.

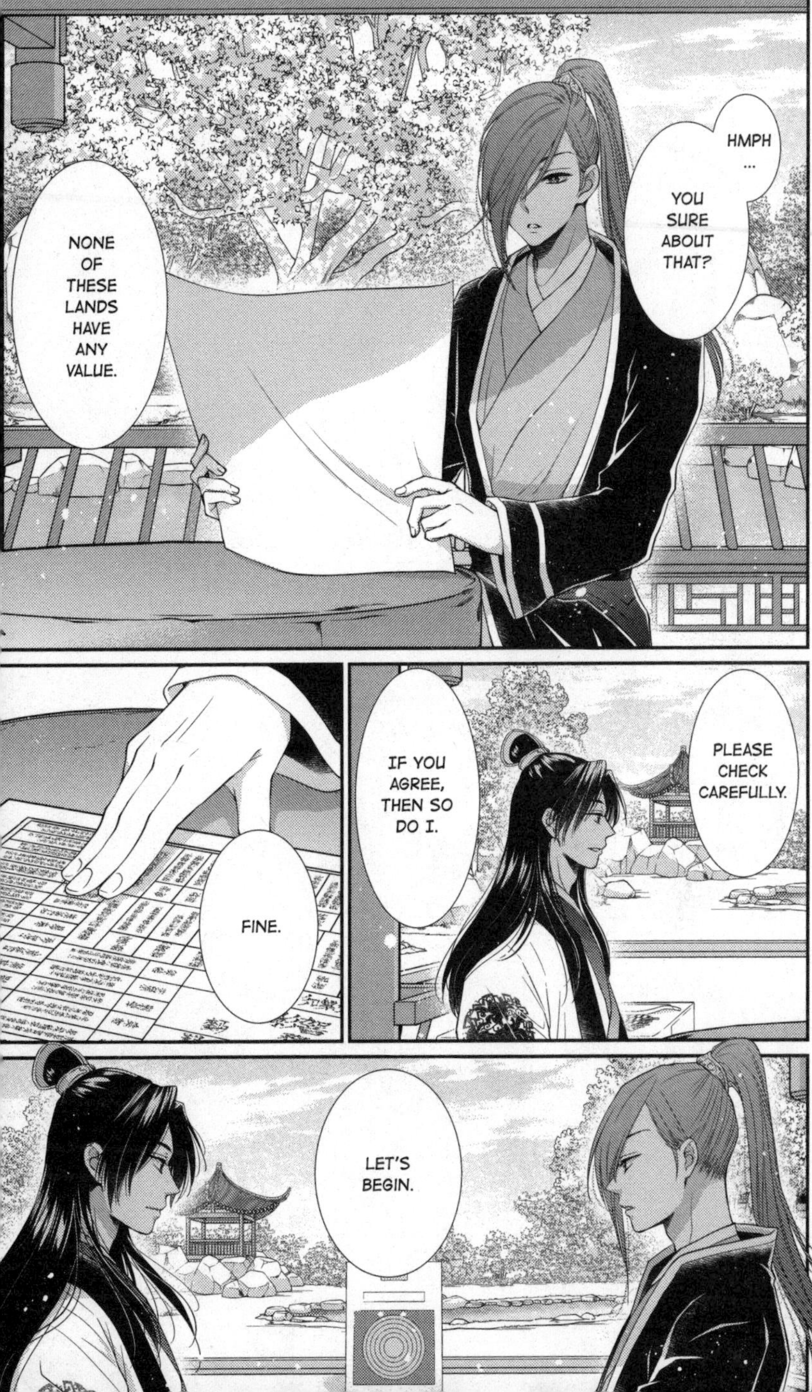
HMPH ... YOU SURE ABOUT THAT?
NONE OF THESE LANDS HAVE ANY VALUE.
PLEASE CHECK CAREFULLY.
IF YOU AGREE, THEN SO DO I.
FINE.
LET'S BEGIN.

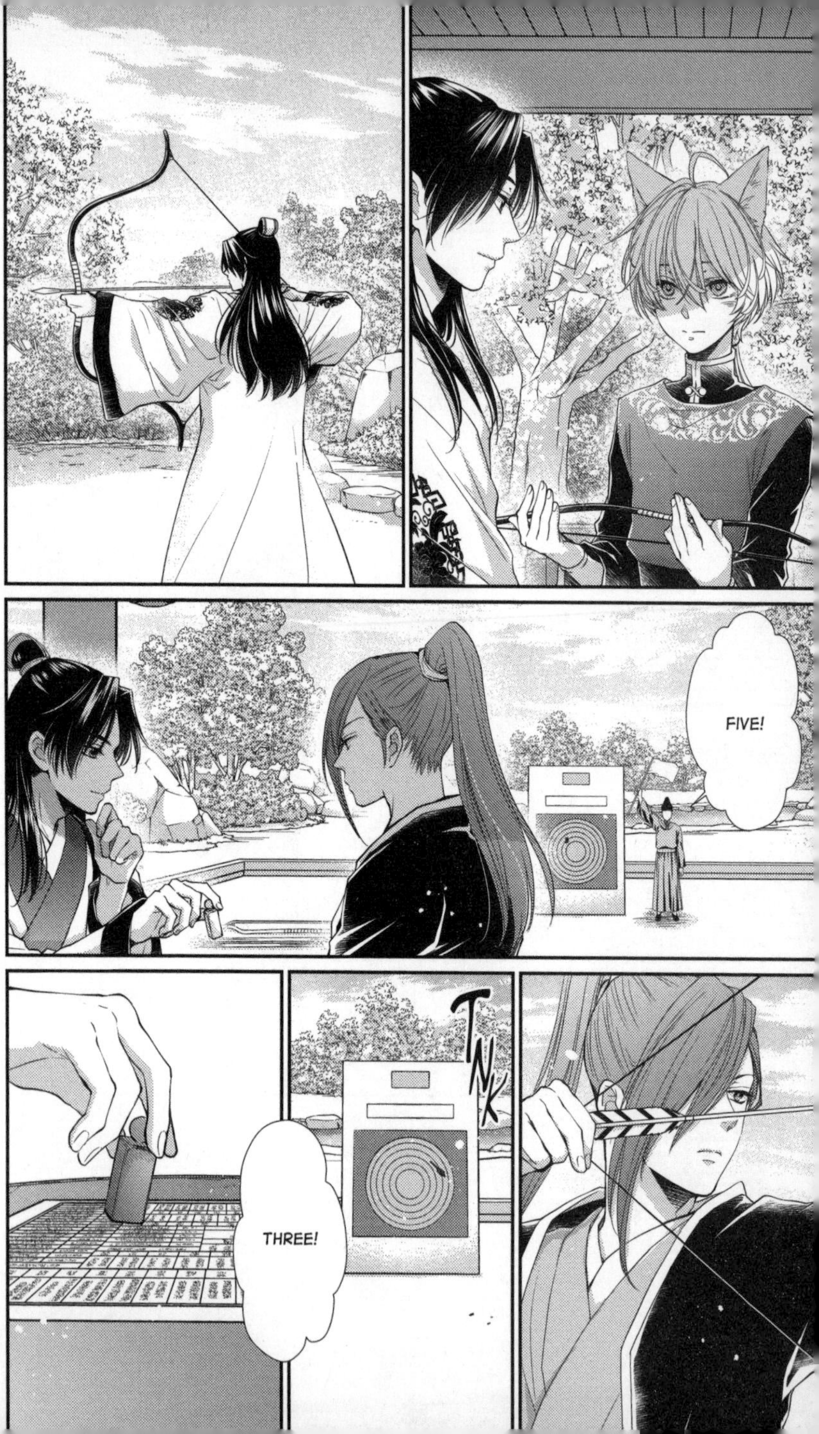
FIVE!
TNK
THREE!

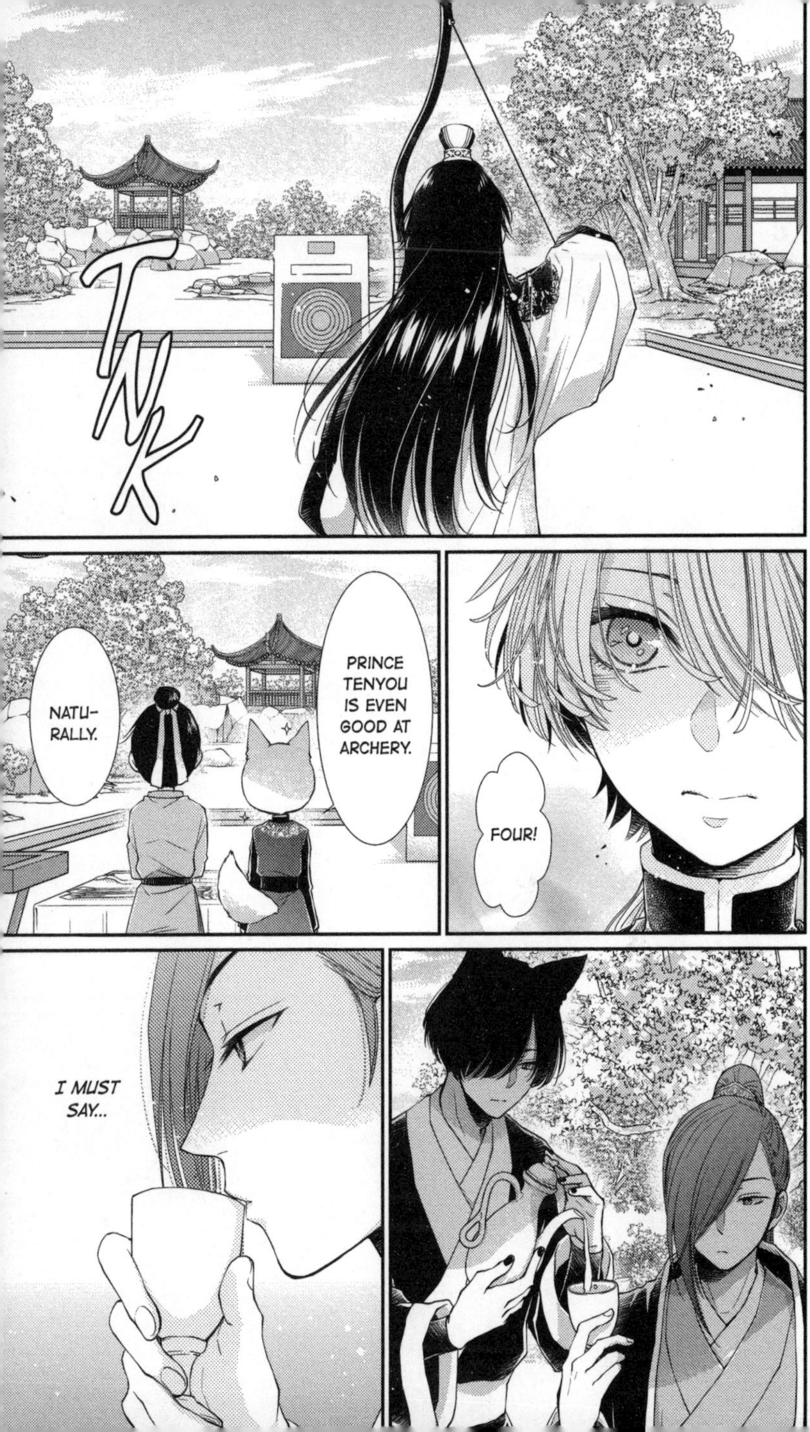
TNK
FOUR!
PRINCE TENYOU IS EVEN GOOD AT ARCHERY.
NATU-RALLY.
I MUST SAY...

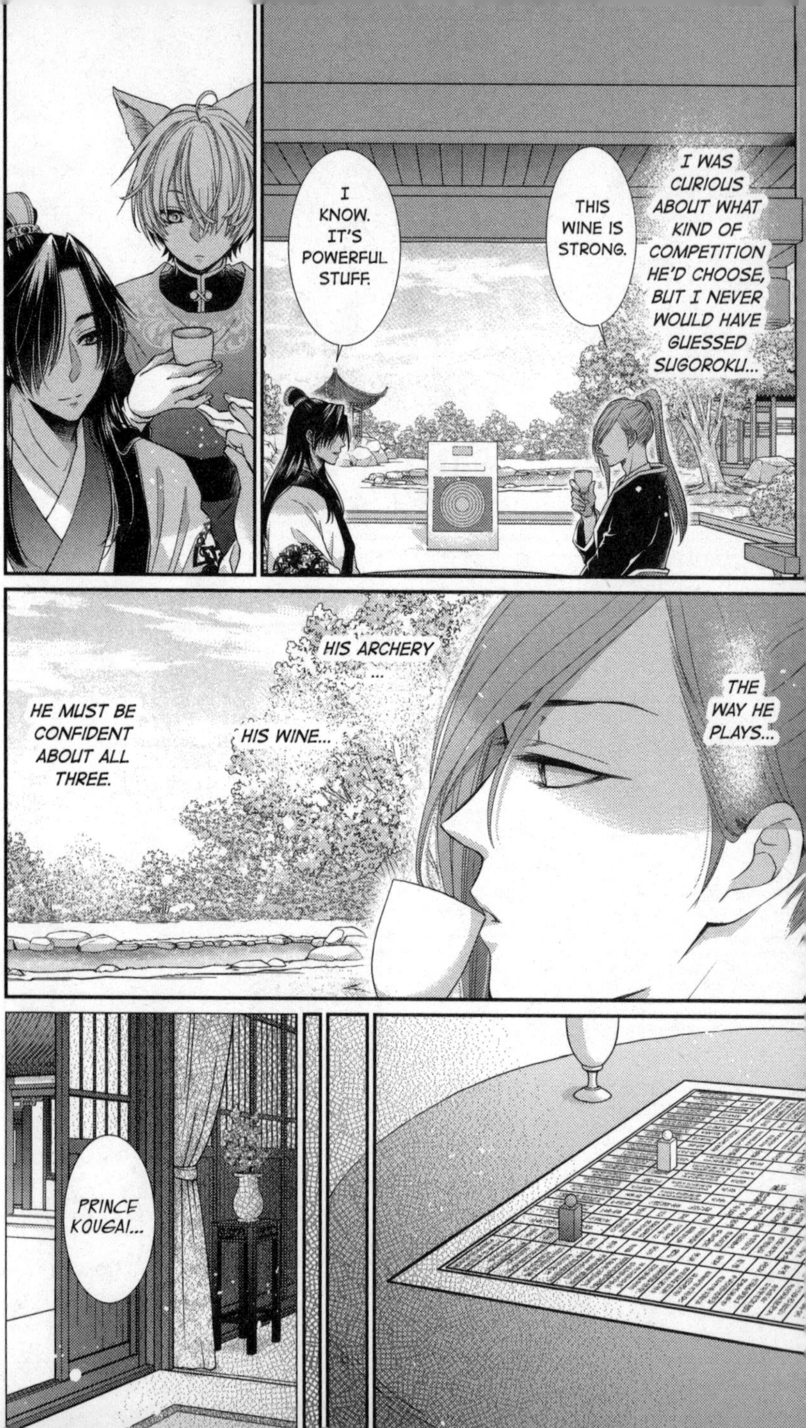
I WAS CURIOUS ABOUT WHAT KIND OF COMPETITION HE'D CHOOSE, BUT I NEVER WOULD HAVE GUESSED SUGOROKU...
THIS WINE IS STRONG.
I KNOW. IT'S POWERFUL STUFF.
THE WAY HE PLAYS...
HIS ARCHERY...
HIS WINE...
HE MUST BE CONFIDENT ABOUT ALL THREE.
PRINCE KOUGAI...

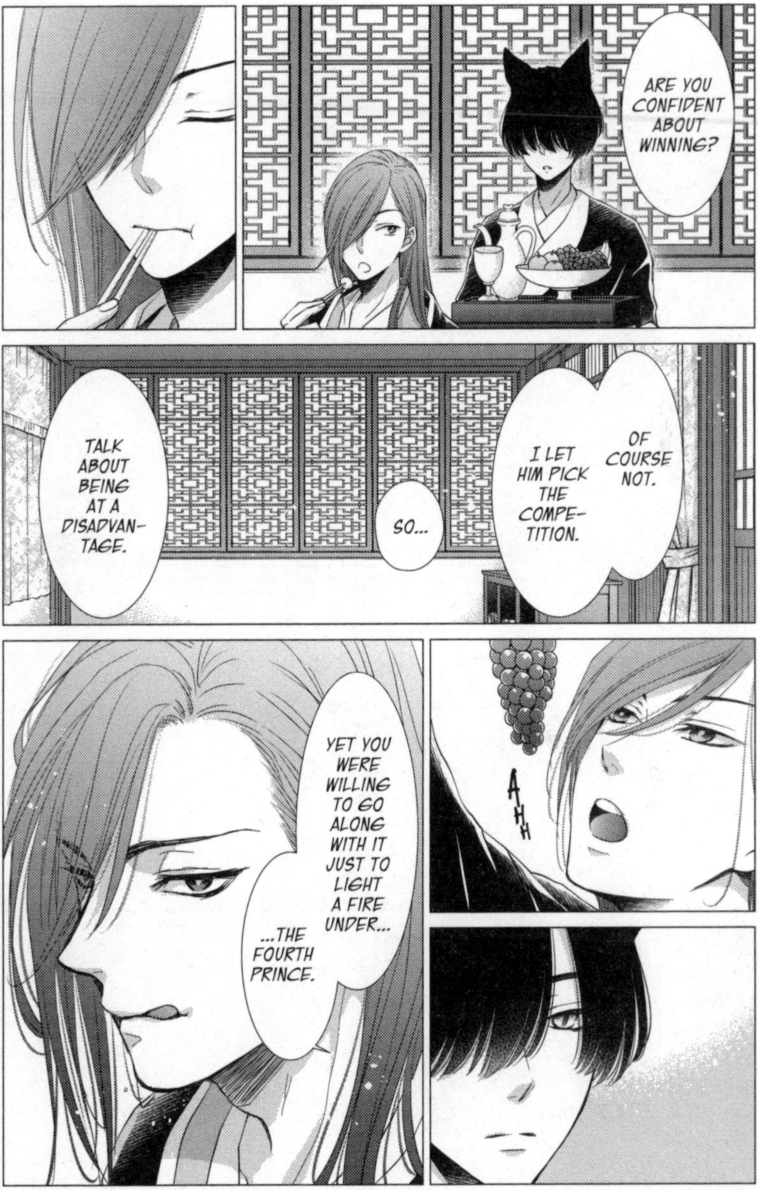
ARE YOU CONFIDENT ABOUT WINNING?
OF COURSE NOT.
I LET HIM PICK THE COMPE-TITION.
SO...
TALK ABOUT BEING AT A DISADVAN-TAGE.
AHH
YET YOU WERE WILLING TO GO ALONG WITH IT JUST TO LIGHT A FIRE UNDER...
...THE FOURTH PRINCE.

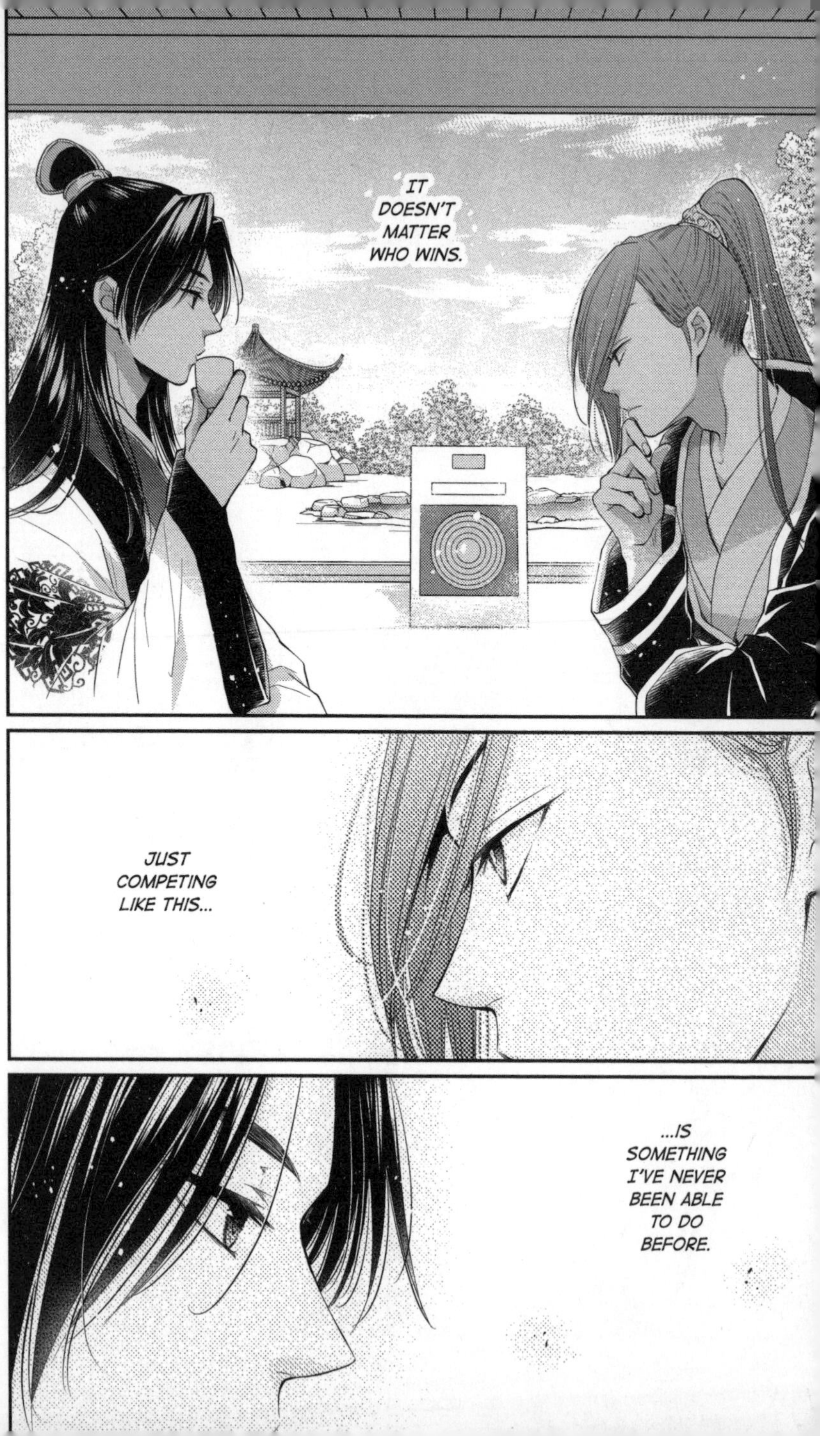
IT DOESN'T MATTER WHO WINS.
JUST COMPETING LIKE THIS...
...IS SOMETHING I'VE NEVER BEEN ABLE TO DO BEFORE.

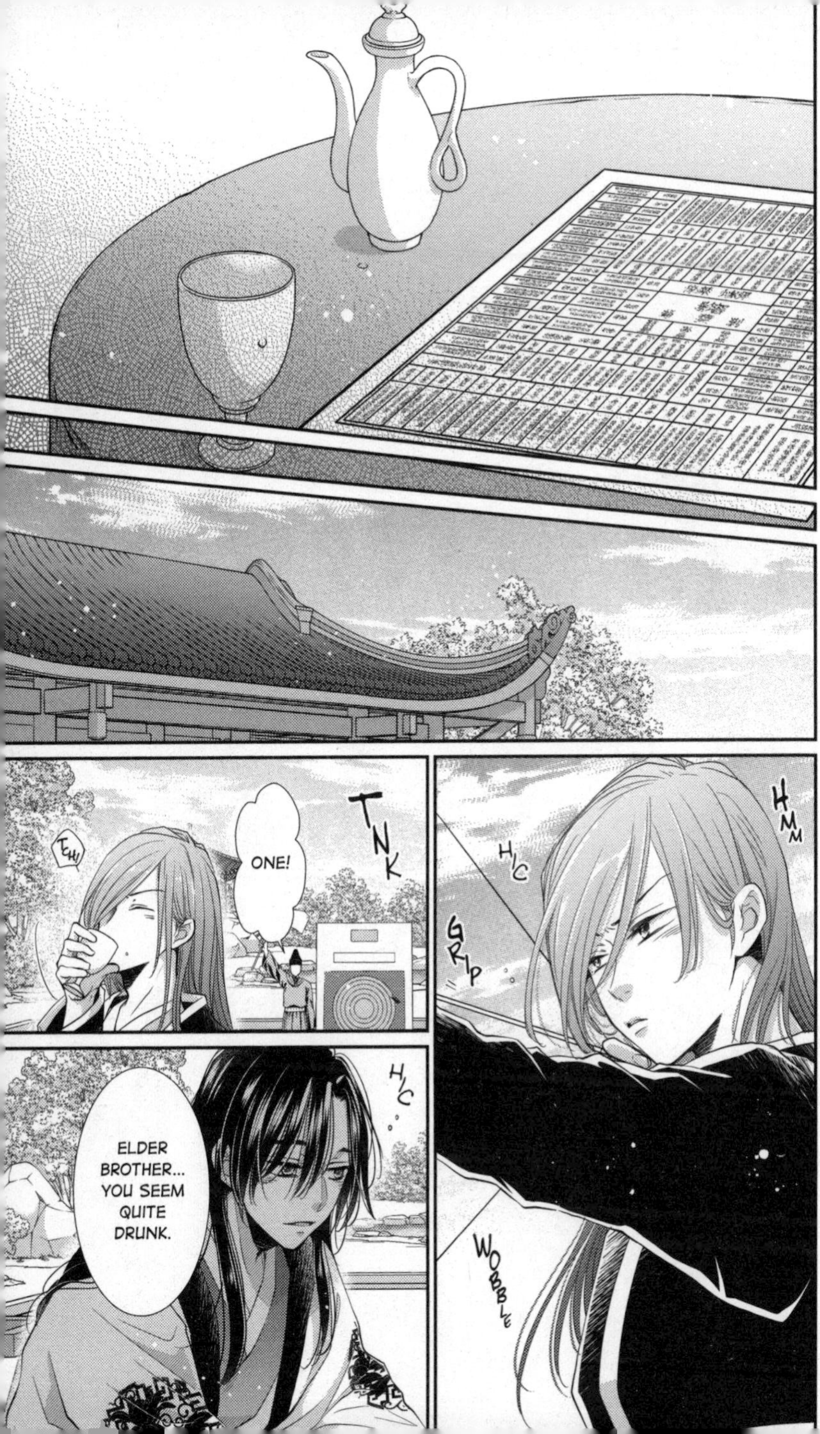
HMM
HIC
GRIP
WOBBLE
TNK
ONE!
TCH!
HIC
ELDER BROTHER... YOU SEEM QUITE DRUNK.

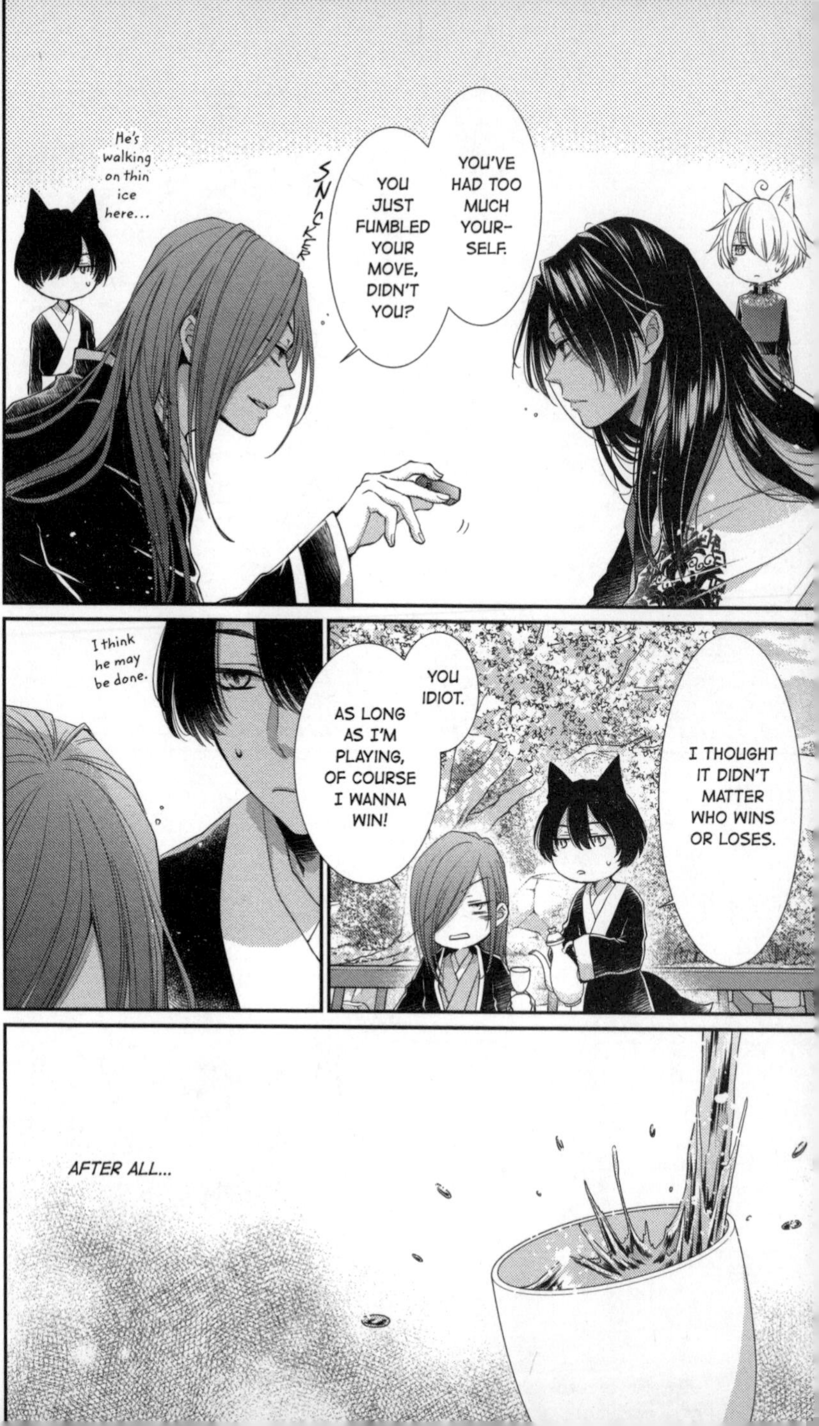
YOU'VE HAD TOO MUCH YOURSELF.
YOU JUST FUMBLED YOUR MOVE, DIDN'T YOU?
SNICKER
He's walking on thin ice here...
I THOUGHT IT DIDN'T MATTER WHO WINS OR LOSES.
YOU IDIOT.
AS LONG AS I'M PLAYING, OF COURSE I WANNA WIN!
I think he may be done.
AFTER ALL...

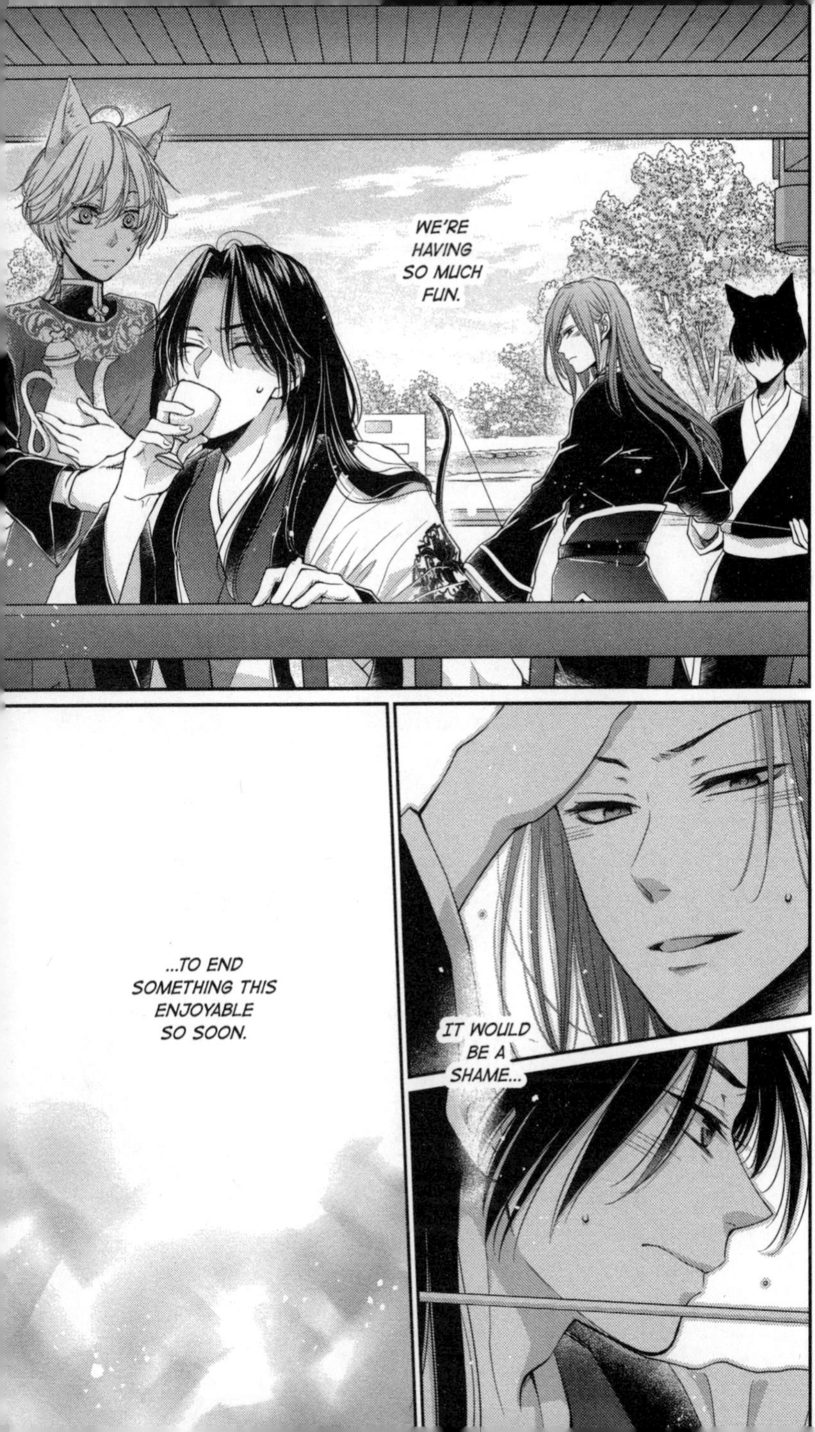
WE'RE HAVING SO MUCH FUN.
IT WOULD BE A SHAME...
...TO END SOMETHING THIS ENJOYABLE SO SOON.

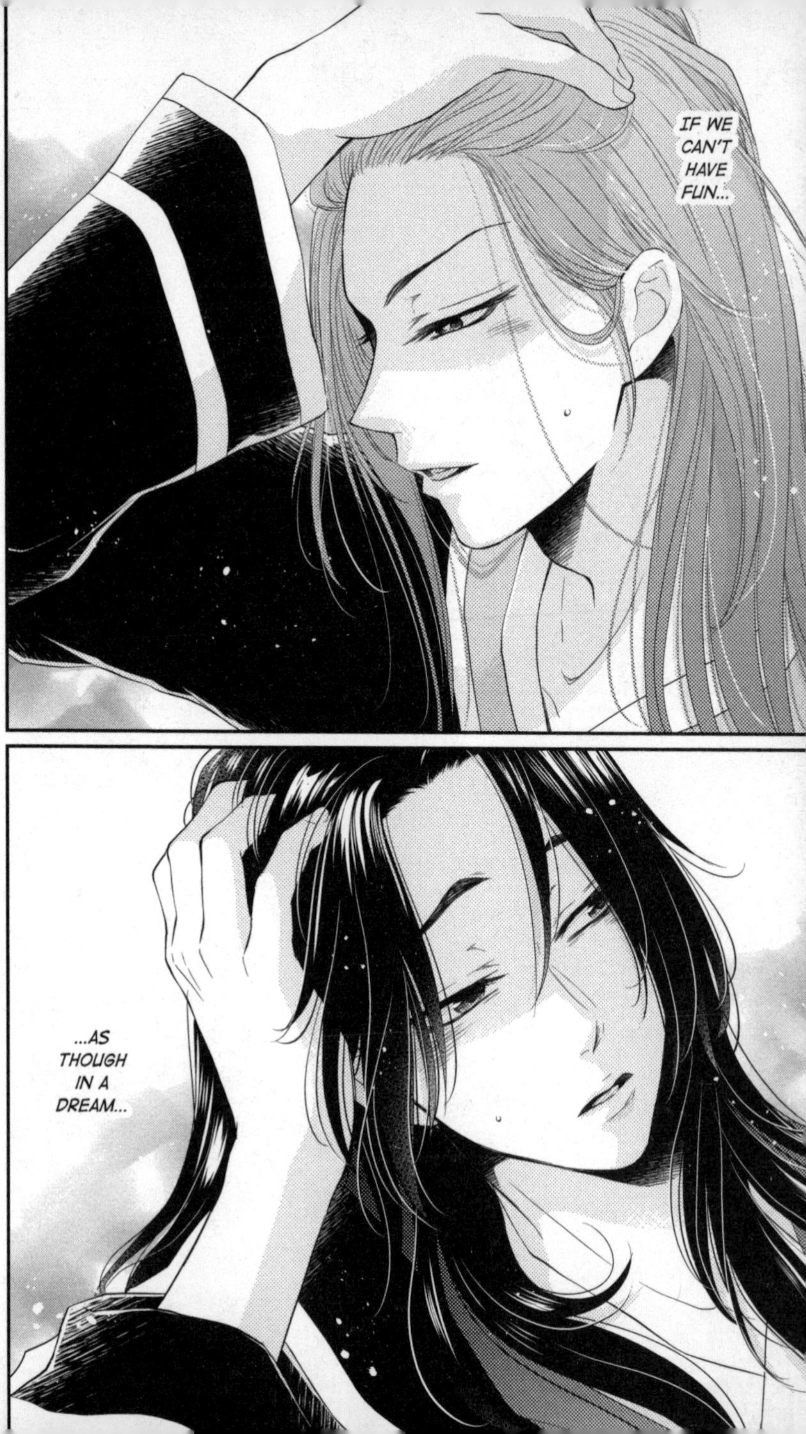
IF WE CAN'T HAVE FUN...
...AS THOUGH IN A DREAM...

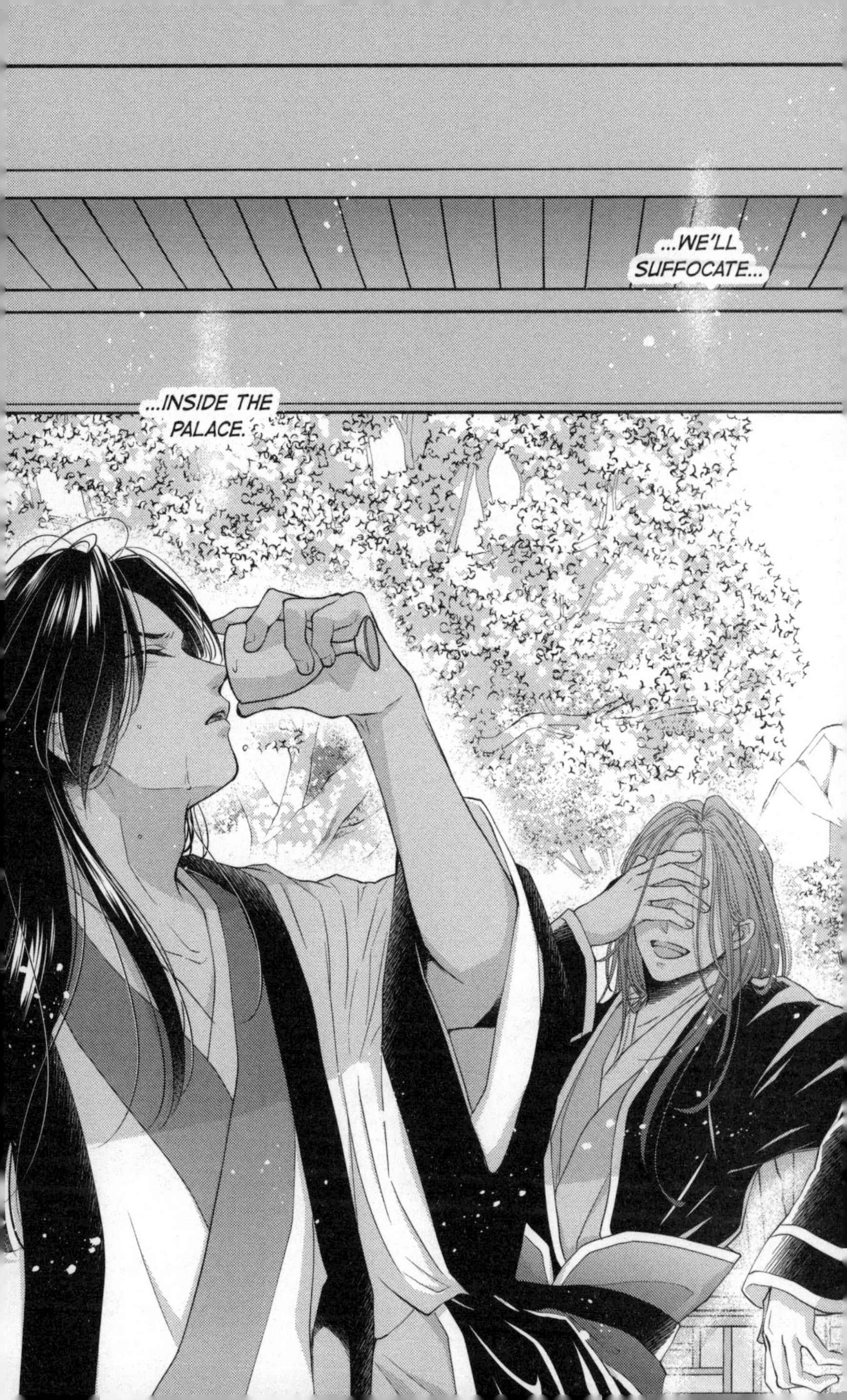
...WE'LL SUFFOCATE...
...INSIDE THE PALACE.

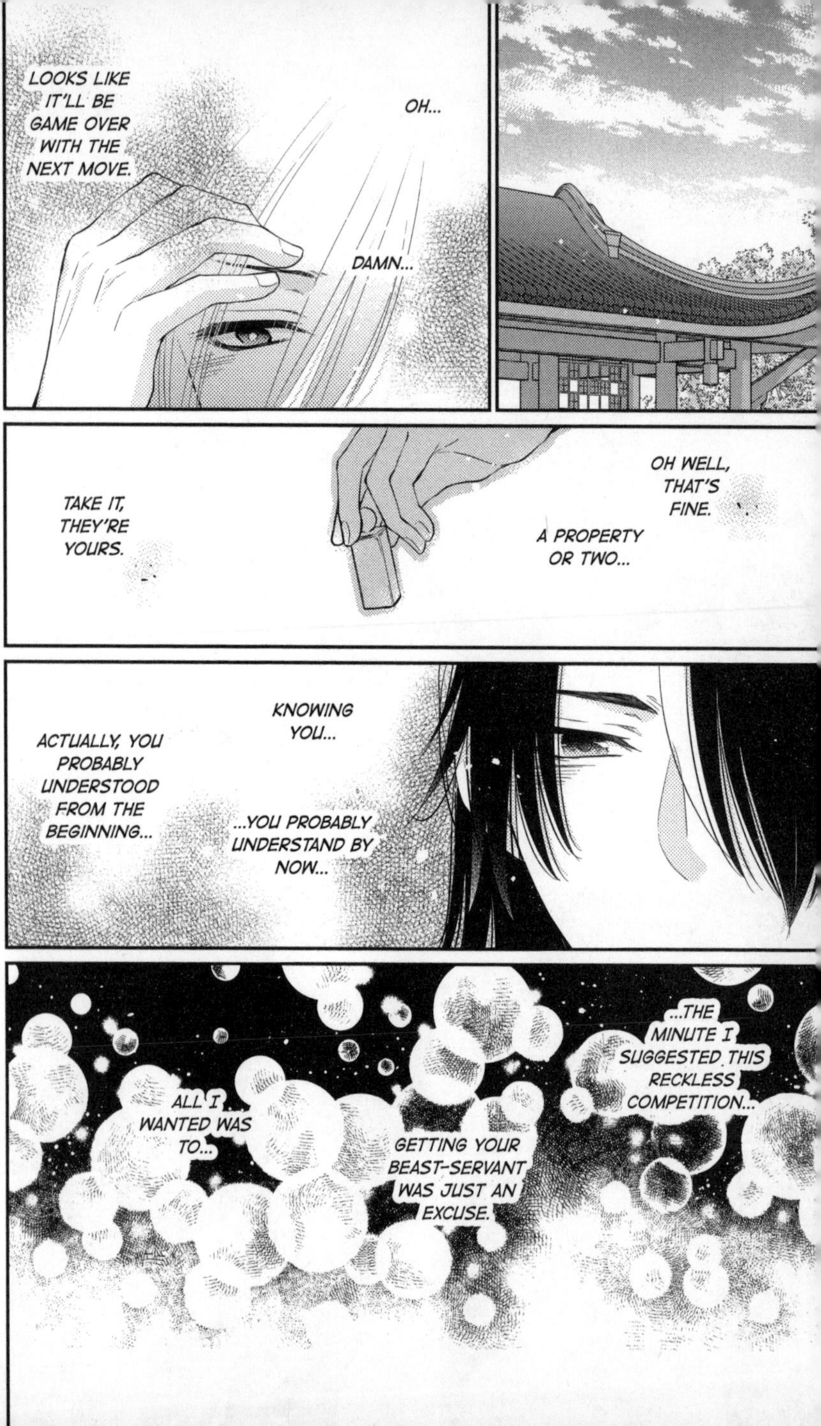
OH...
DAMN...
LOOKS LIKE IT'LL BE GAME OVER WITH THE NEXT MOVE.
OH WELL, THAT'S FINE.
A PROPERTY OR TWO...
TAKE IT, THEY'RE YOURS.
KNOWING YOU...
...YOU PROBABLY UNDERSTAND BY NOW...
ACTUALLY, YOU PROBABLY UNDERSTOOD FROM THE BEGINNING...
...THE MINUTE I SUGGESTED THIS RECKLESS COMPETITION...
GETTING YOUR BEAST-SERVANT WAS JUST AN EXCUSE.
ALL I WANTED WAS TO...

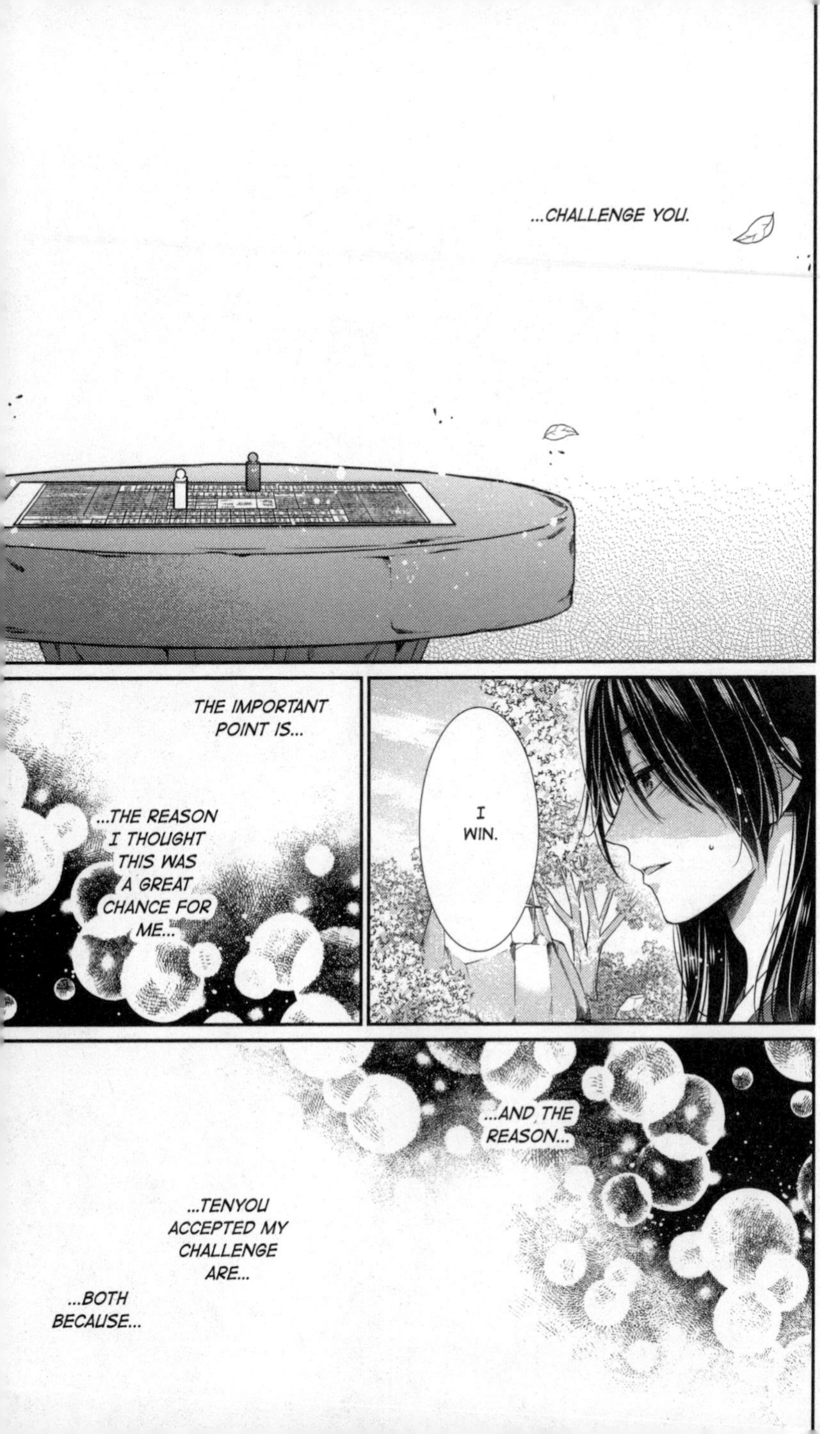
...CHALLENGE YOU.
I WIN.
THE IMPORTANT POINT IS...
...THE REASON I THOUGHT THIS WAS A GREAT CHANCE FOR ME...
...AND THE REASON...
...TENYOU ACCEPTED MY CHALLENGE ARE...
...BOTH BECAUSE...

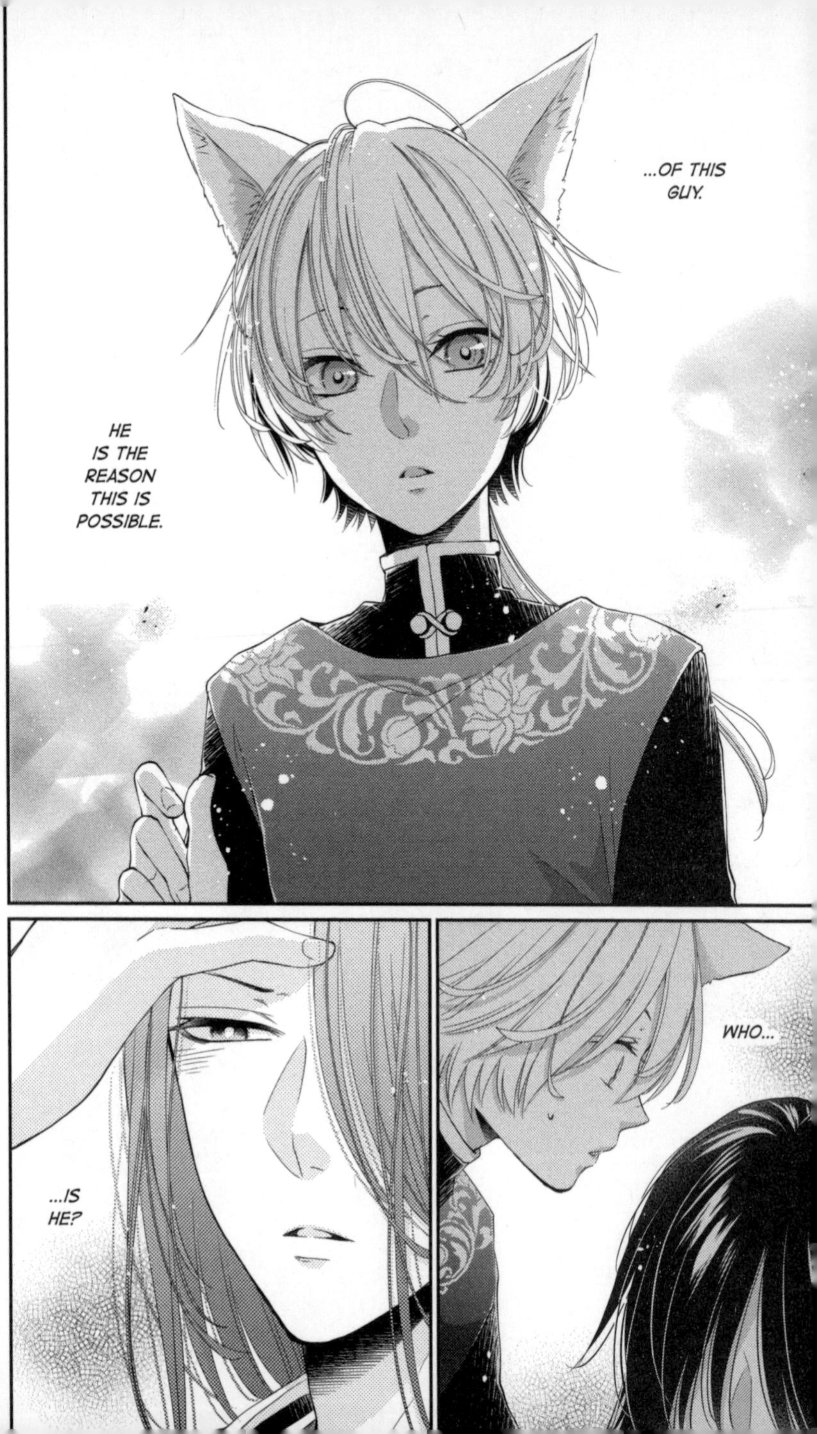
...OF THIS GUY.
HE IS THE REASON THIS IS POSSIBLE.
WHO...
...IS HE?

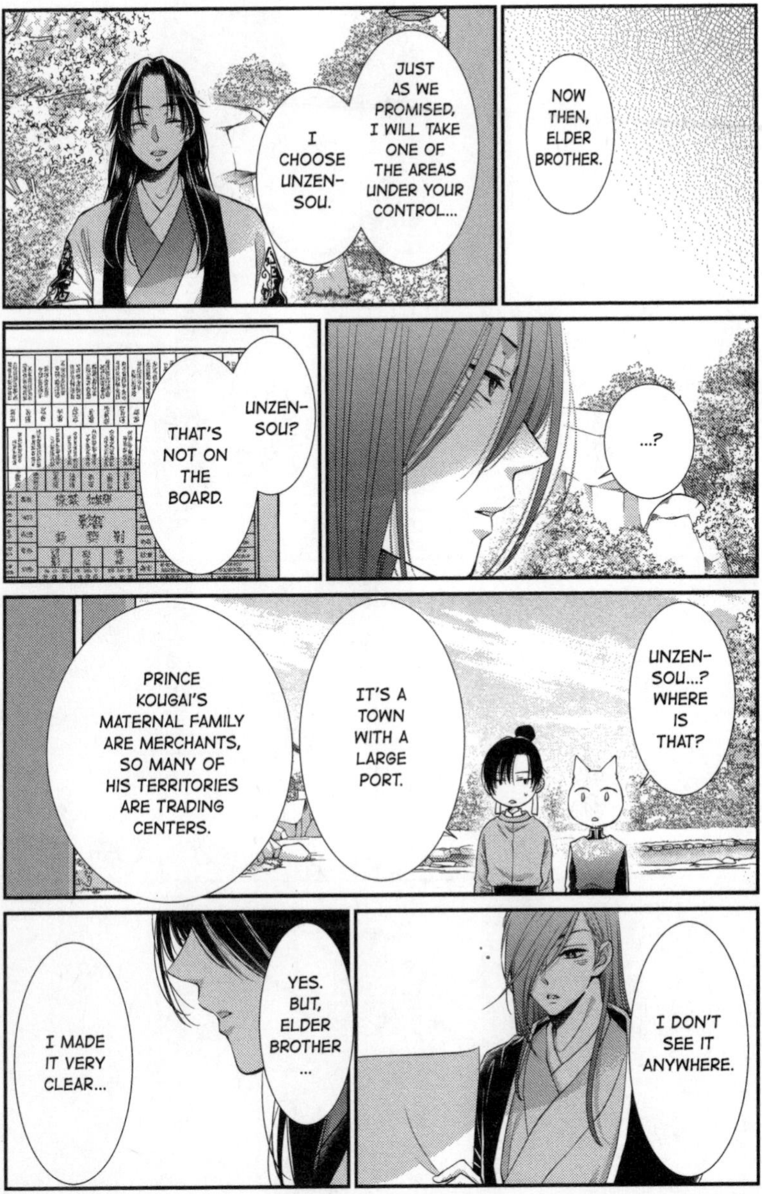
NOW THEN, ELDER BROTHER.
JUST AS WE PROMISED, I WILL TAKE ONE OF THE AREAS UNDER YOUR CONTROL...
I CHOOSE UNZEN-SOU.
...?
UNZEN-SOU?
THAT'S NOT ON THE BOARD.
UNZEN-SOU...? WHERE IS THAT?
IT'S A TOWN WITH A LARGE PORT.
PRINCE KOUGAI'S MATERNAL FAMILY ARE MERCHANTS, SO MANY OF HIS TERRITORIES ARE TRADING CENTERS.
I DON'T SEE IT ANYWHERE.
YES. BUT, ELDER BROTHER...
I MADE IT VERY CLEAR...

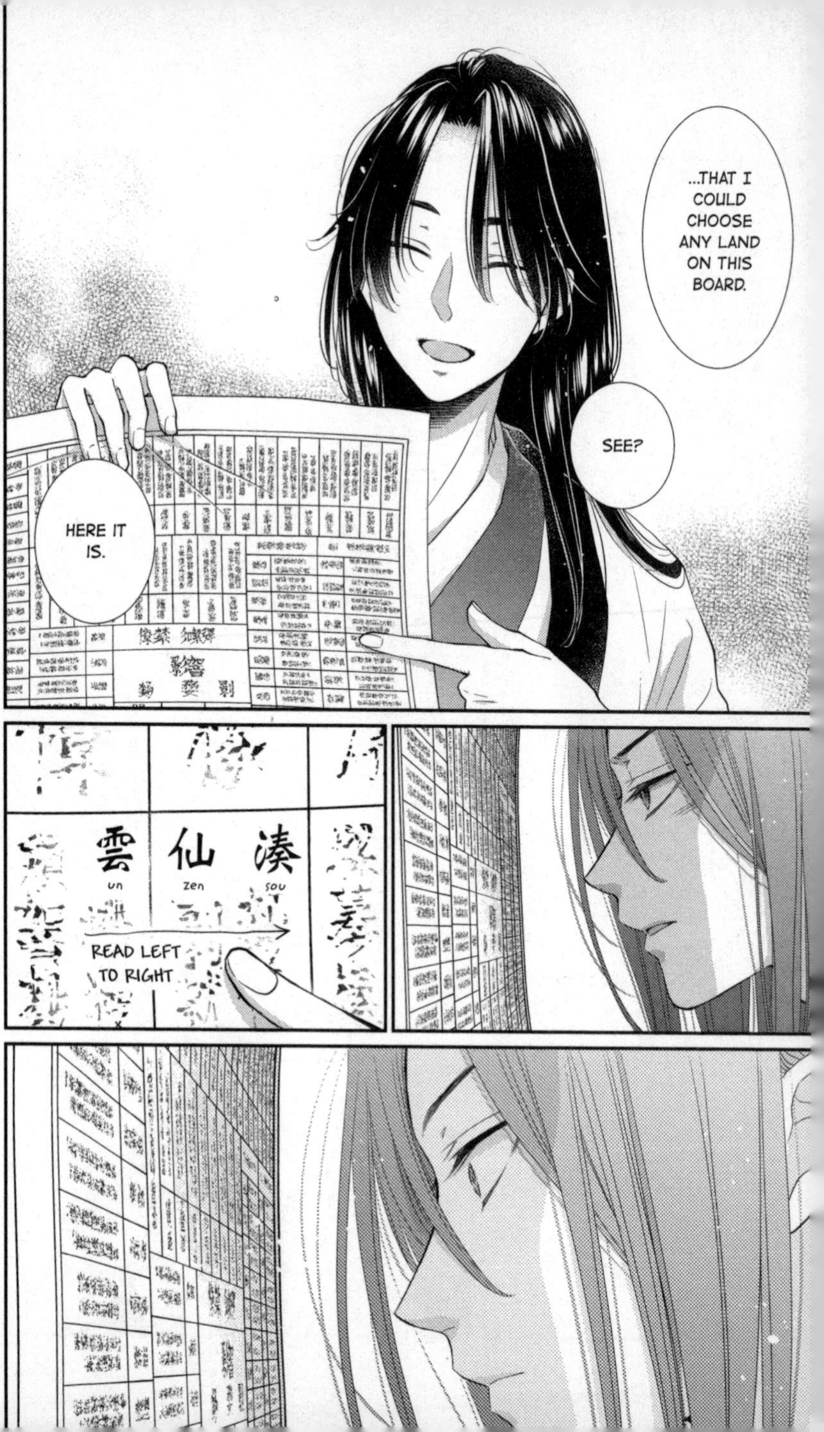
...THAT I COULD CHOOSE ANY LAND ON THIS BOARD.
SEE?
HERE IT IS.
雲 un
仙 zen
湊 sou
READ LEFT TO RIGHT

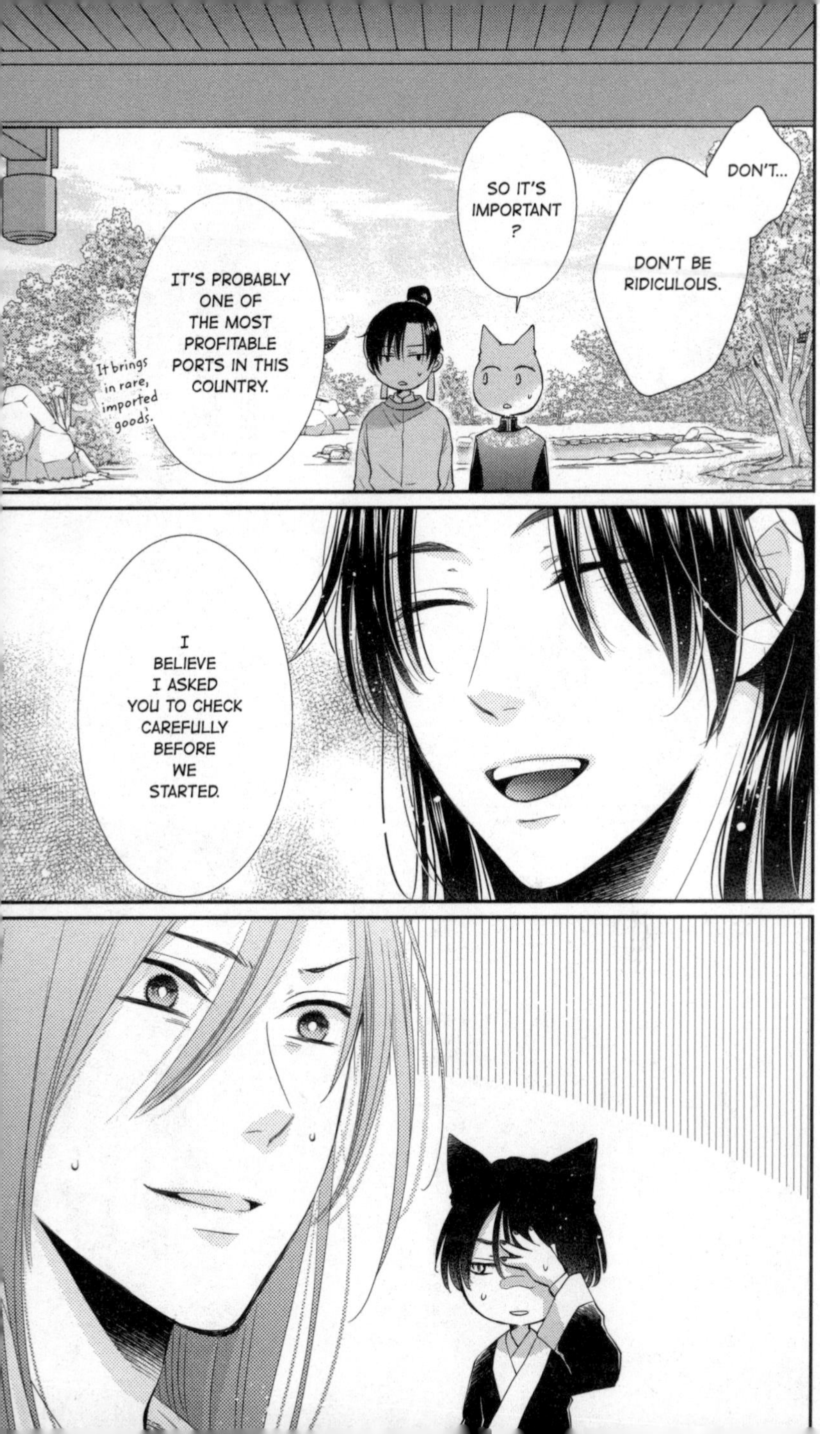
DON'T...
DON'T BE RIDICULOUS.
SO IT'S IMPORTANT ?
IT'S PROBABLY ONE OF THE MOST PROFITABLE PORTS IN THIS COUNTRY.
It brings in rare, imported goods.
I BELIEVE I ASKED YOU TO CHECK CAREFULLY BEFORE WE STARTED.

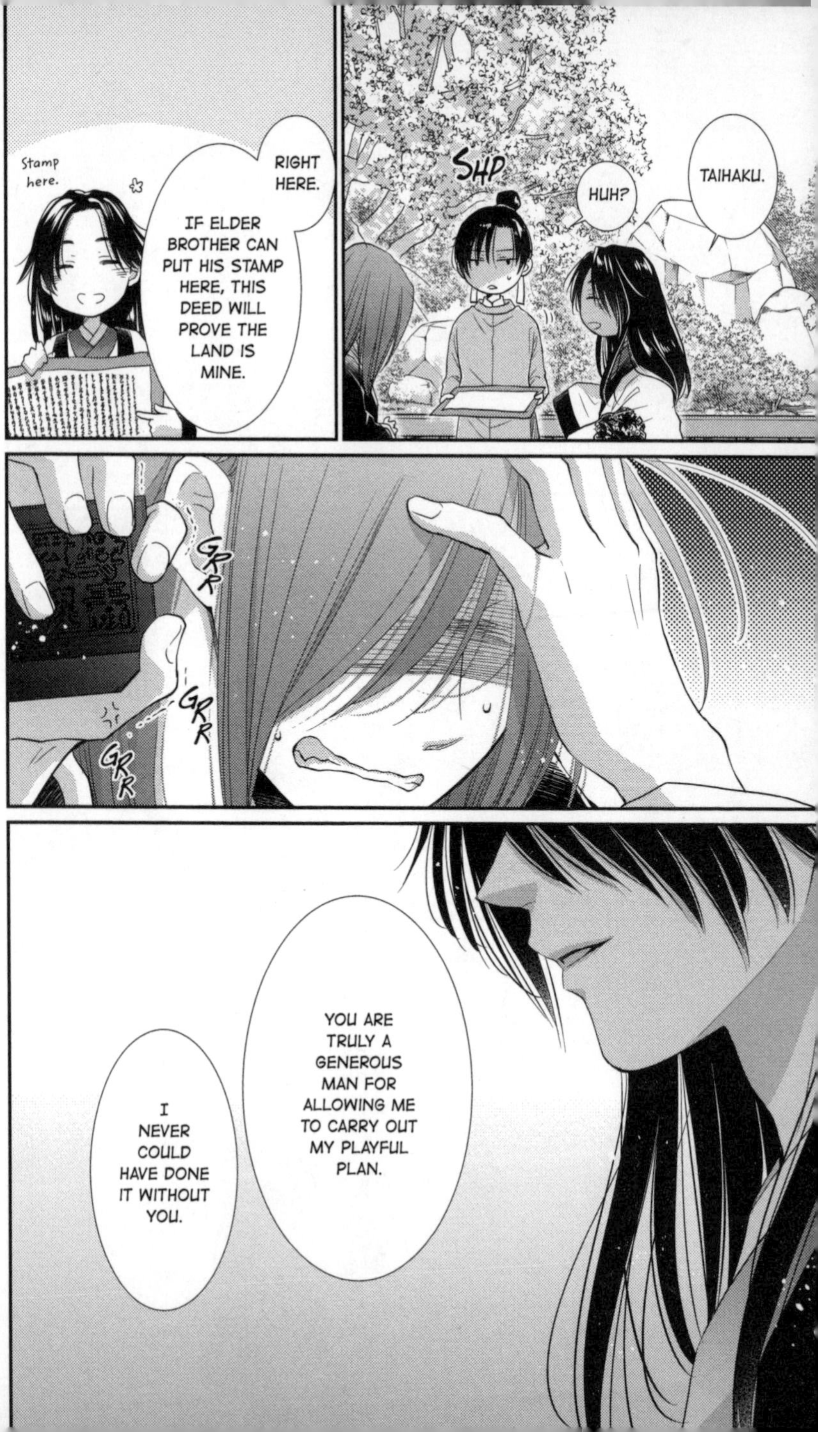
TAIHAKU.
HUH?
SHP
RIGHT HERE.
IF ELDER BROTHER CAN PUT HIS STAMP HERE, THIS DEED WILL PROVE THE LAND IS MINE.
Stamp here.
GRR
GRR
GRR
YOU ARE TRULY A GENEROUS MAN FOR ALLOWING ME TO CARRY OUT MY PLAYFUL PLAN.
I NEVER COULD HAVE DONE IT WITHOUT YOU.

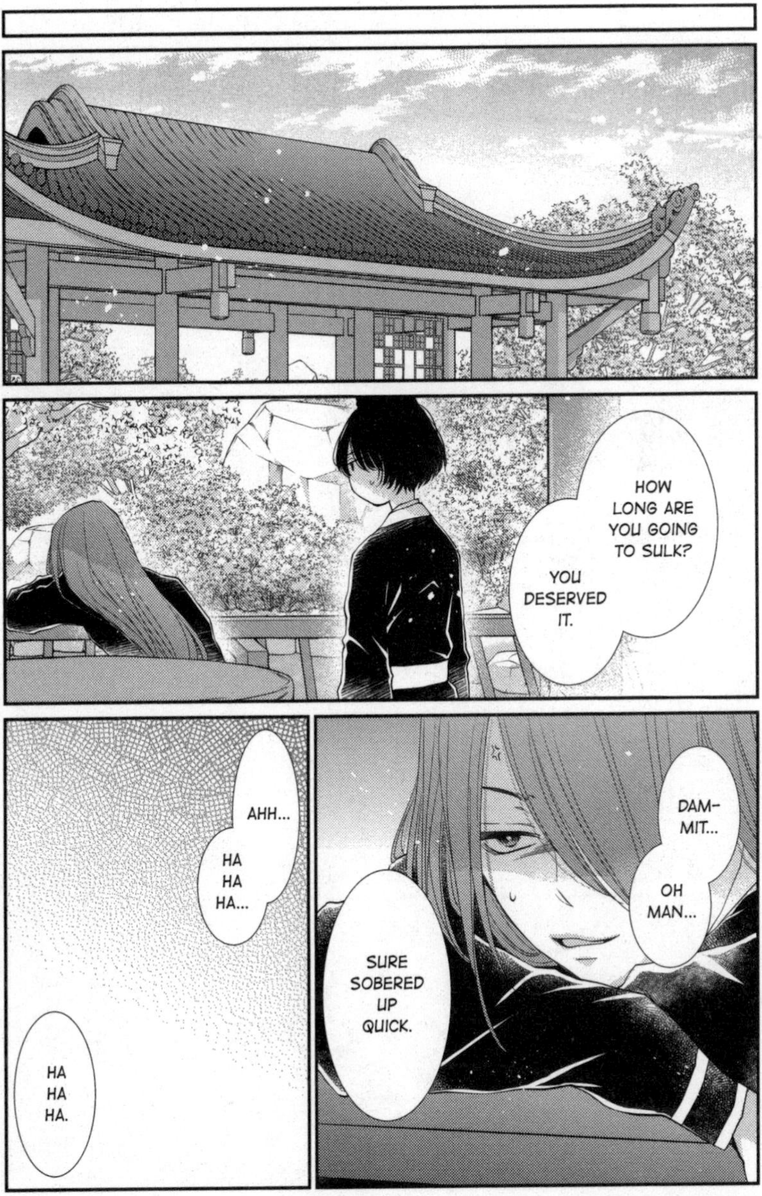
HOW LONG ARE YOU GOING TO SULK?
YOU DESERVED IT.
DAM-MIT...
OH MAN...
SURE SOBERED UP QUICK.
AHH...
HA HA HA...
HA HA HA.

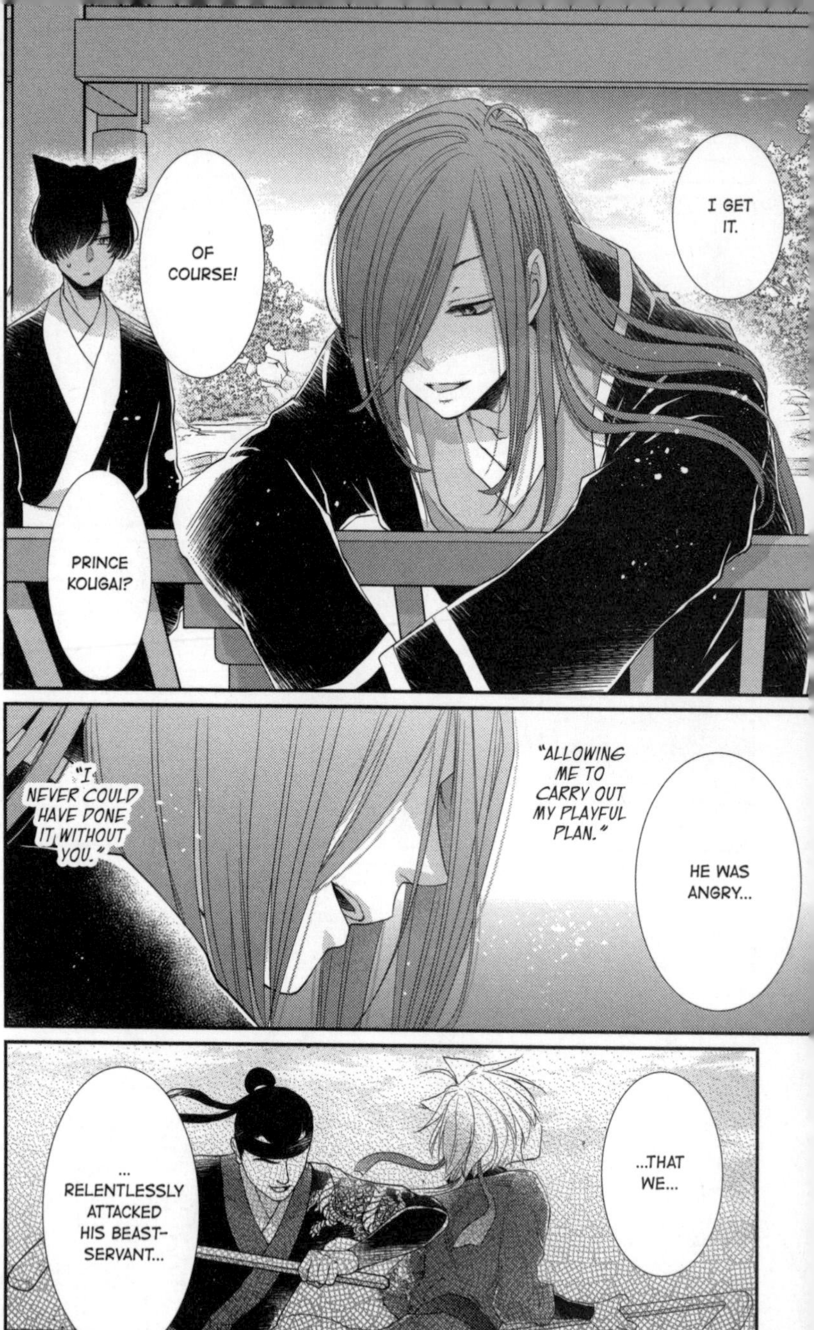

I GET IT.
OF COURSE!
PRINCE KOUGAI?
"ALLOWING ME TO CARRY OUT MY PLAYFUL PLAN."
"I NEVER COULD HAVE DONE IT WITHOUT YOU."
HE WAS ANGRY...
...THAT WE...
...RELENTLESSLY ATTACKED HIS BEAST-SERVANT...

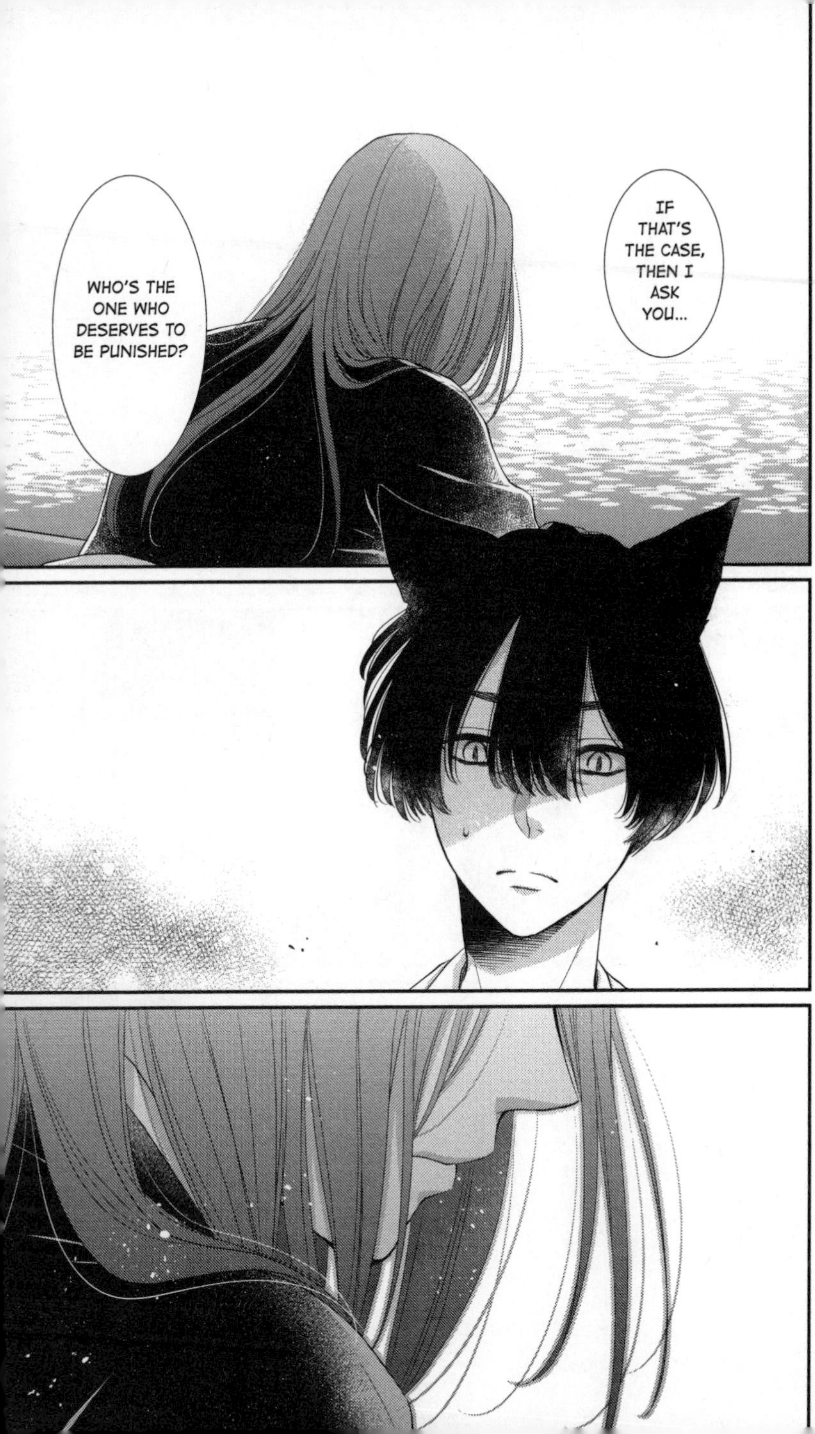
IF THAT'S THE CASE, THEN I ASK YOU...
WHO'S THE ONE WHO DESERVES TO BE PUNISHED?

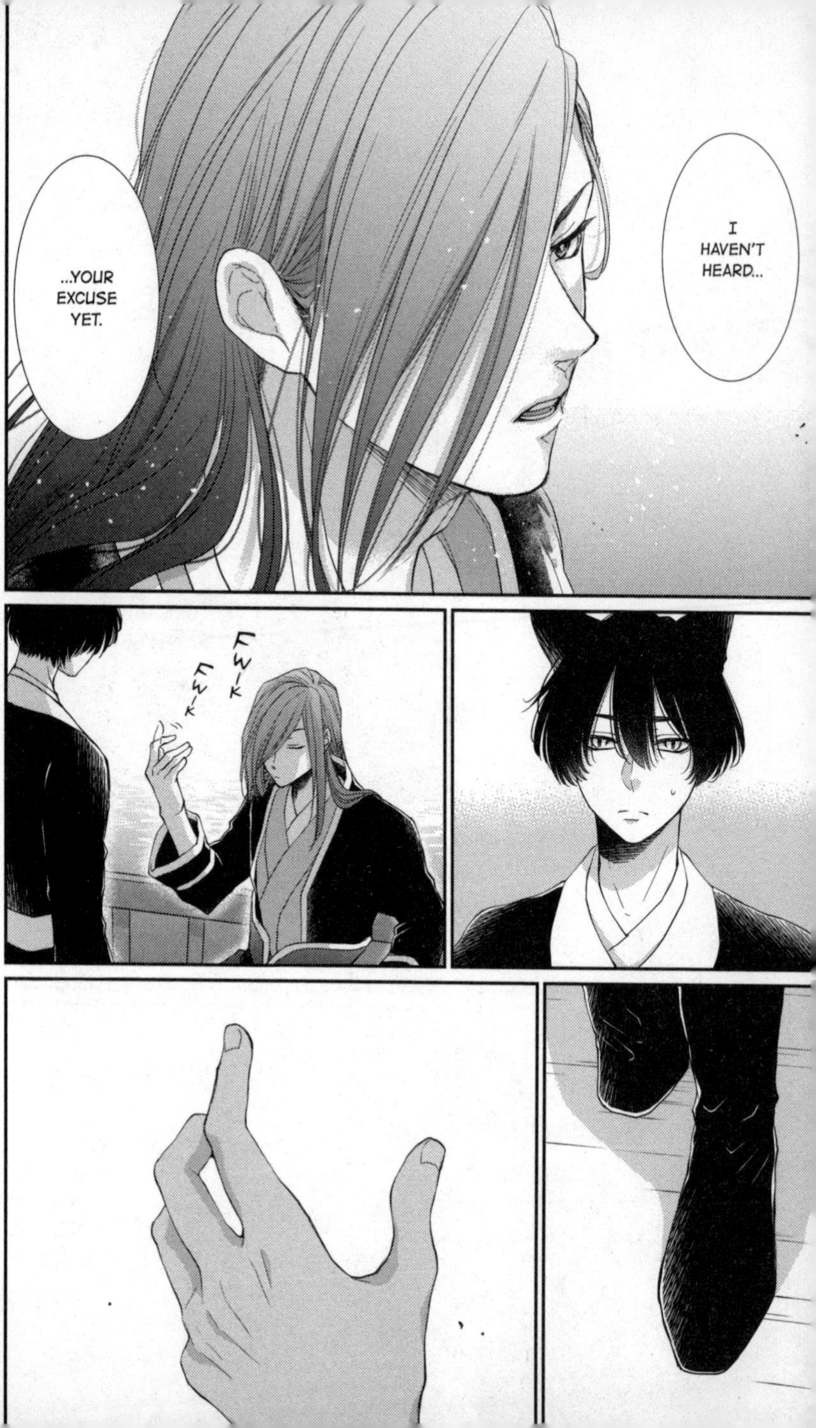
I HAVEN'T HEARD...
...YOUR EXCUSE YET.
FWIK
FWIK

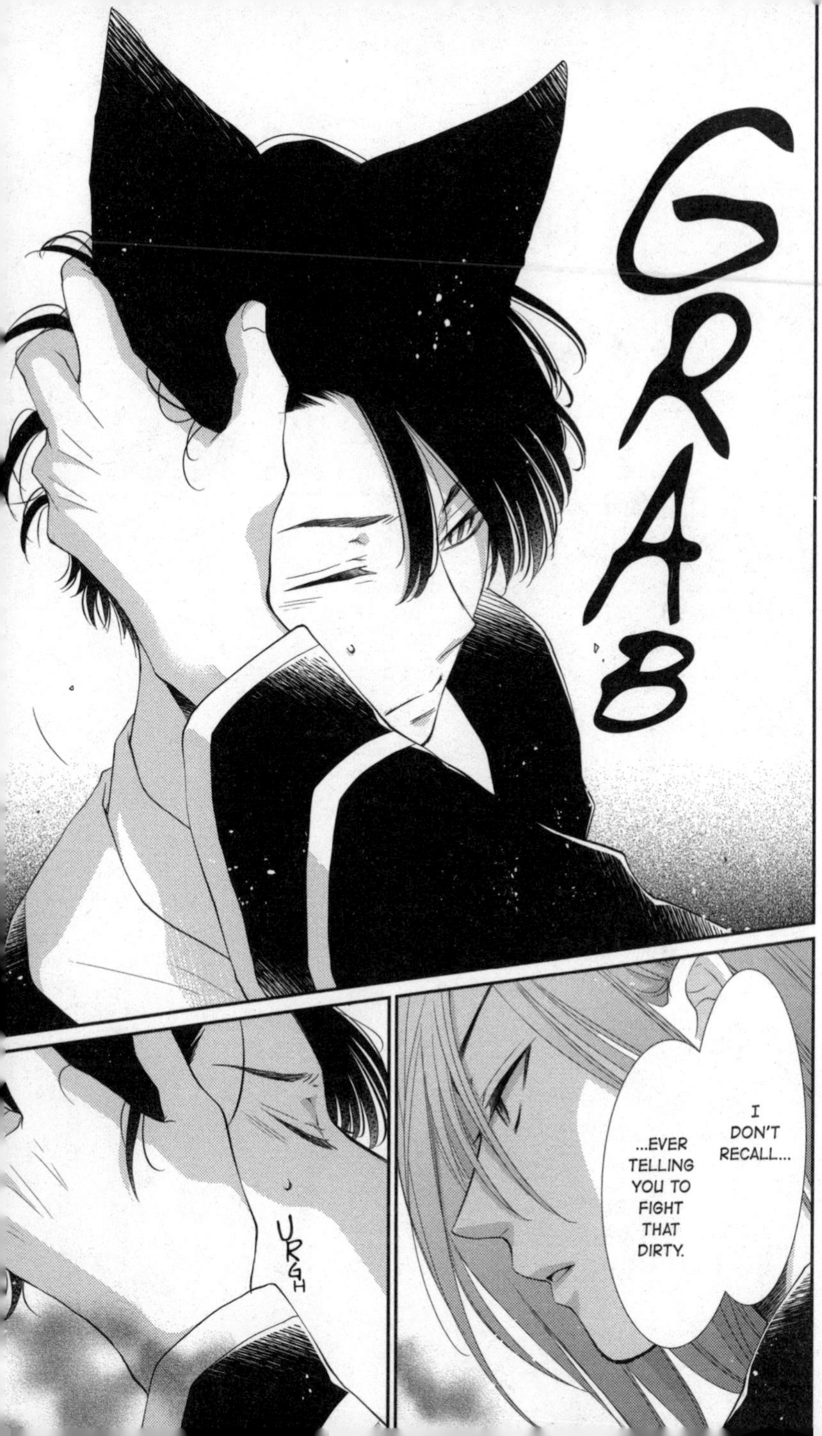
GRAB
I DON'T RECALL...
...EVER TELLING YOU TO FIGHT THAT DIRTY.
URGH

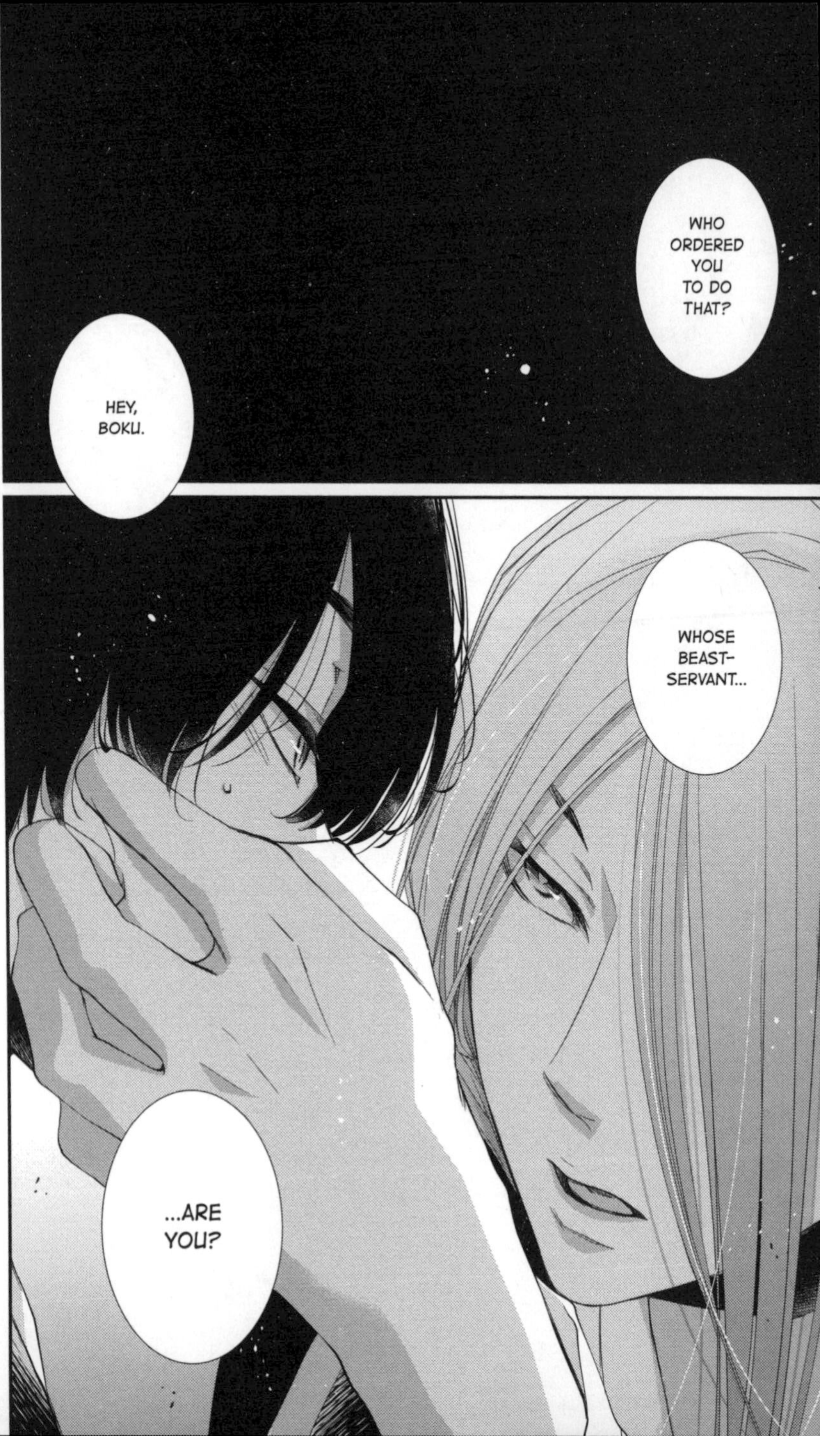
WHO ORDERED YOU TO DO THAT?
HEY, BOKU.
WHOSE BEAST-SERVANT...
...ARE YOU?

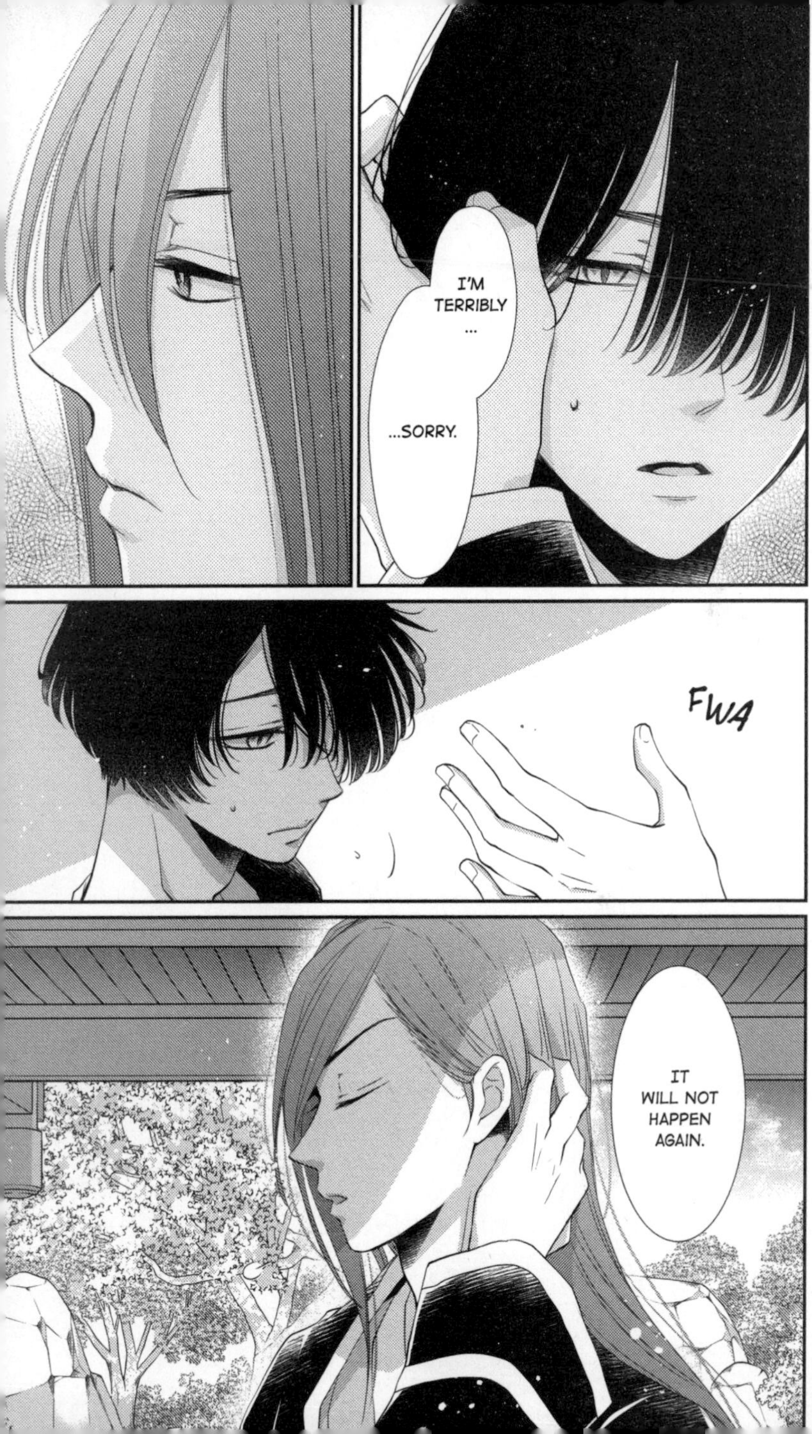
I'M TERRIBLY ...
...SORRY.
FWA
IT WILL NOT HAPPEN AGAIN.

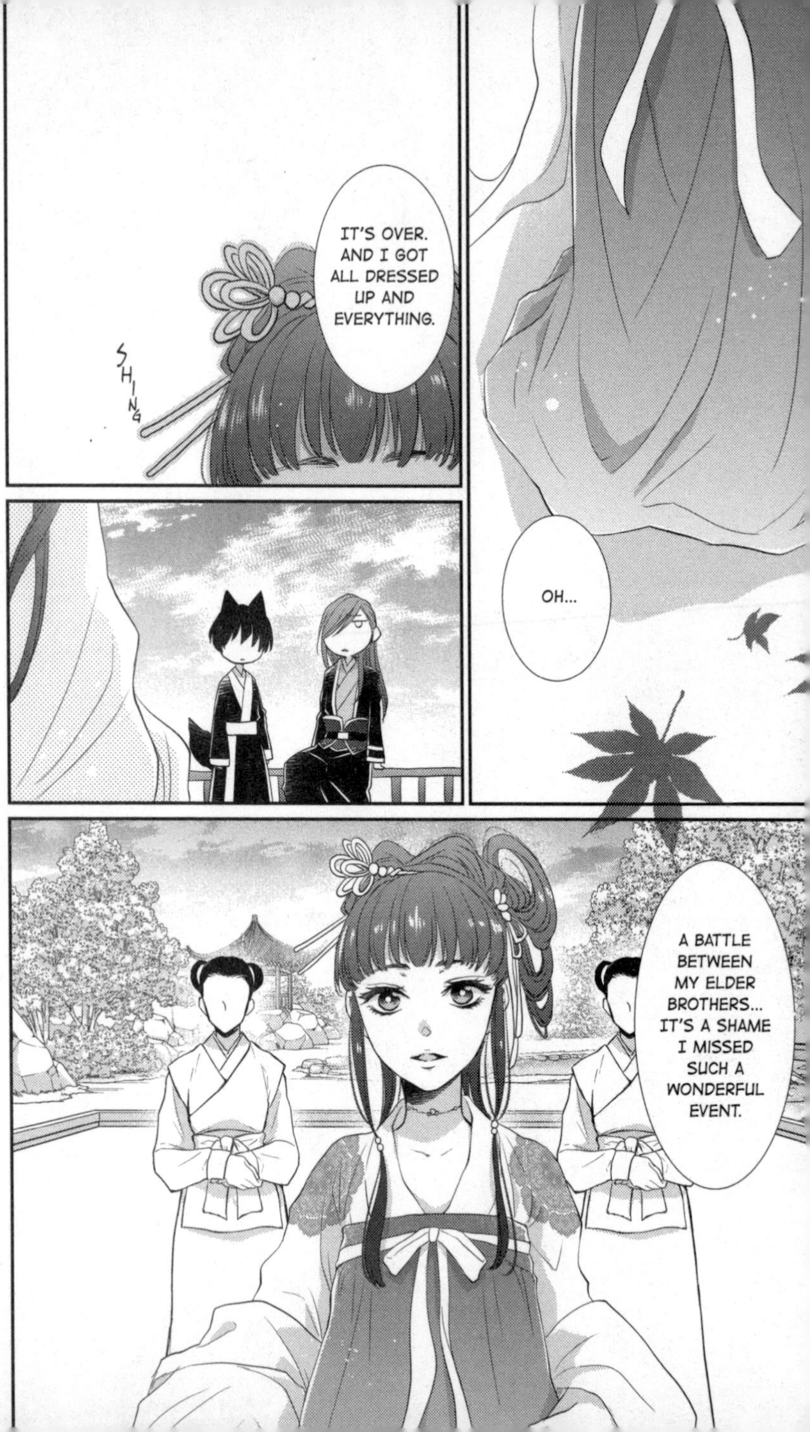
OH...
IT'S OVER. AND I GOT ALL DRESSED UP AND EVERYTHING.
SHING
A BATTLE BETWEEN MY ELDER BROTHERS... IT'S A SHAME I MISSED SUCH A WONDERFUL EVENT.

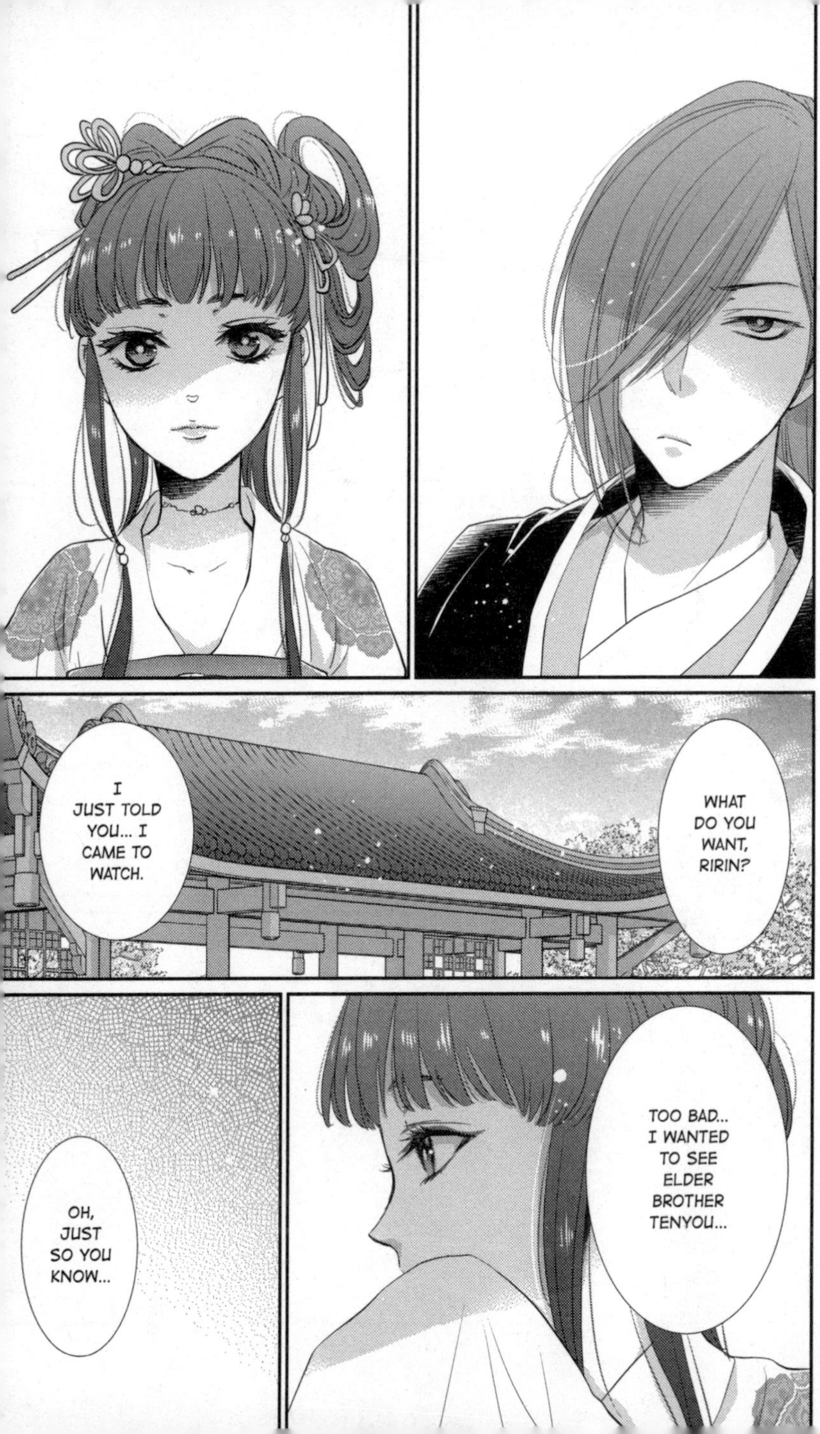
WHAT DO YOU WANT, RIRIN?
I JUST TOLD YOU... I CAME TO WATCH.
TOO BAD... I WANTED TO SEE ELDER BROTHER TENYOU...
OH, JUST SO YOU KNOW...

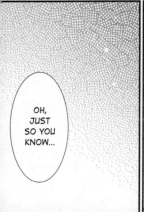

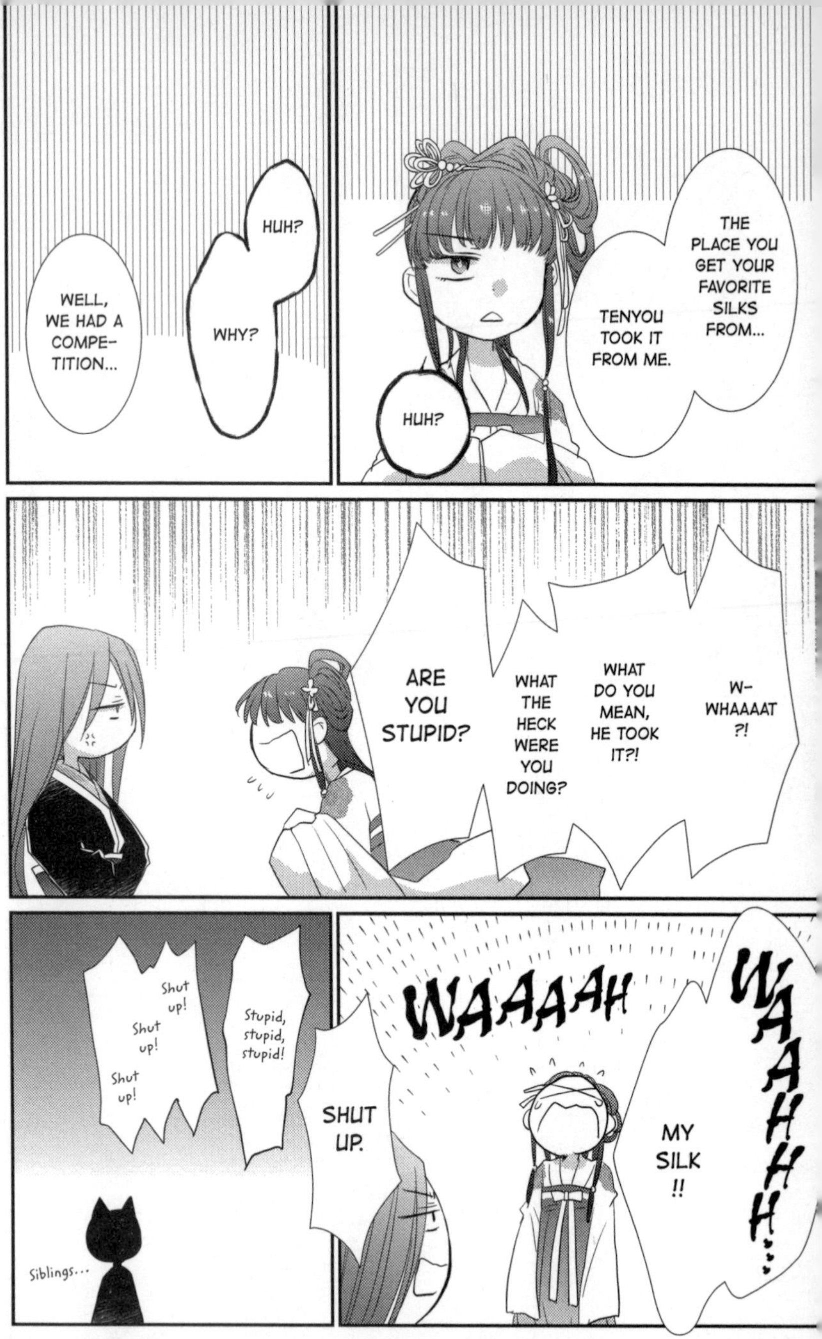
THE PLACE YOU GET YOUR FAVORITE SILKS FROM...
TENYOU TOOK IT FROM ME.
HUH?
HUH?
WHY?
WELL, WE HAD A COMPE-TITION...
W-WHAAAAT?!
WHAT DO YOU MEAN, HE TOOK IT?!
WHAT THE HECK WERE YOU DOING?
ARE YOU STUPID?
WAAHHHH...
MY SILK!!
WAAAAH
SHUT UP.
Stupid, stupid, stupid!
Shut up!
Shut up!
Shut up!
Siblings...

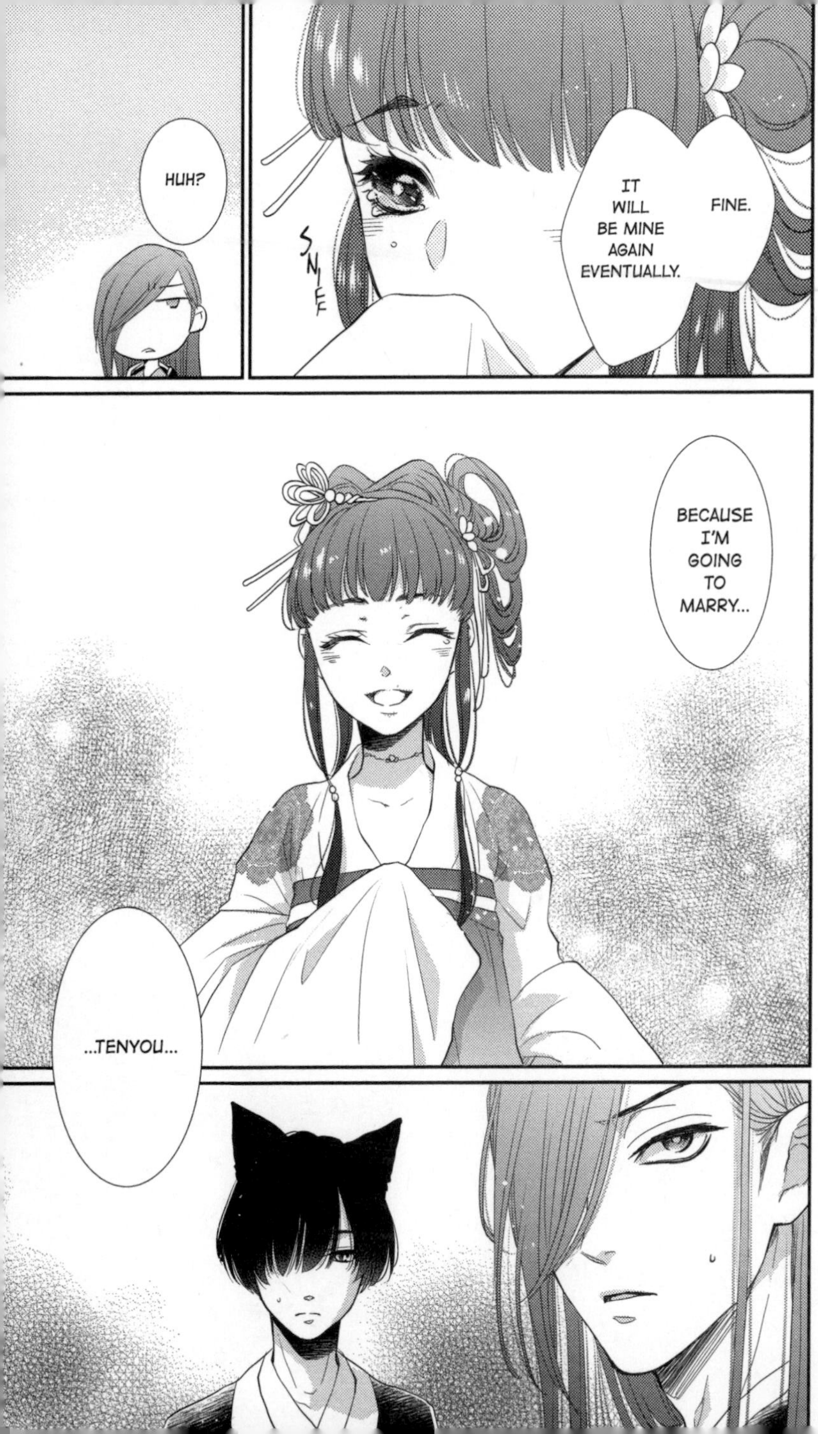
FINE.
IT WILL BE MINE AGAIN EVENTUALLY.
SNIFF
HUH?
BECAUSE I'M GOING TO MARRY...
...TENYOU...

THE
KING'S
Beast

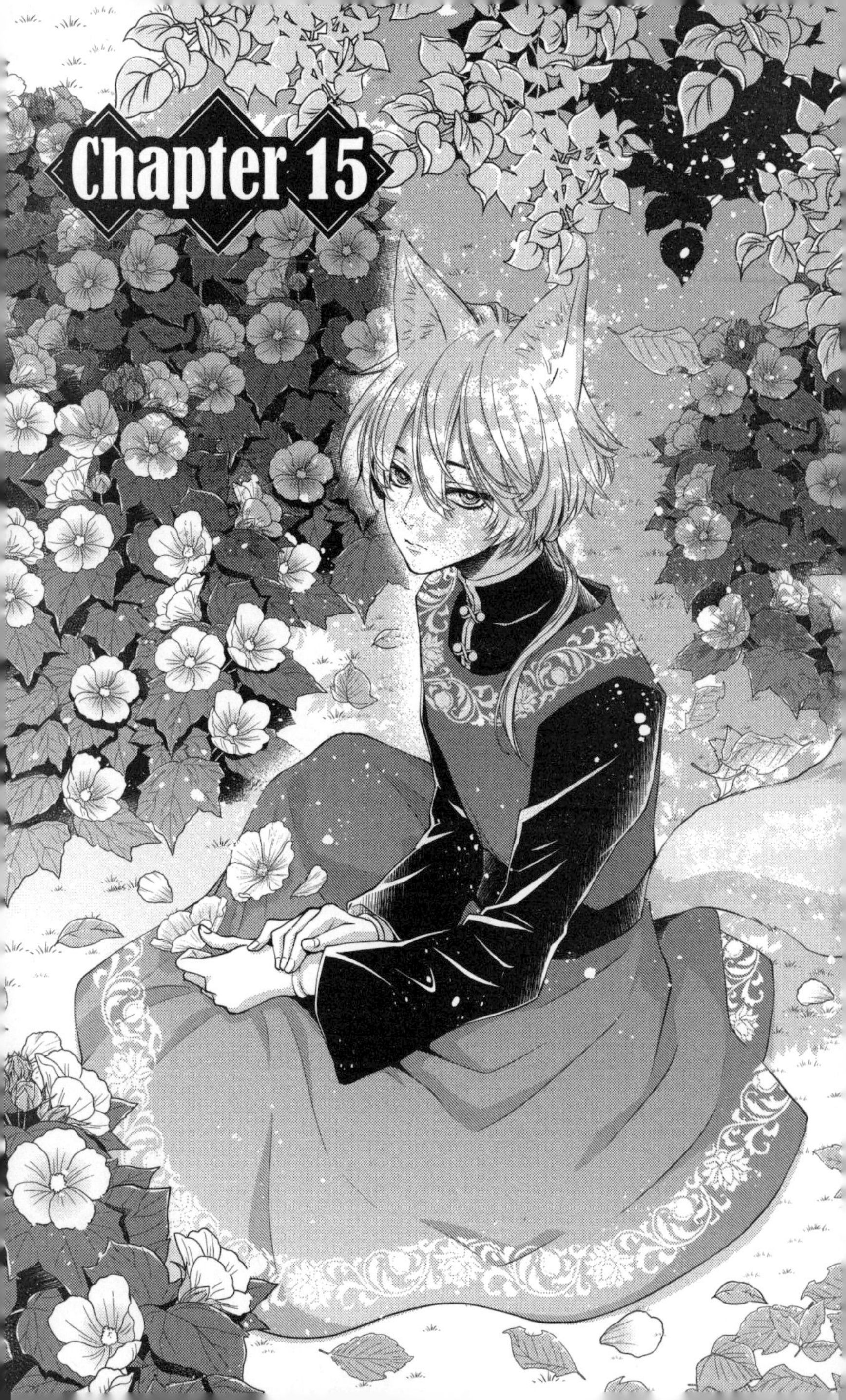
Chapter 15

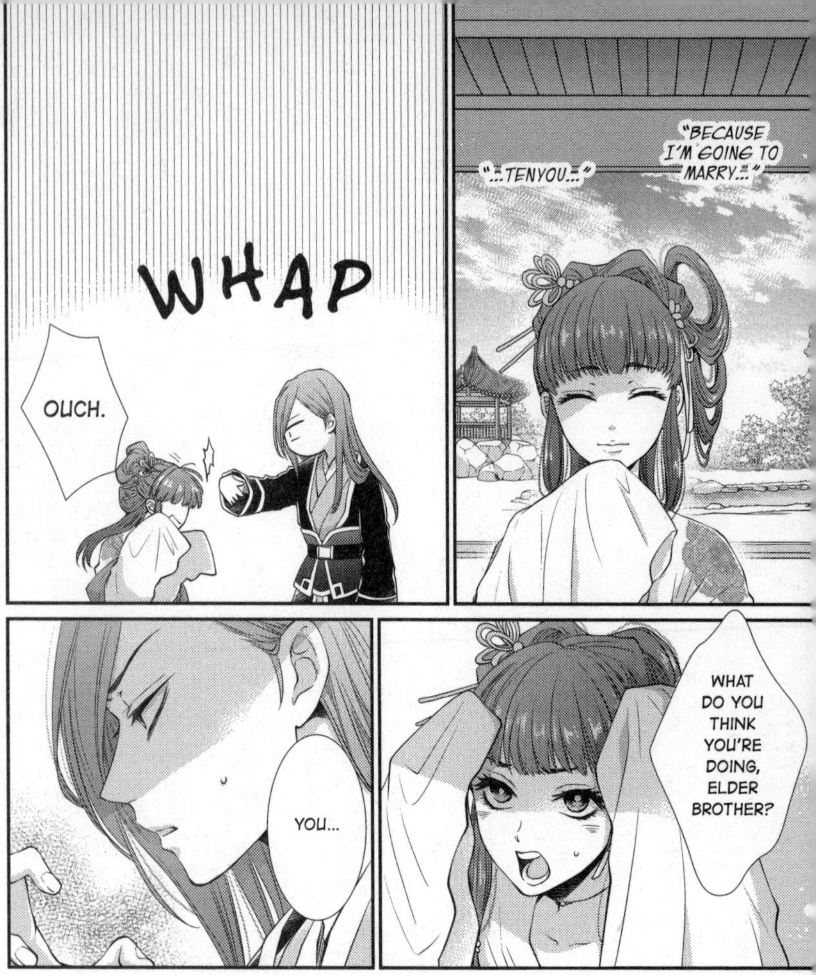
"BECAUSE I'M GOING TO MARRY..."
"...TENYOU..."
WHAP
OUCH.
WHAT DO YOU THINK YOU'RE DOING, ELDER BROTHER?
YOU...

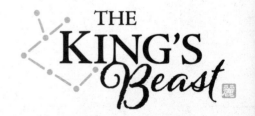

THE KING'S Beast

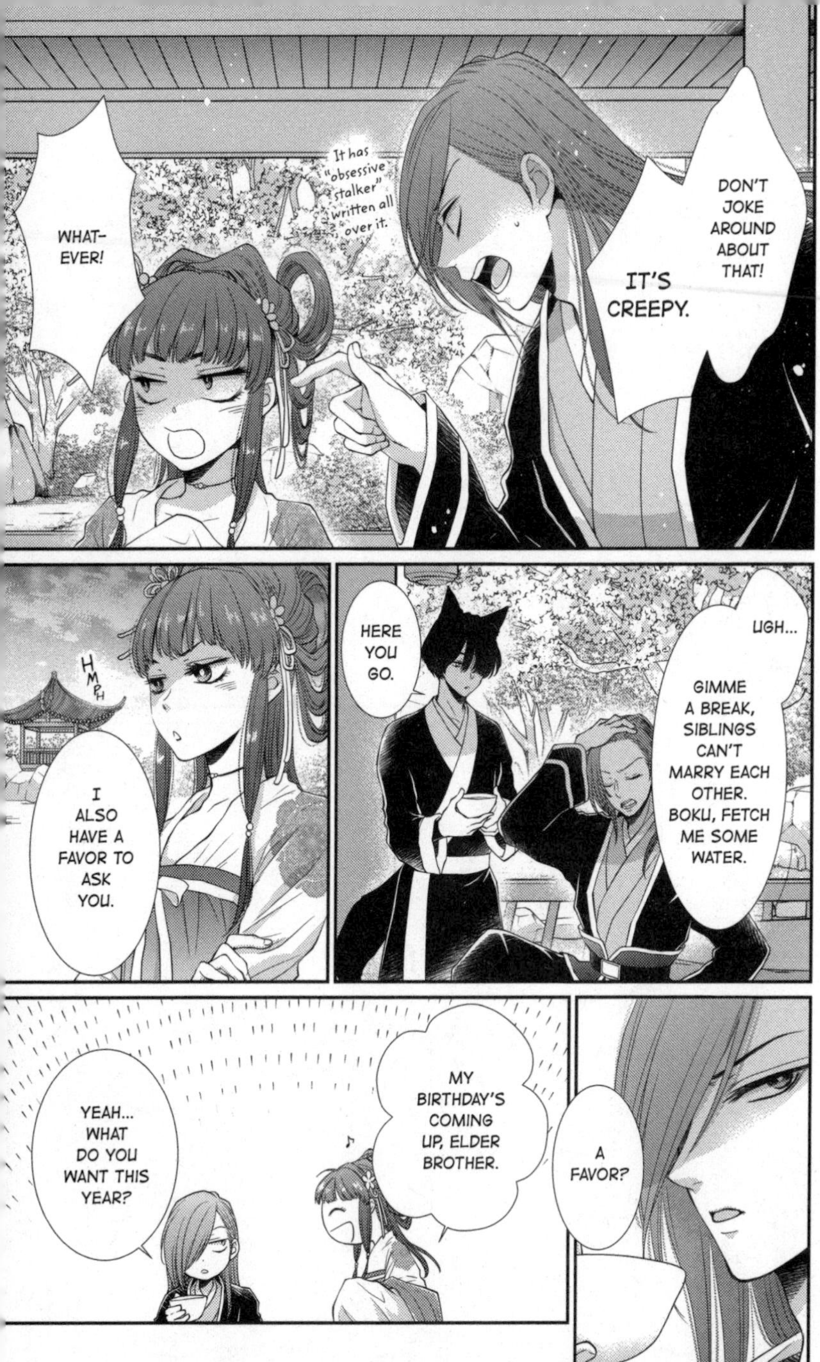
DON'T JOKE AROUND ABOUT THAT!
IT'S CREEPY.
It has "obsessive stalker" written all over it.
WHAT-EVER!
UGH...
GIMME A BREAK, SIBLINGS CAN'T MARRY EACH OTHER. BOKU, FETCH ME SOME WATER.
HERE YOU GO.
HMPH
I ALSO HAVE A FAVOR TO ASK YOU.
A FAVOR?
MY BIRTHDAY'S COMING UP, ELDER BROTHER.
YEAH... WHAT DO YOU WANT THIS YEAR?

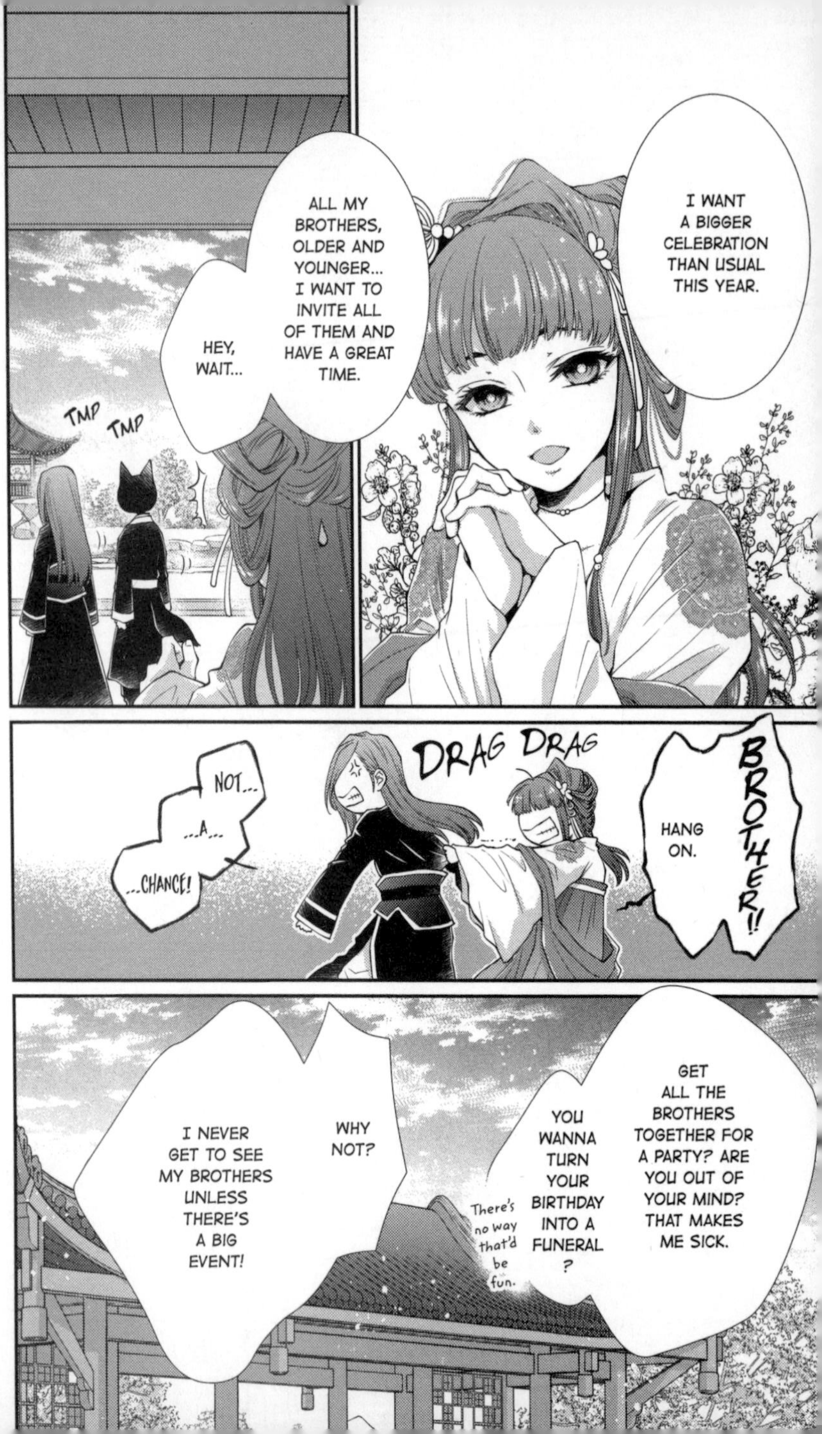
I WANT A BIGGER CELEBRATION THAN USUAL THIS YEAR.
ALL MY BROTHERS, OLDER AND YOUNGER... I WANT TO INVITE ALL OF THEM AND HAVE A GREAT TIME.
HEY, WAIT...
TMP
TMP
BROTHER!!
HANG ON.
DRAG DRAG
NOT...
...A...
...CHANCE!
GET ALL THE BROTHERS TOGETHER FOR A PARTY? ARE YOU OUT OF YOUR MIND? THAT MAKES ME SICK.
YOU WANNA TURN YOUR BIRTHDAY INTO A FUNERAL?
There's no way that'd be fun.
WHY NOT?
I NEVER GET TO SEE MY BROTHERS UNLESS THERE'S A BIG EVENT!

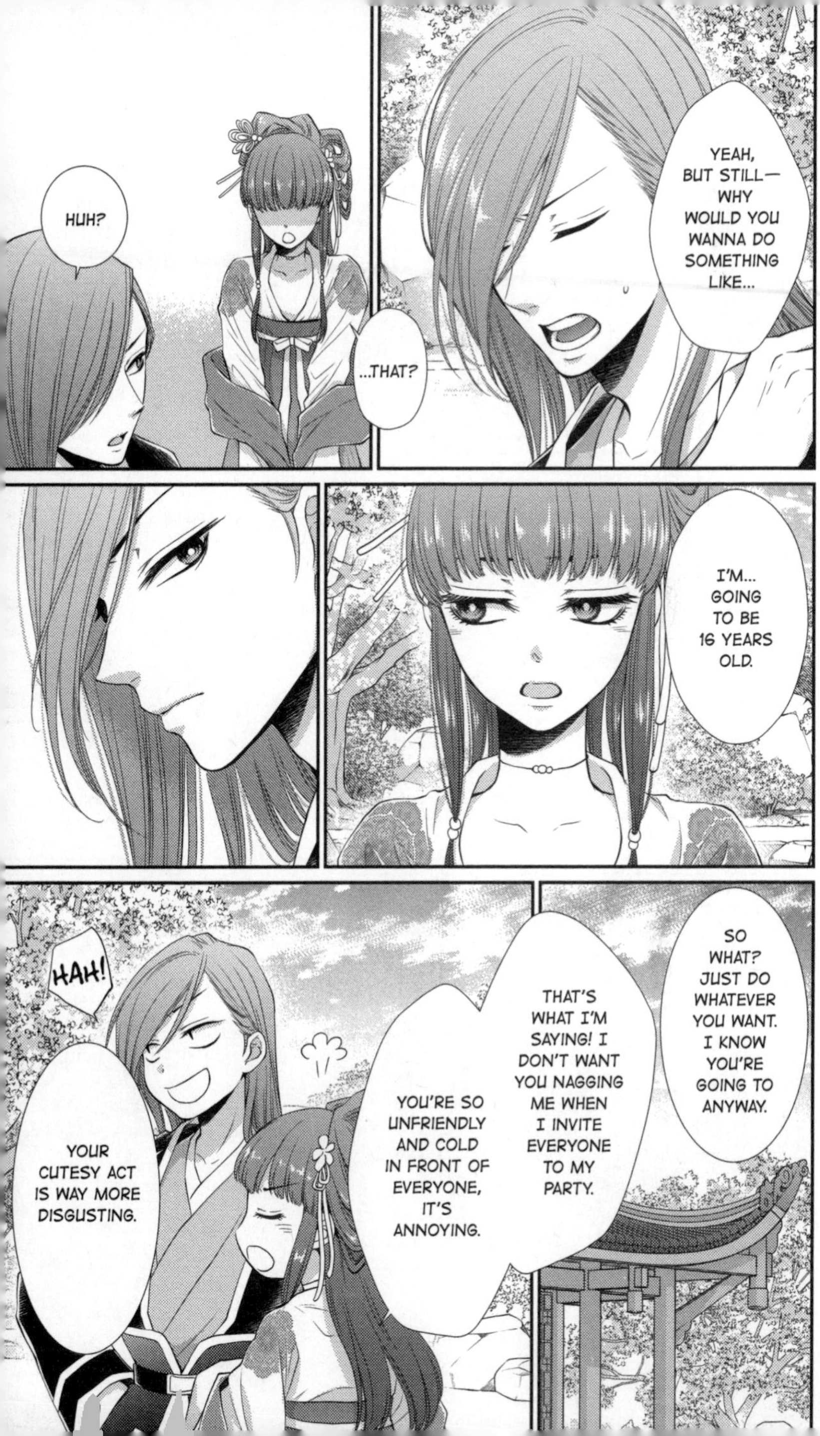

YEAH, BUT STILL— WHY WOULD YOU WANNA DO SOMETHING LIKE...
...THAT?
HUH?
I'M... GOING TO BE 16 YEARS OLD.
SO WHAT? JUST DO WHATEVER YOU WANT. I KNOW YOU'RE GOING TO ANYWAY.
THAT'S WHAT I'M SAYING! I DON'T WANT YOU NAGGING ME WHEN I INVITE EVERYONE TO MY PARTY.
YOU'RE SO UNFRIENDLY AND COLD IN FRONT OF EVERYONE, IT'S ANNOYING.
HAH!
YOUR CUTESY ACT IS WAY MORE DISGUSTING.

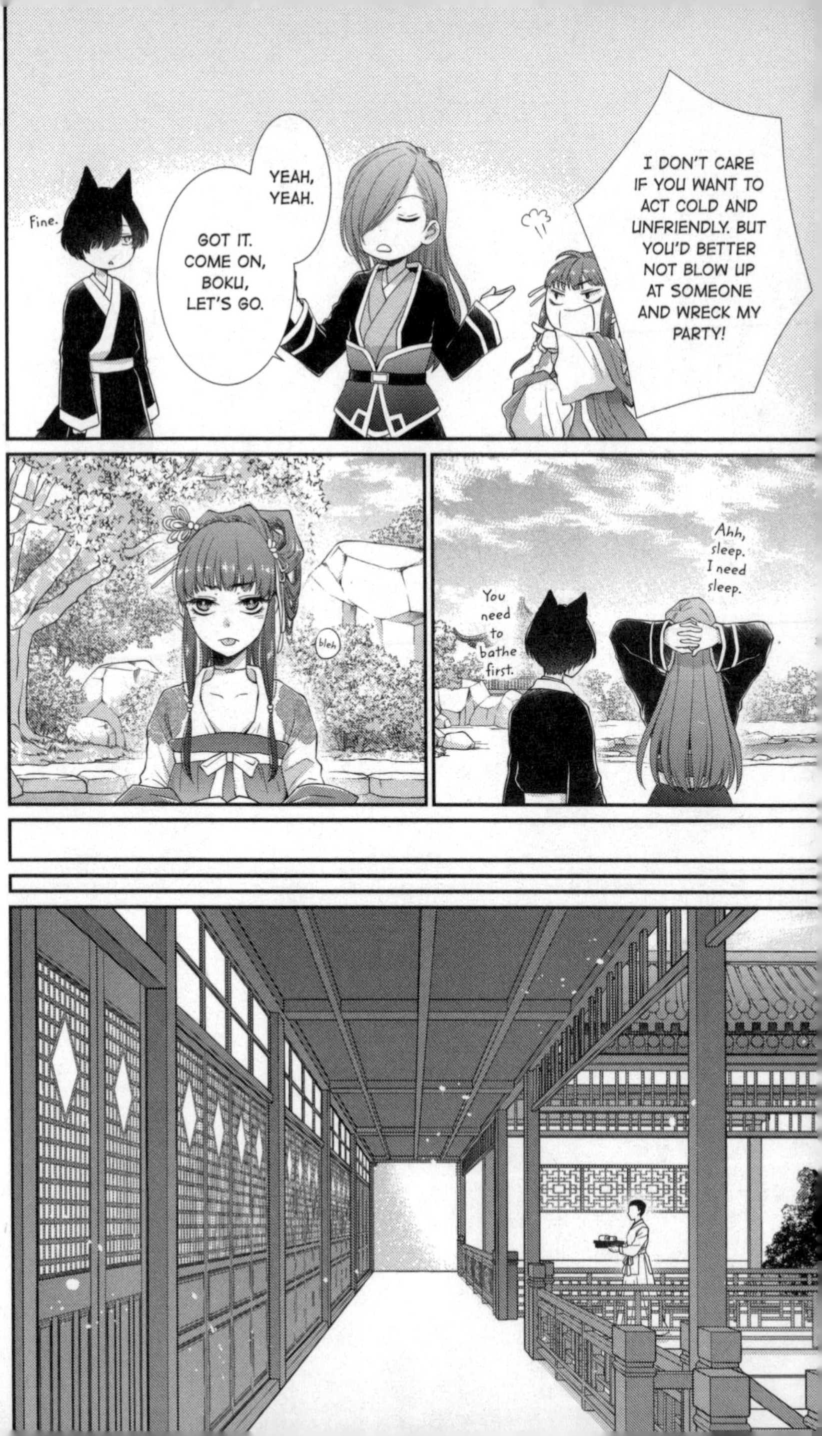
I DON'T CARE IF YOU WANT TO ACT COLD AND UNFRIENDLY. BUT YOU'D BETTER NOT BLOW UP AT SOMEONE AND WRECK MY PARTY!
YEAH, YEAH.
GOT IT. COME ON, BOKU, LET'S GO.
Fine.
Ahh, sleep. I need sleep.
You need to bathe first.
bleh

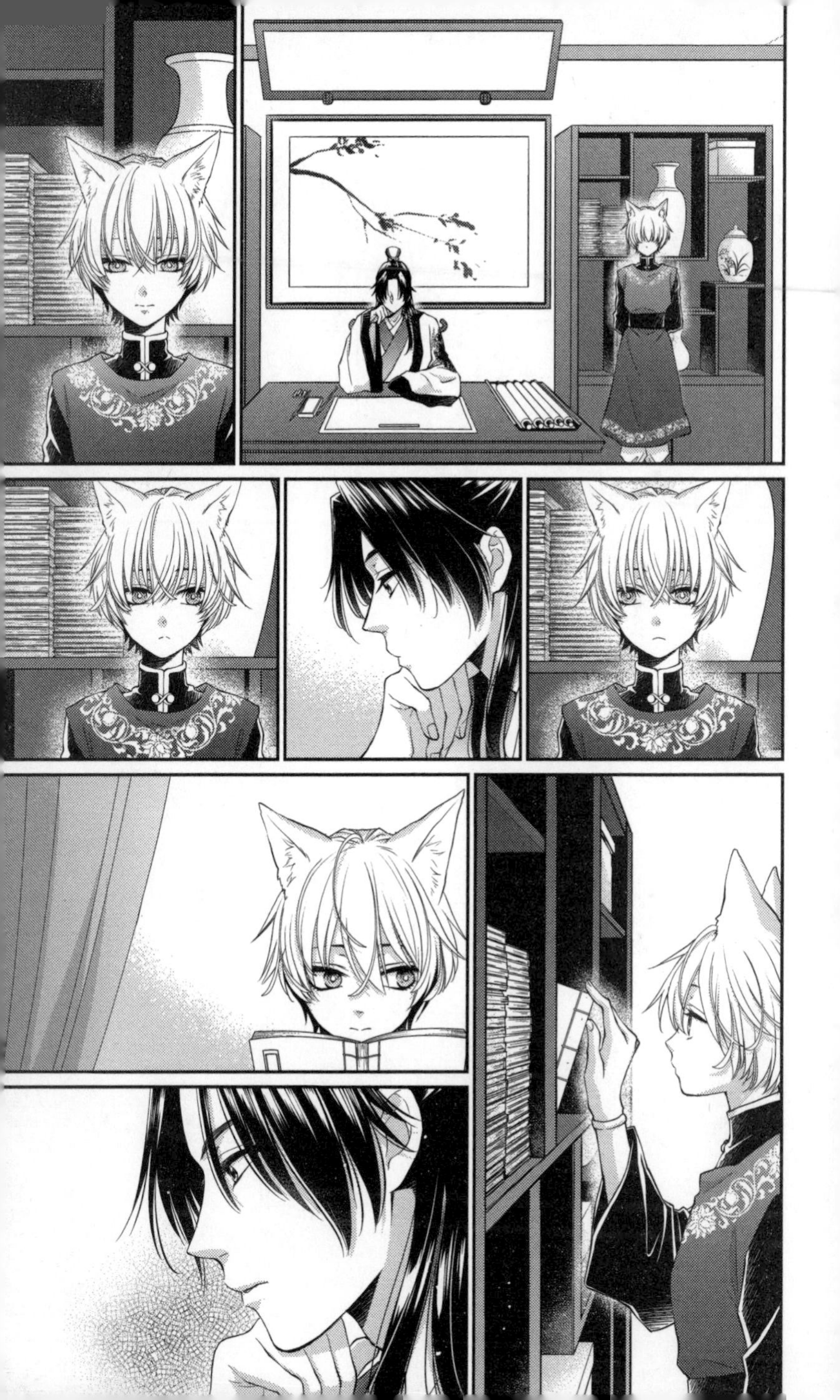

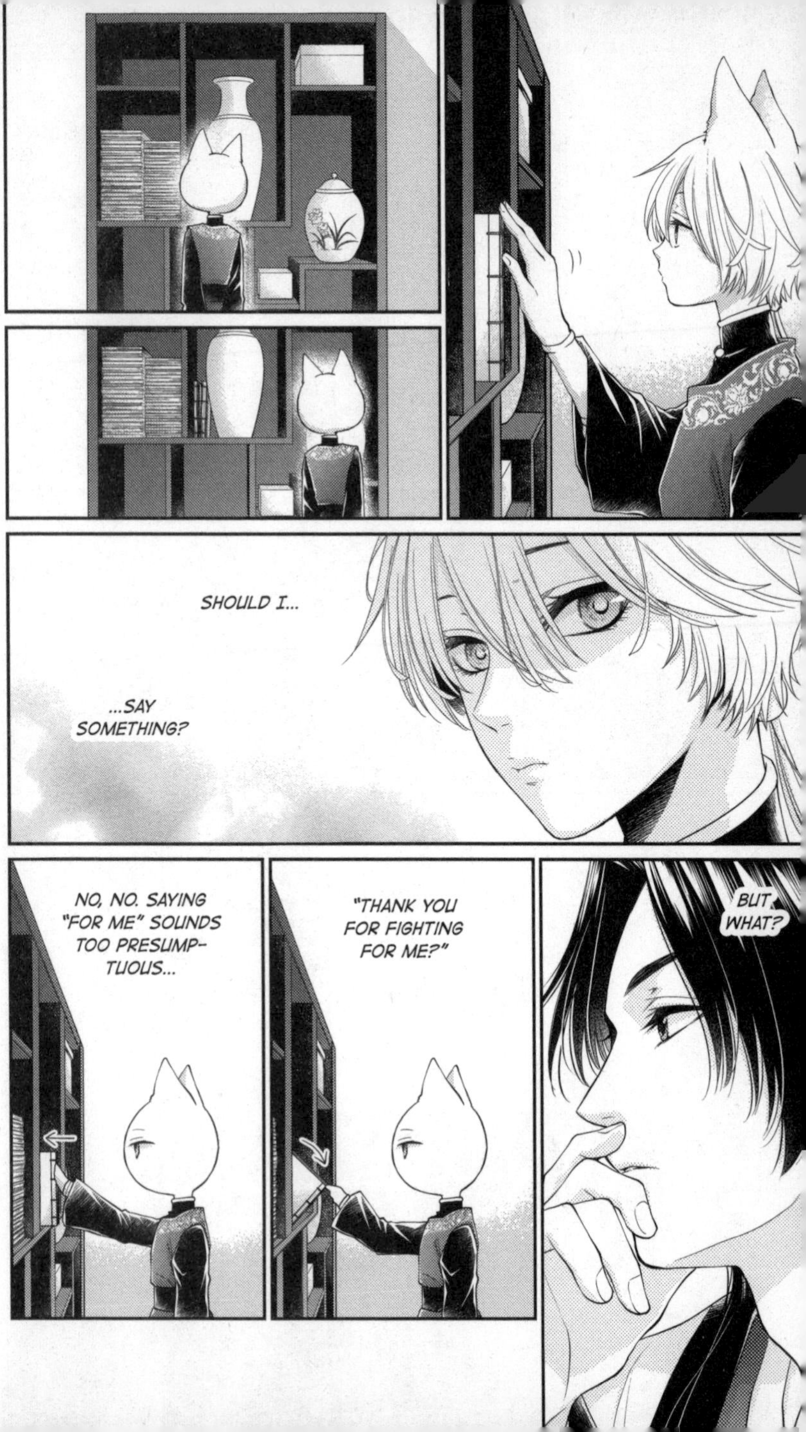

SHOULD I...
...SAY SOMETHING?
BUT WHAT?
"THANK YOU FOR FIGHTING FOR ME?"
NO, NO. SAYING "FOR ME" SOUNDS TOO PRESUMP-TUOUS...

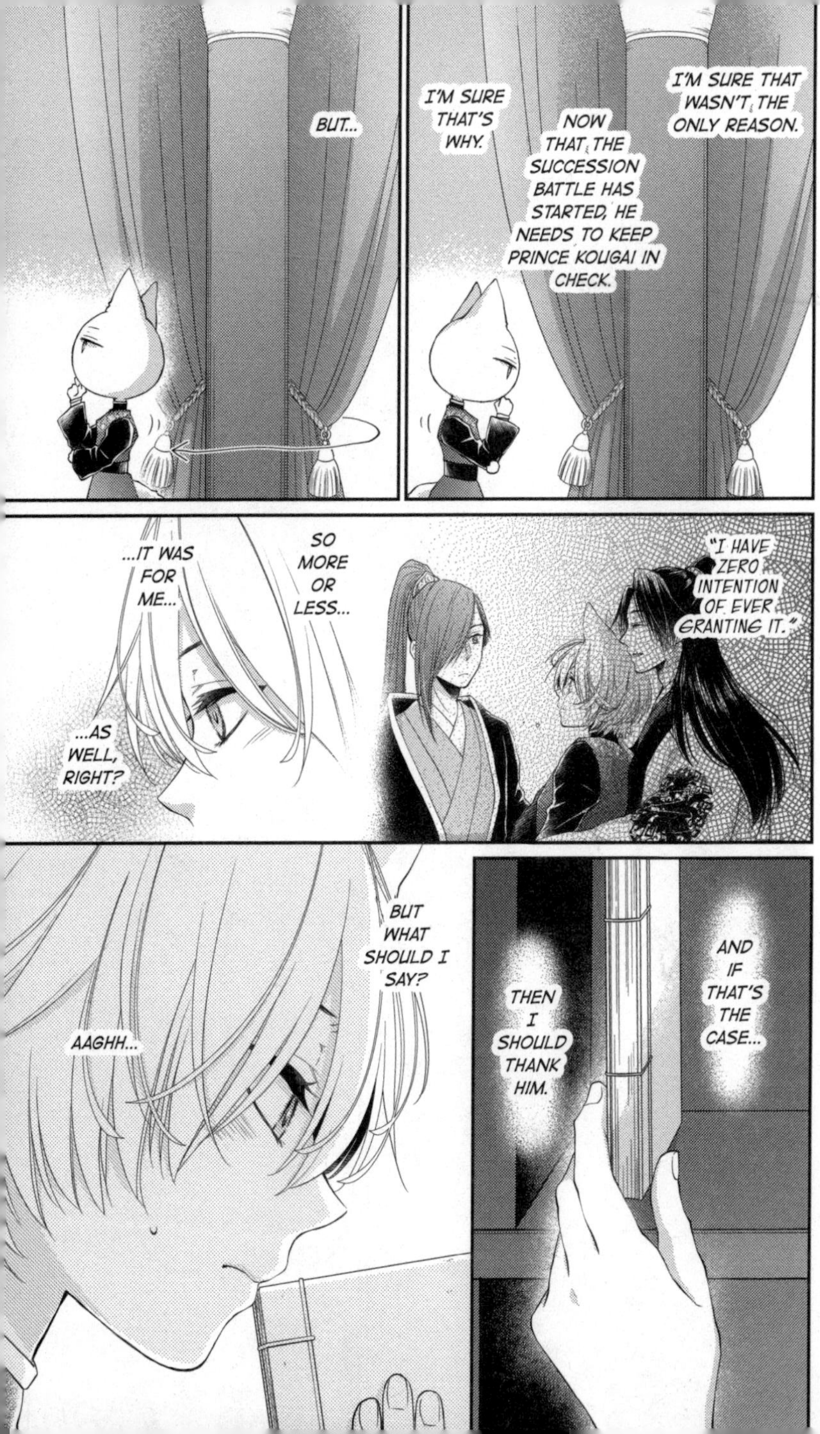
I'M SURE THAT WASN'T THE ONLY REASON.
NOW THAT THE SUCCESSION BATTLE HAS STARTED, HE NEEDS TO KEEP PRINCE KOUGAI IN CHECK.
I'M SURE THAT'S WHY.
BUT...
"I HAVE ZERO INTENTION OF EVER GRANTING IT."
SO MORE OR LESS...
...IT WAS FOR ME...
...AS WELL, RIGHT?
AND IF THAT'S THE CASE...
THEN I SHOULD THANK HIM.
BUT WHAT SHOULD I SAY?
AAGHH...

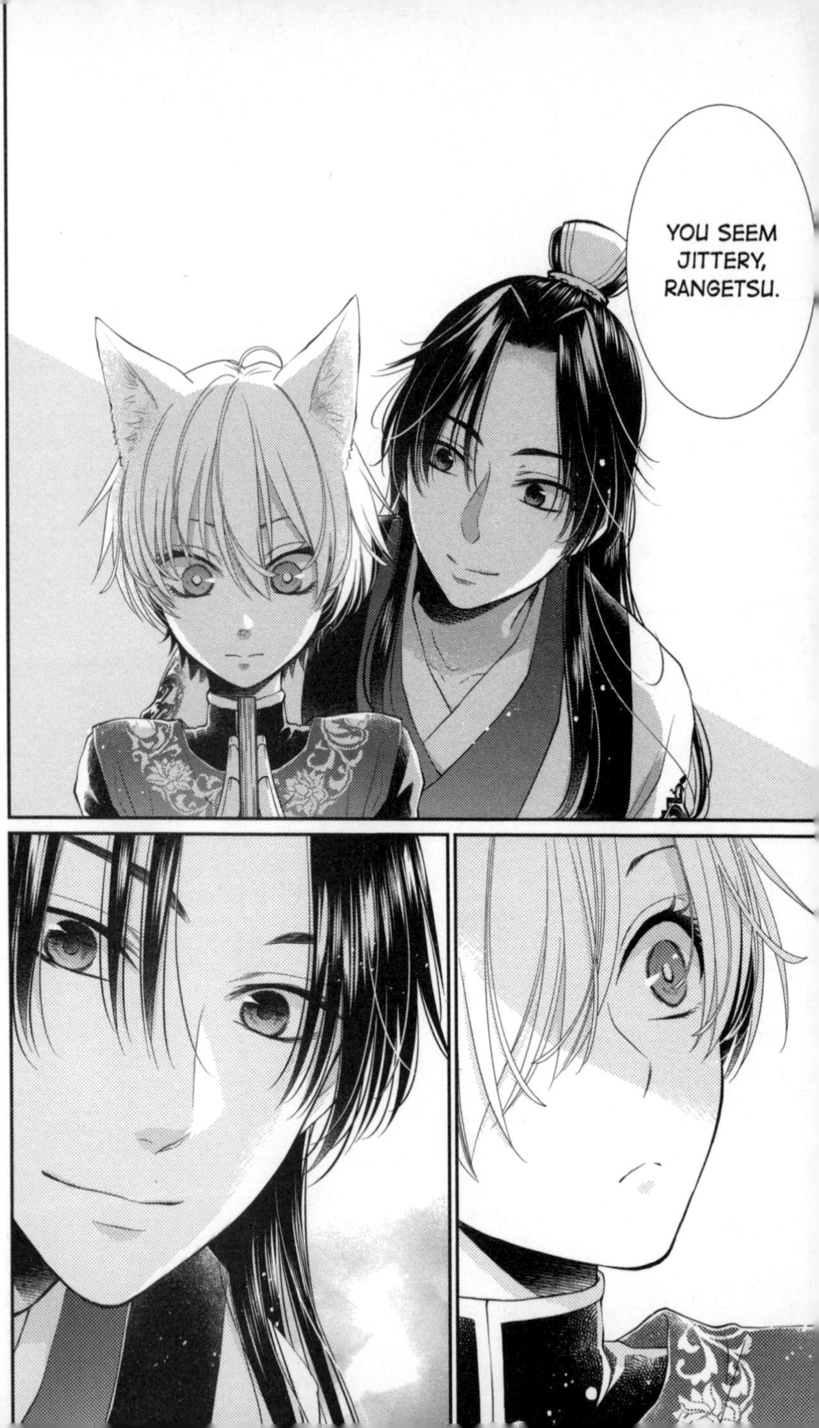
YOU SEEM JITTERY, RANGETSU.

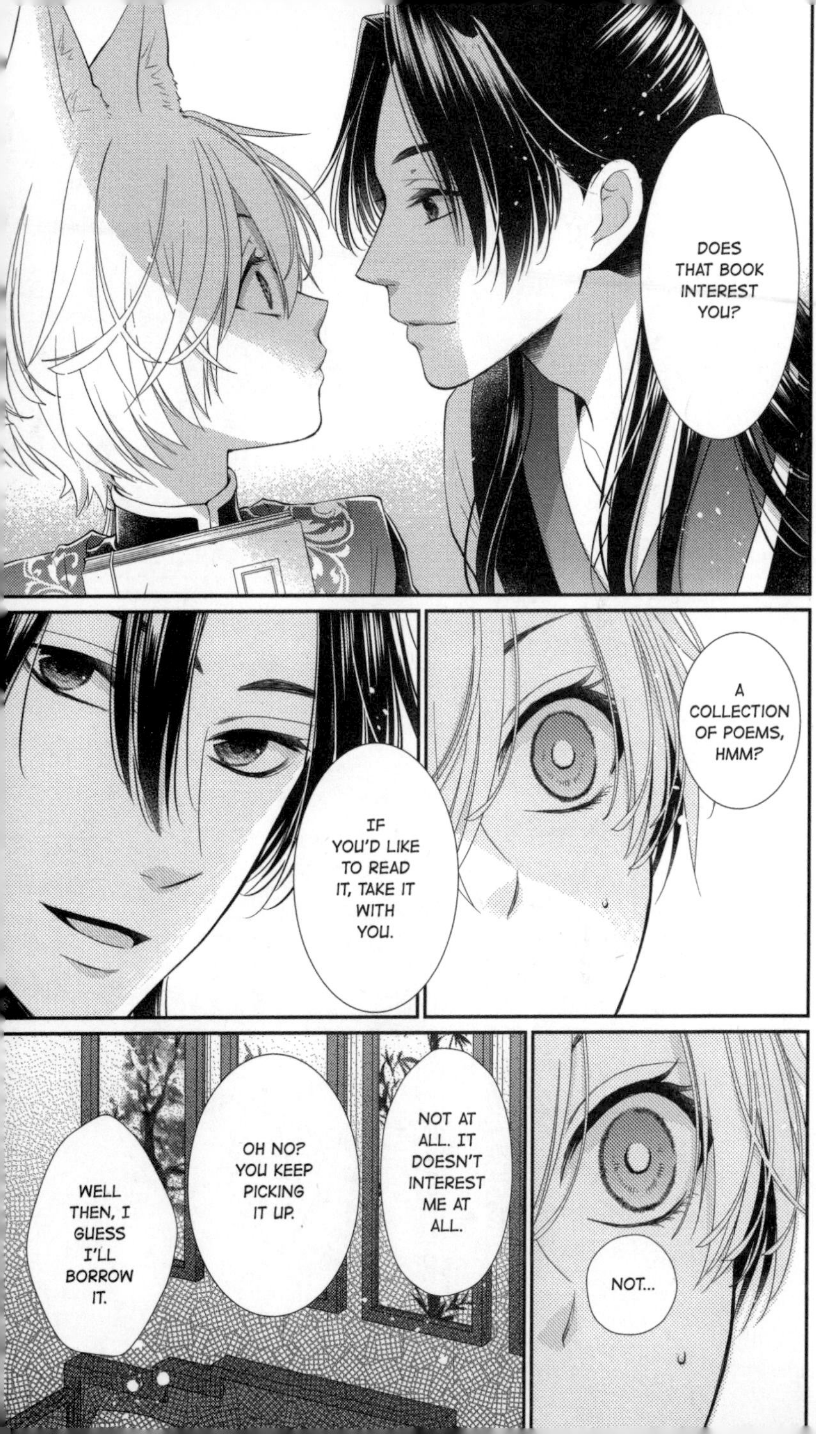
DOES THAT BOOK INTEREST YOU?
A COLLECTION OF POEMS, HMM?
IF YOU'D LIKE TO READ IT, TAKE IT WITH YOU.
NOT...
NOT AT ALL. IT DOESN'T INTEREST ME AT ALL.
OH NO? YOU KEEP PICKING IT UP.
WELL THEN, I GUESS I'LL BORROW IT.

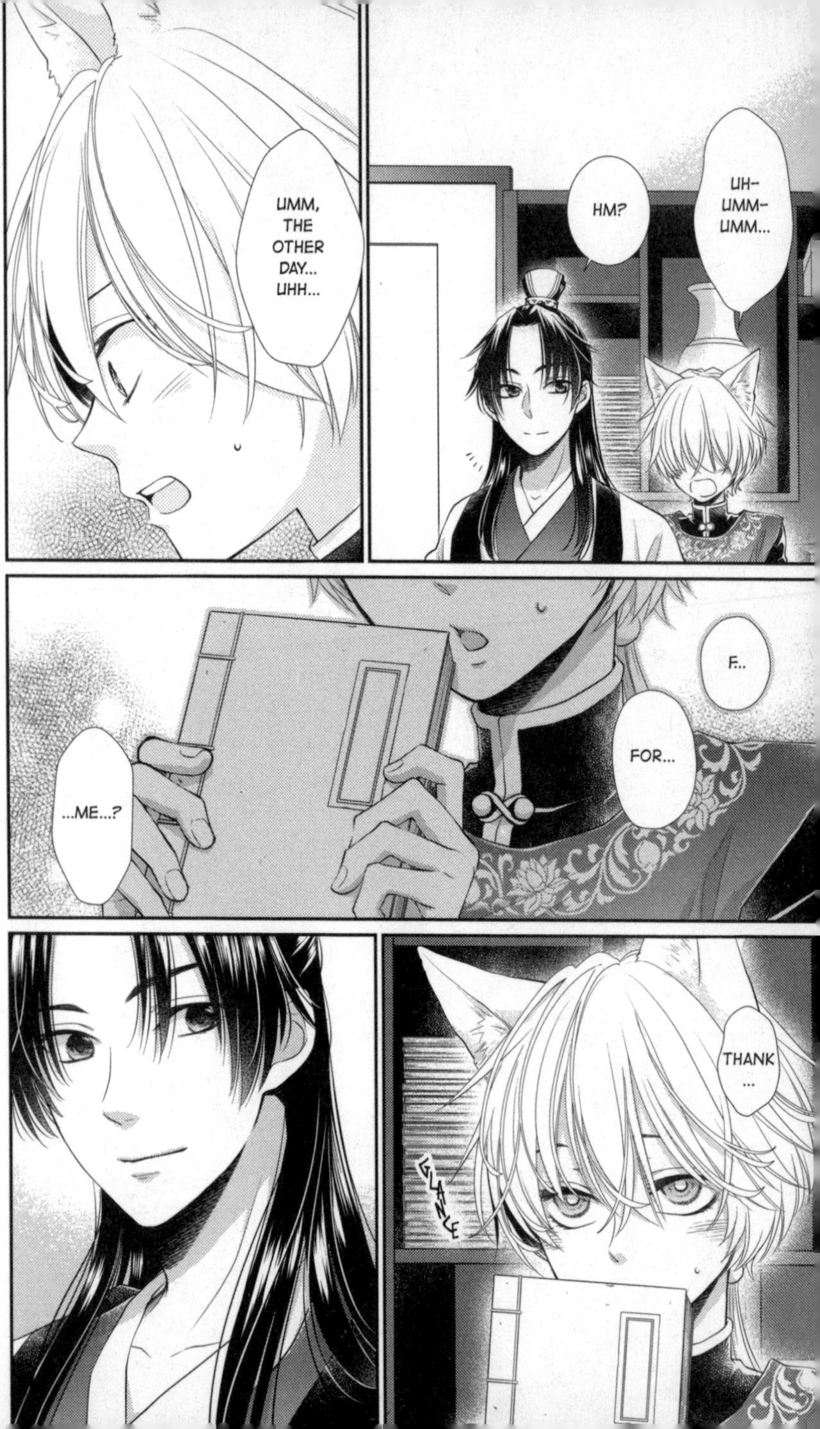
UH-
UMM-
UMM...
HM?
UMM, THE OTHER DAY... UHH...
F...
FOR...
...ME...?
THANK ...
GLANCE

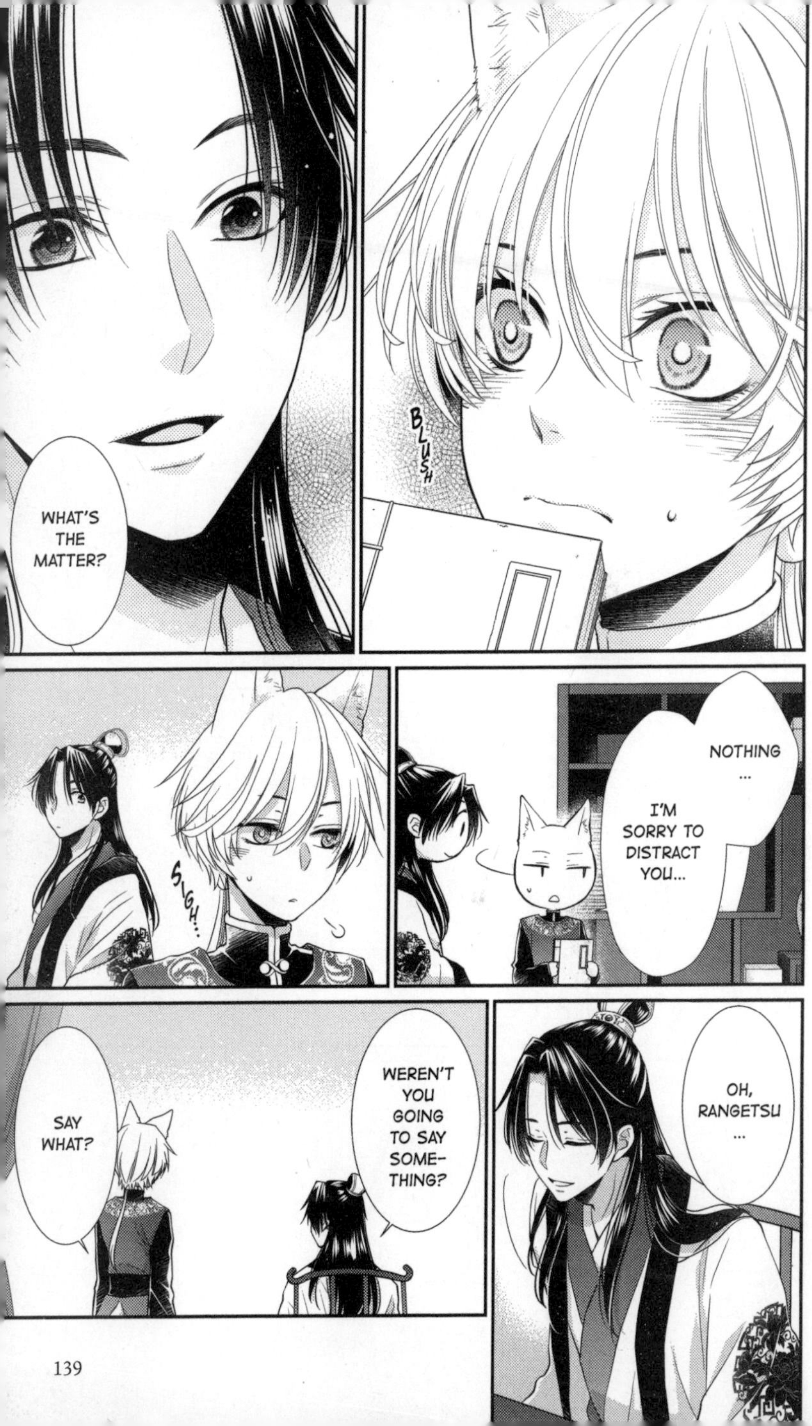
BLUSH
WHAT'S THE MATTER?
NOTHING ...
I'M SORRY TO DISTRACT YOU...
SIGH...
OH, RANGETSU ...
WEREN'T YOU GOING TO SAY SOME-THING?
SAY WHAT?

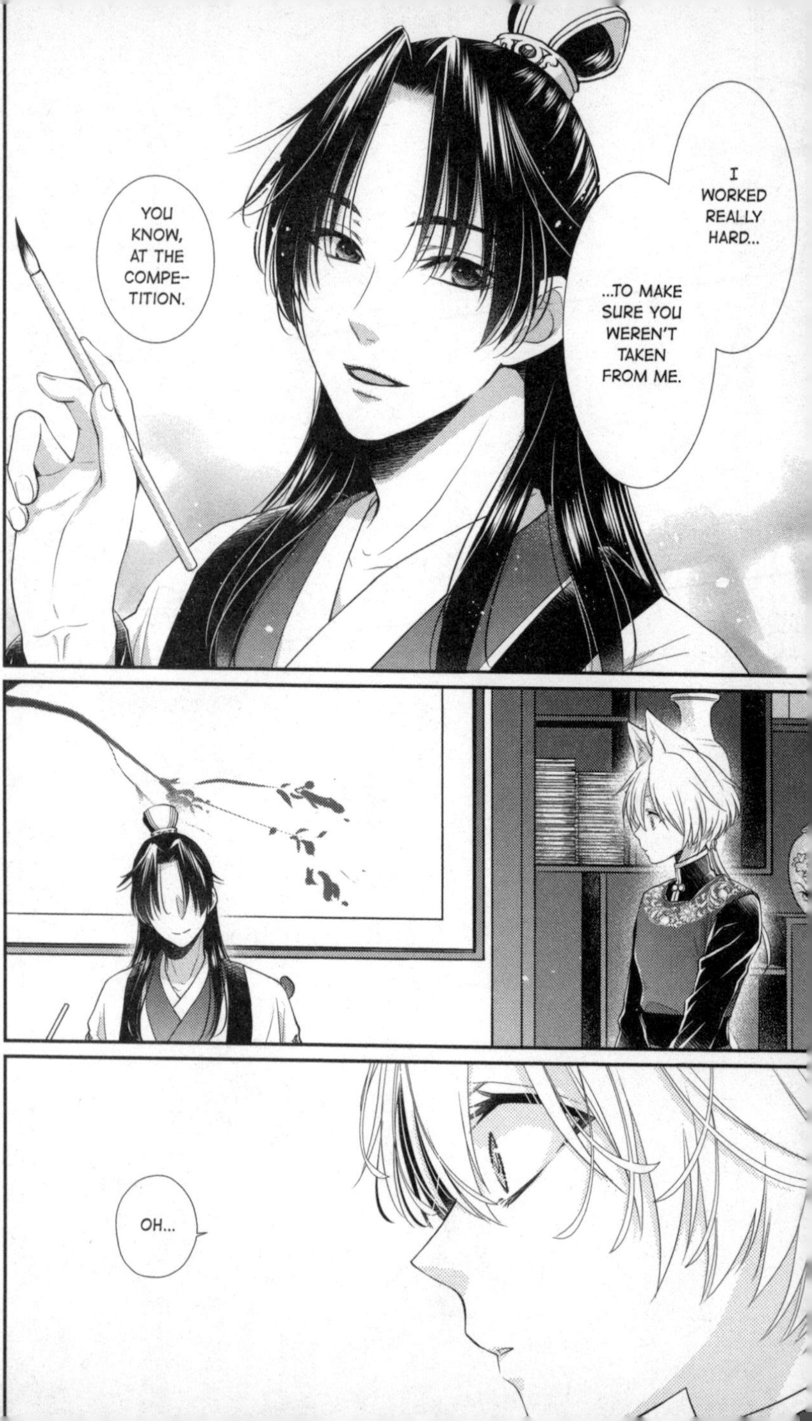
I WORKED REALLY HARD...
...TO MAKE SURE YOU WEREN'T TAKEN FROM ME.
YOU KNOW, AT THE COMPE-TITION.
OH...

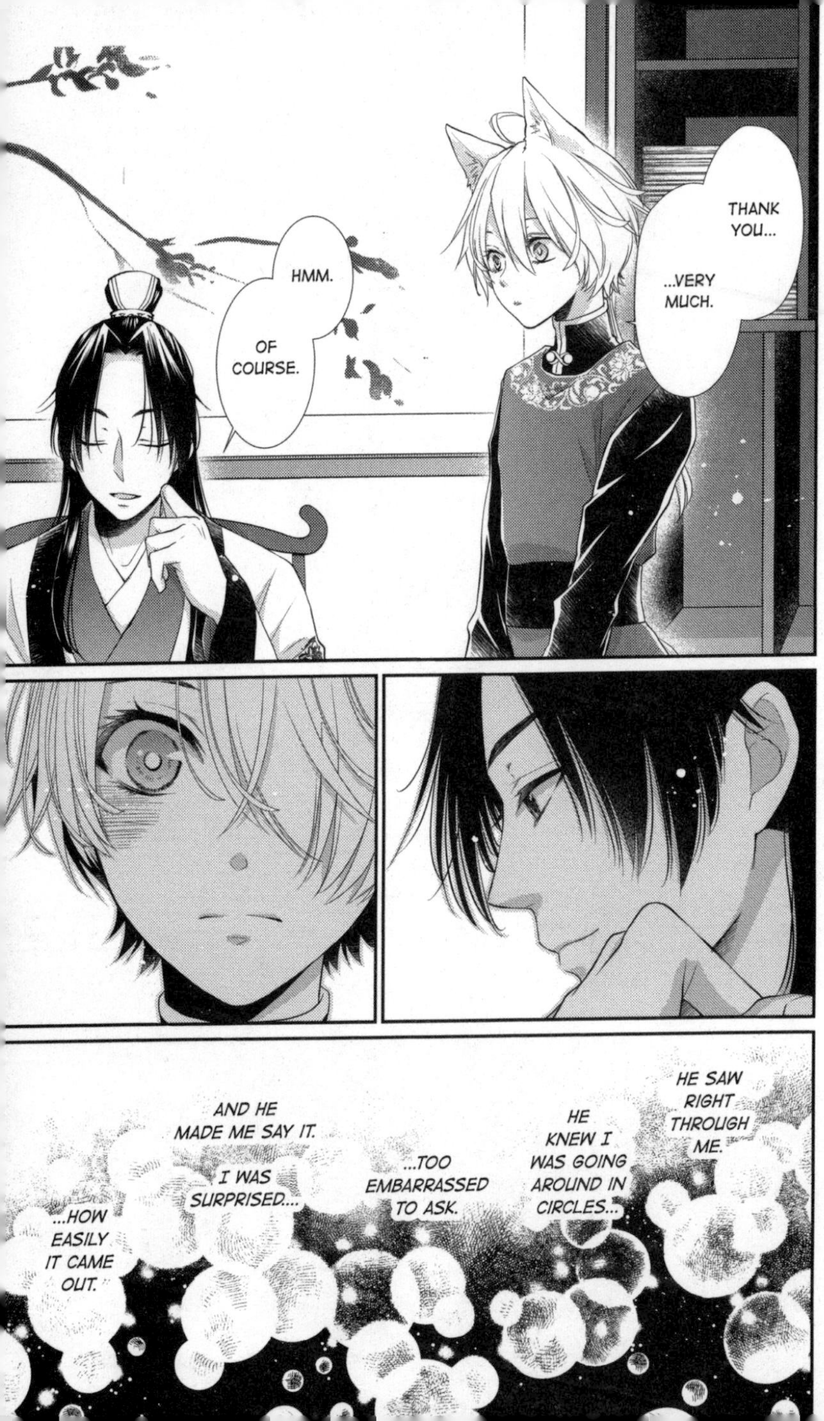
THANK YOU...
...VERY MUCH.
HMM.
OF COURSE.
HE SAW RIGHT THROUGH ME.
HE KNEW I WAS GOING AROUND IN CIRCLES...
...TOO EMBARRASSED TO ASK.
AND HE MADE ME SAY IT.
I WAS SURPRISED....
...HOW EASILY IT CAME OUT.

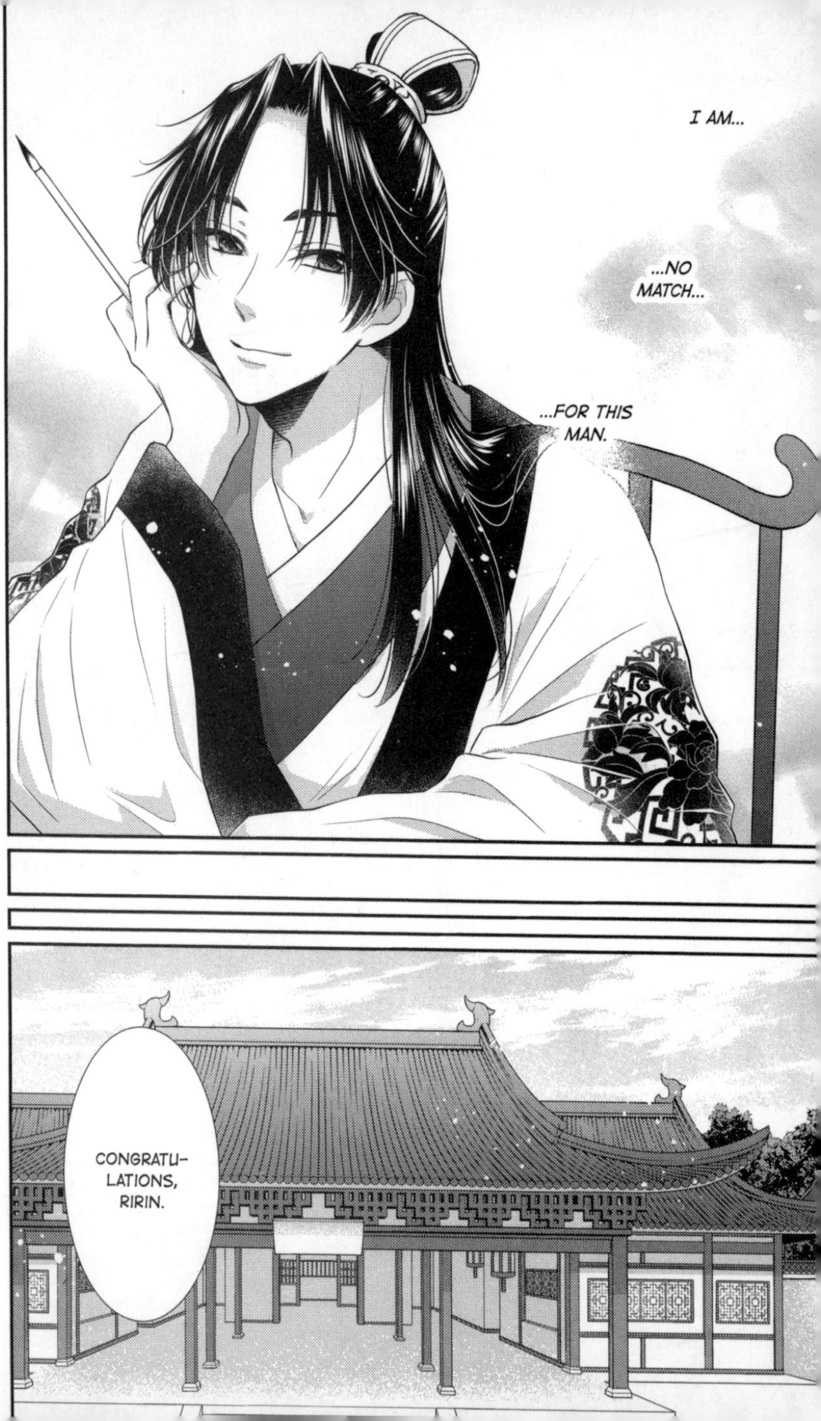
I AM...
...NO MATCH...
...FOR THIS MAN.
CONGRATU-LATIONS, RIRIN.

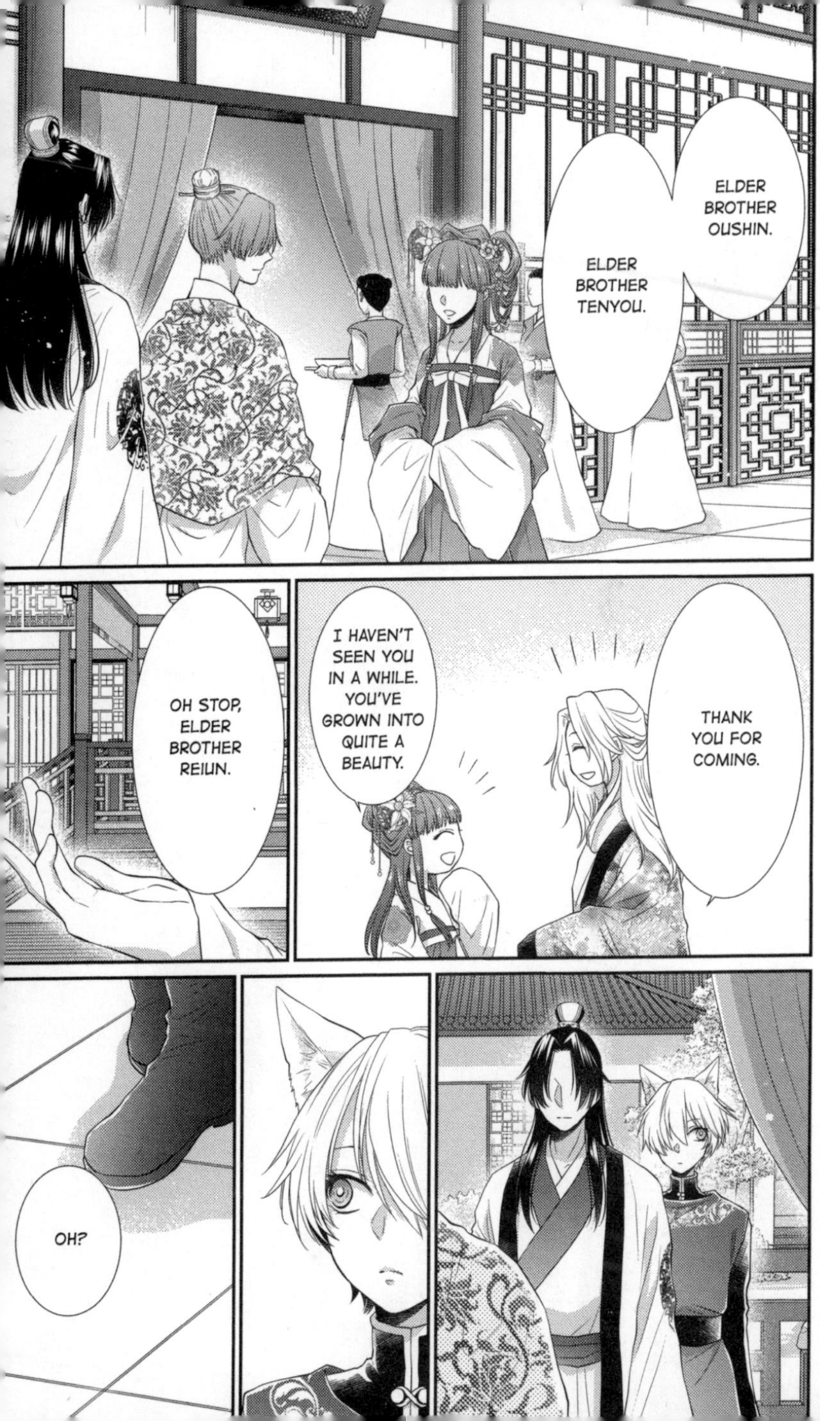
ELDER BROTHER OUSHIN.
ELDER BROTHER TENYOU.
THANK YOU FOR COMING.
I HAVEN'T SEEN YOU IN A WHILE. YOU'VE GROWN INTO QUITE A BEAUTY.
OH STOP, ELDER BROTHER REIUN.
OH?

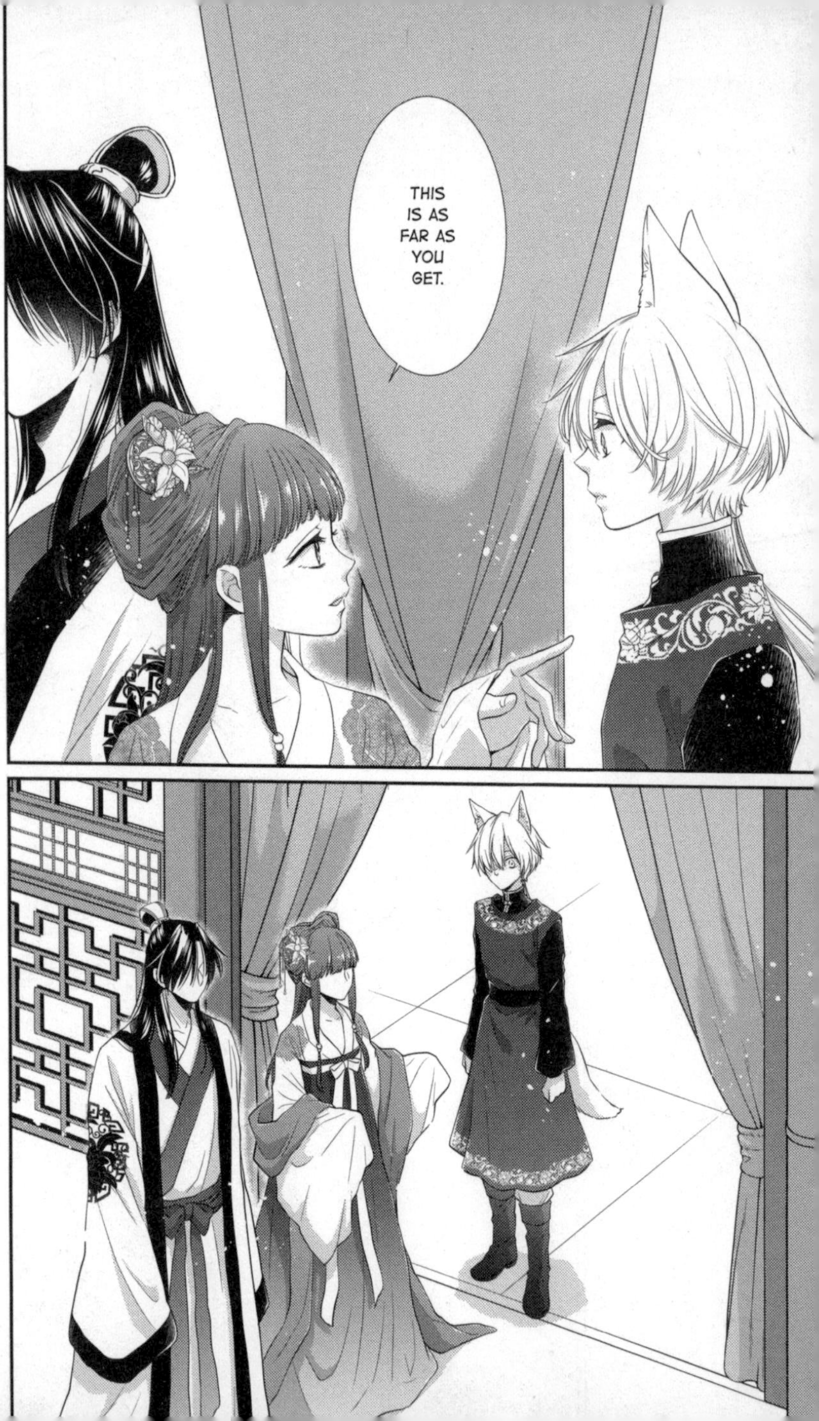
THIS IS AS FAR AS YOU GET.

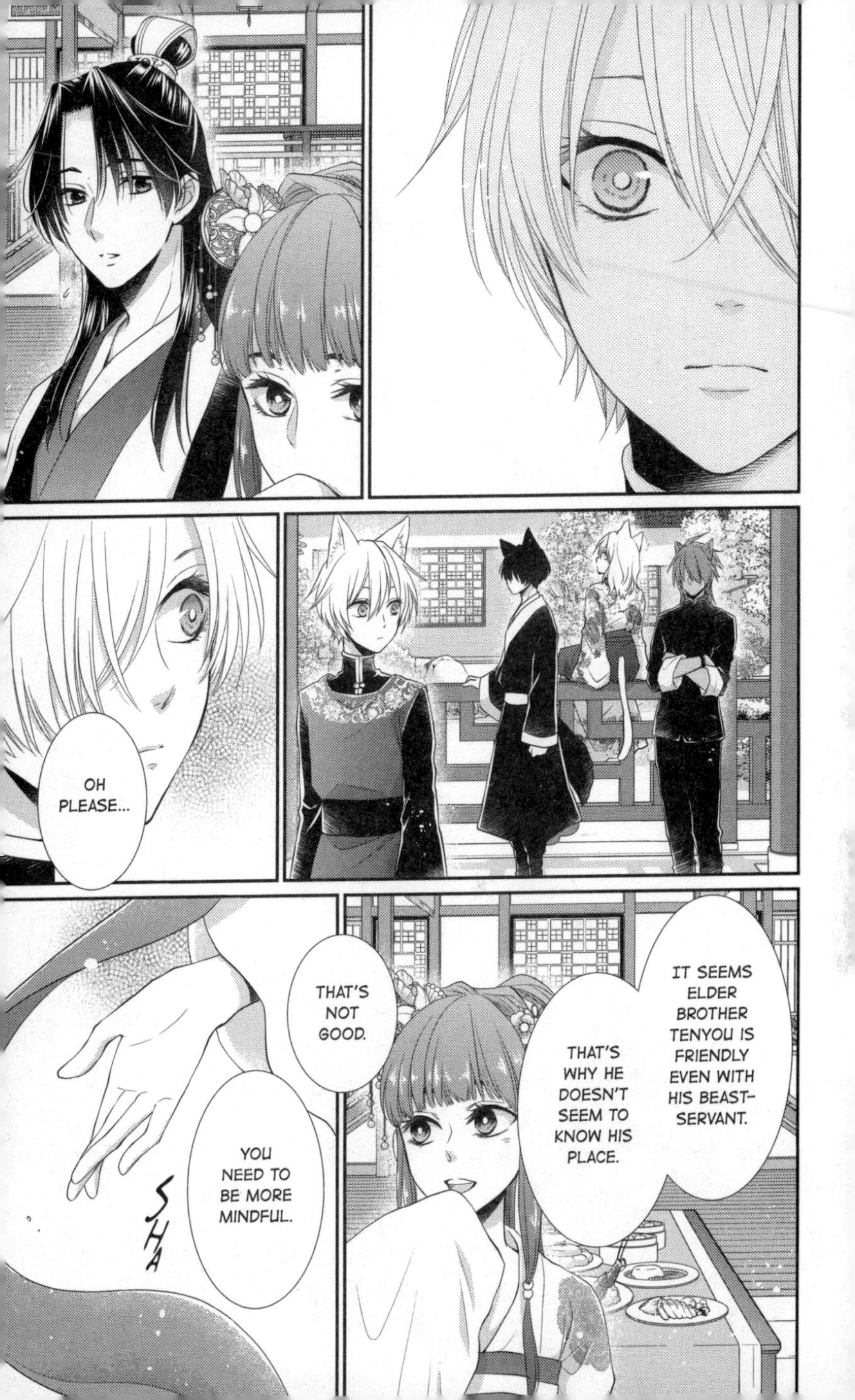
OH PLEASE...
IT SEEMS ELDER BROTHER TENYOU IS FRIENDLY EVEN WITH HIS BEAST-SERVANT.
THAT'S WHY HE DOESN'T SEEM TO KNOW HIS PLACE.
THAT'S NOT GOOD.
YOU NEED TO BE MORE MINDFUL.
SHA

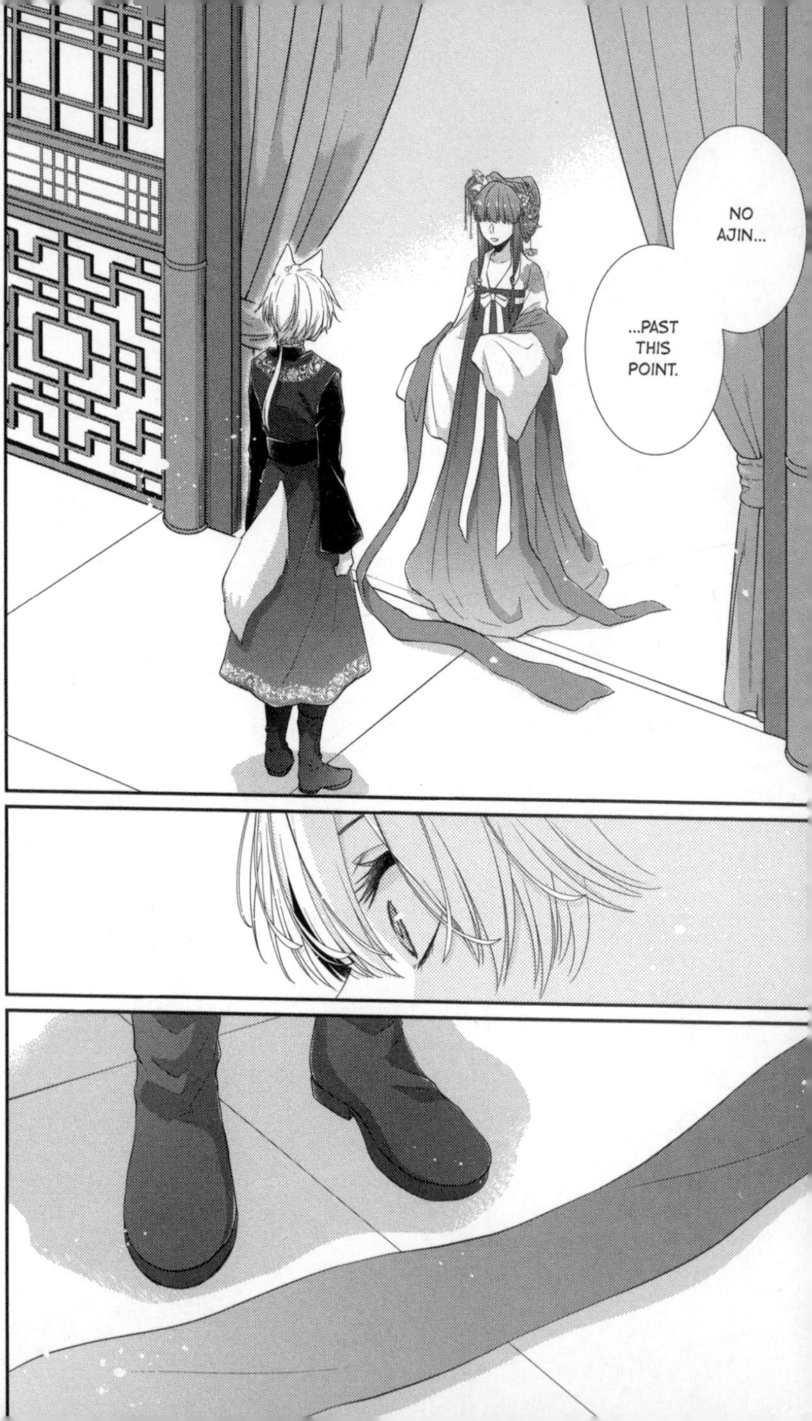
NO AJIN...
...PAST THIS POINT.

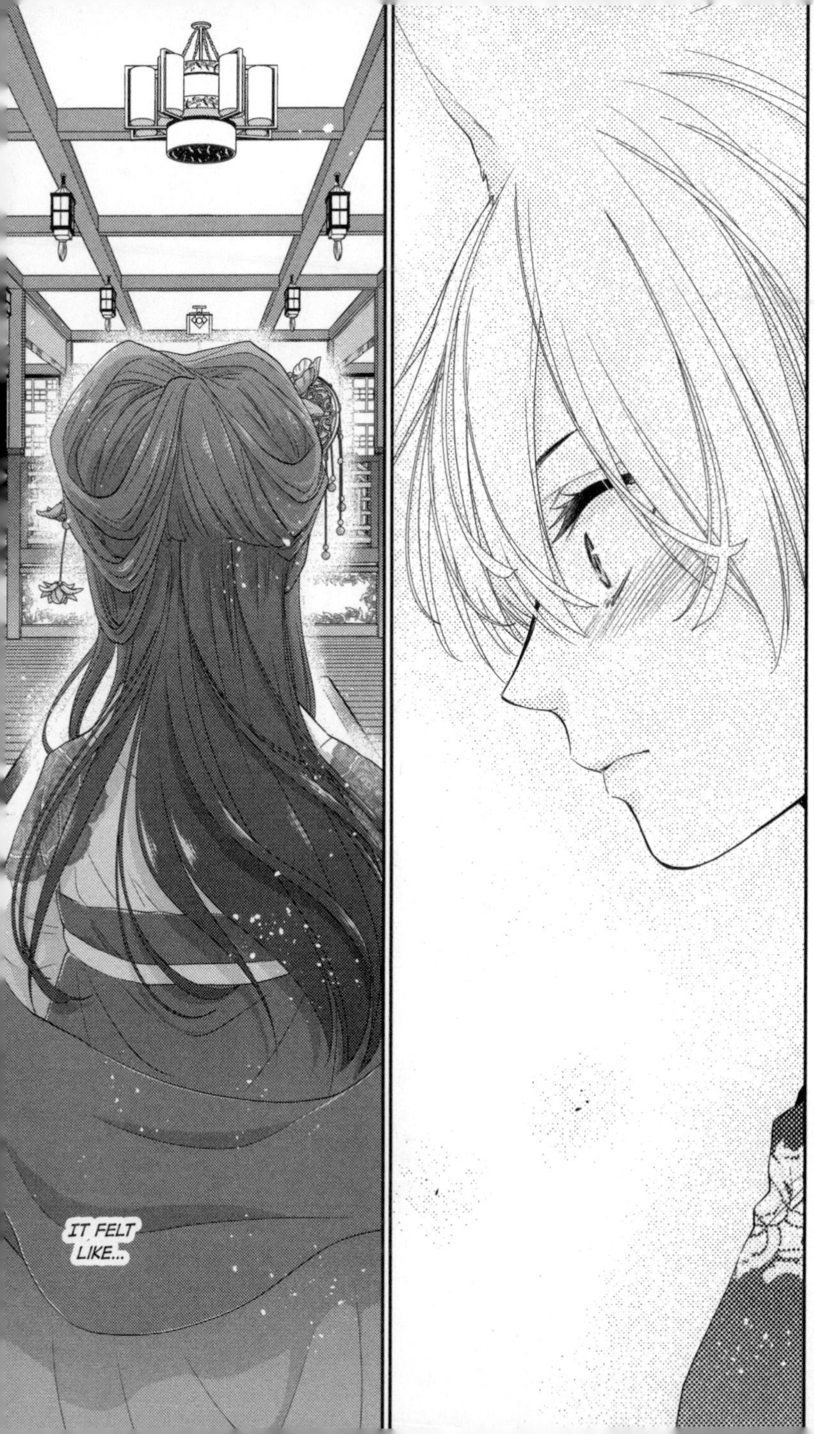
IT FELT LIKE...

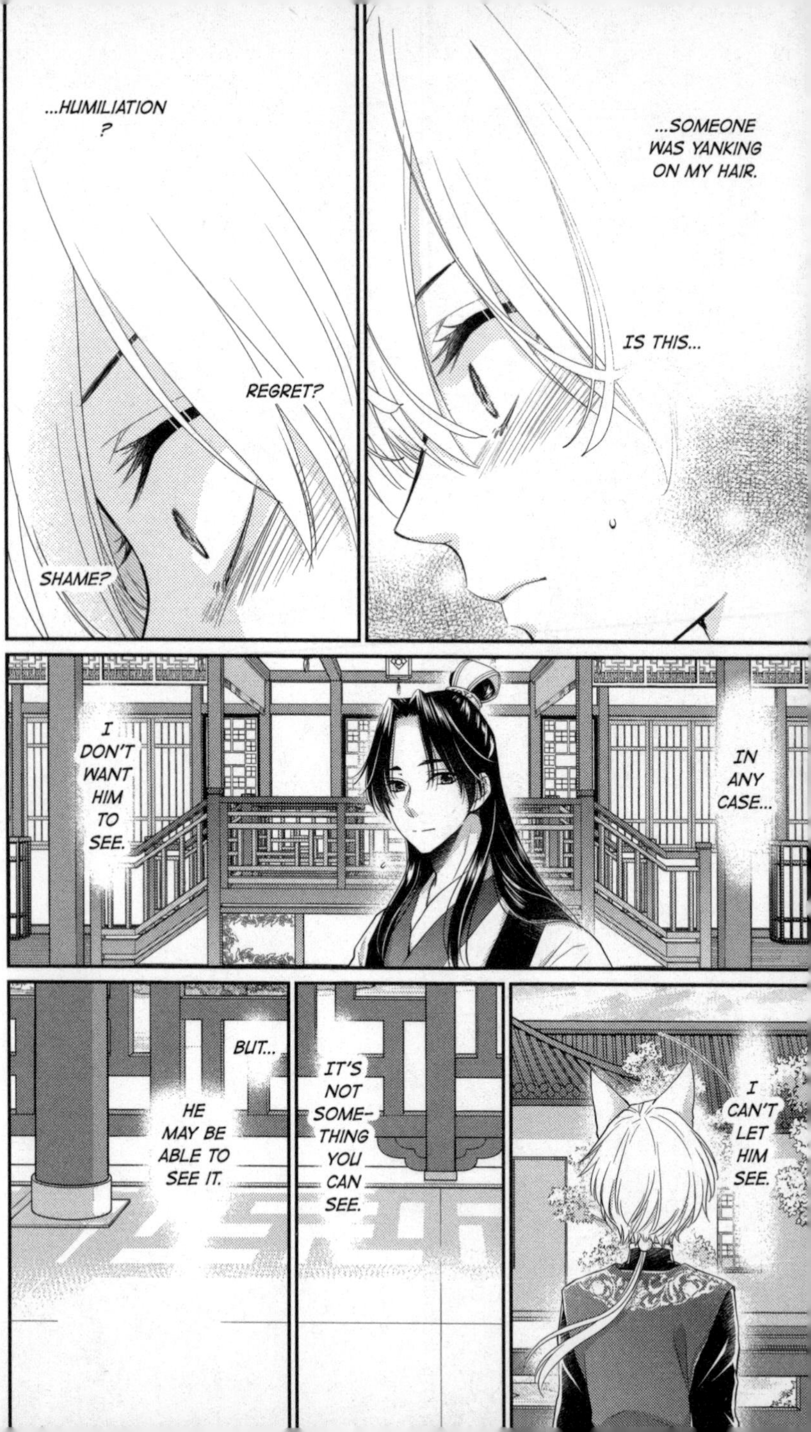
...SOMEONE WAS YANKING ON MY HAIR.
IS THIS...
...HUMILIATION?
REGRET?
SHAME?
IN ANY CASE...
I DON'T WANT HIM TO SEE.
I CAN'T LET HIM SEE.
IT'S NOT SOMETHING YOU CAN SEE.
BUT...
HE MAY BE ABLE TO SEE IT.

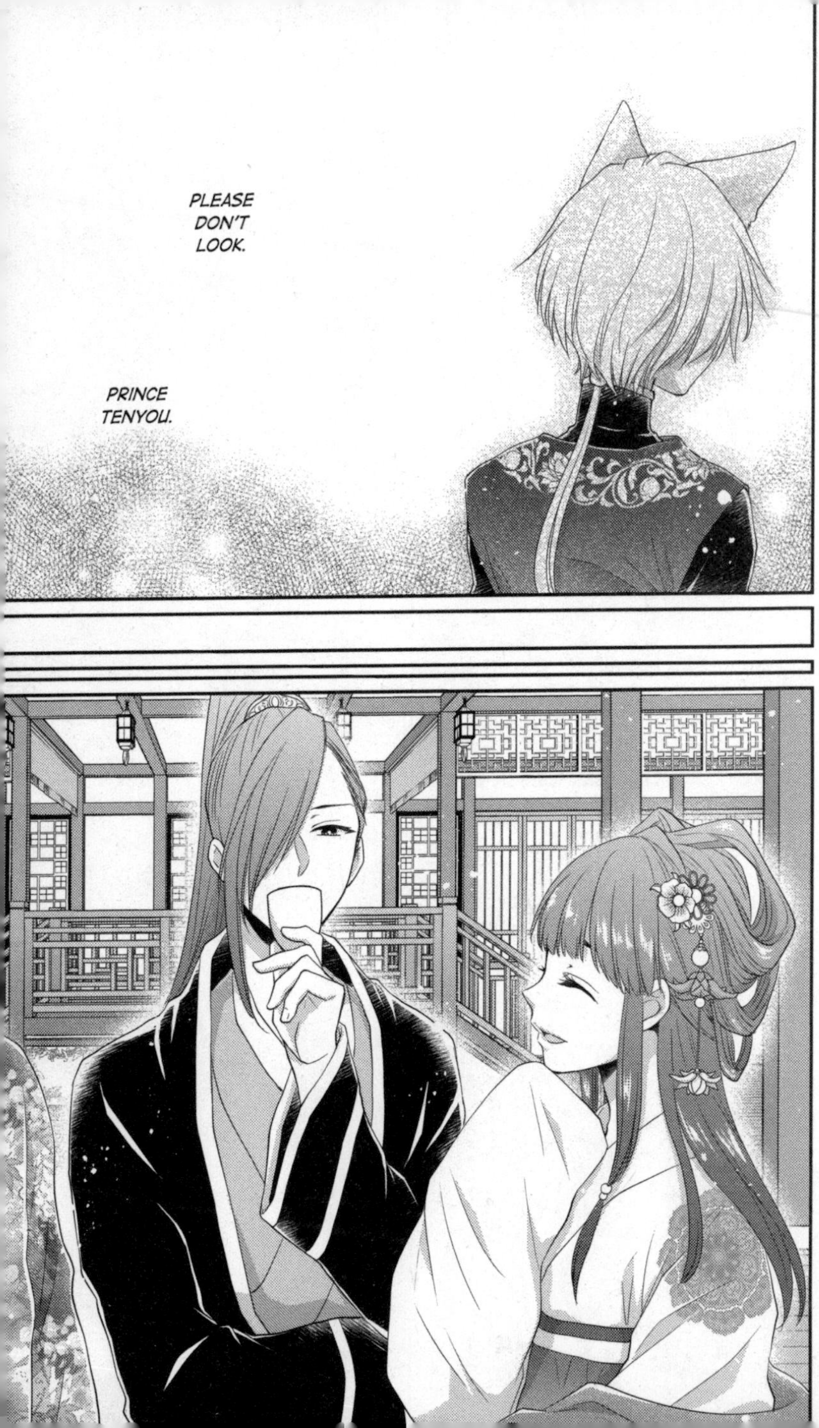
PLEASE DON'T LOOK.
PRINCE TENYOU.

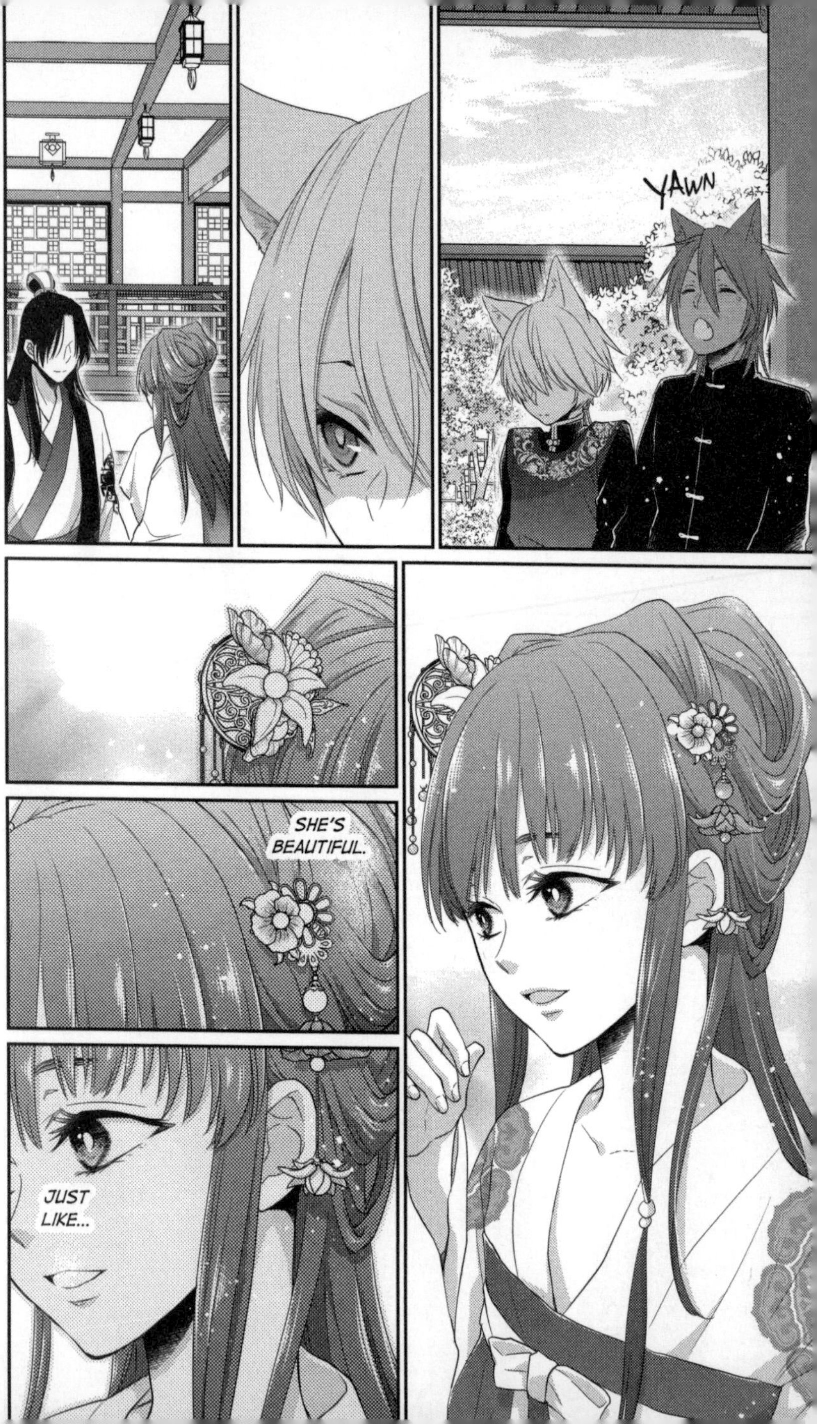
YAWN
SHE'S BEAUTIFUL.
JUST LIKE...

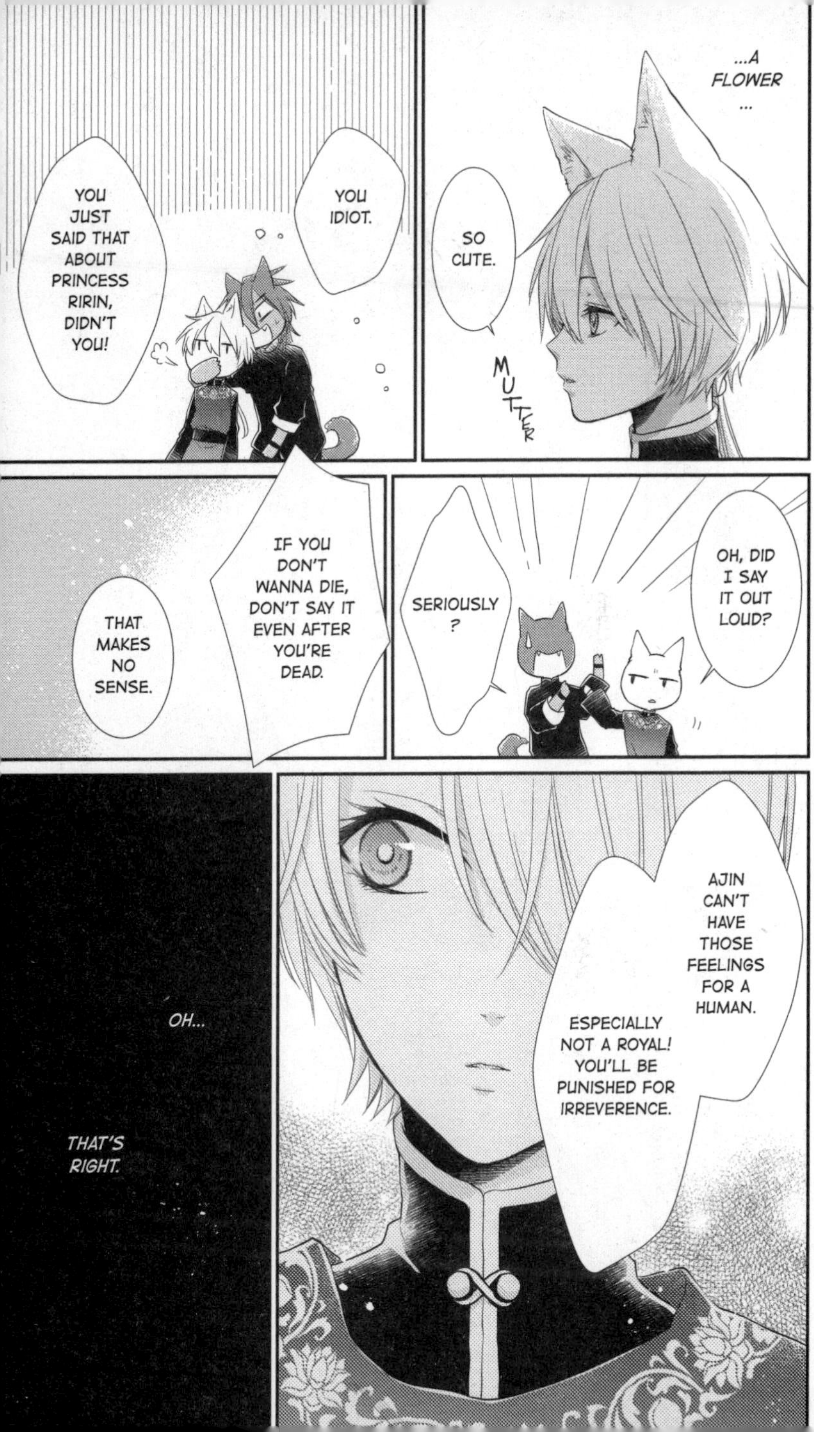
...A FLOWER ...
SO CUTE.
MUTTER
YOU IDIOT.
YOU JUST SAID THAT ABOUT PRINCESS RIRIN, DIDN'T YOU!
OH, DID I SAY IT OUT LOUD?
SERIOUSLY?
IF YOU DON'T WANNA DIE, DON'T SAY IT EVEN AFTER YOU'RE DEAD.
THAT MAKES NO SENSE.
AJIN CAN'T HAVE THOSE FEELINGS FOR A HUMAN.
ESPECIALLY NOT A ROYAL! YOU'LL BE PUNISHED FOR IRREVERENCE.
OH...
THAT'S RIGHT.

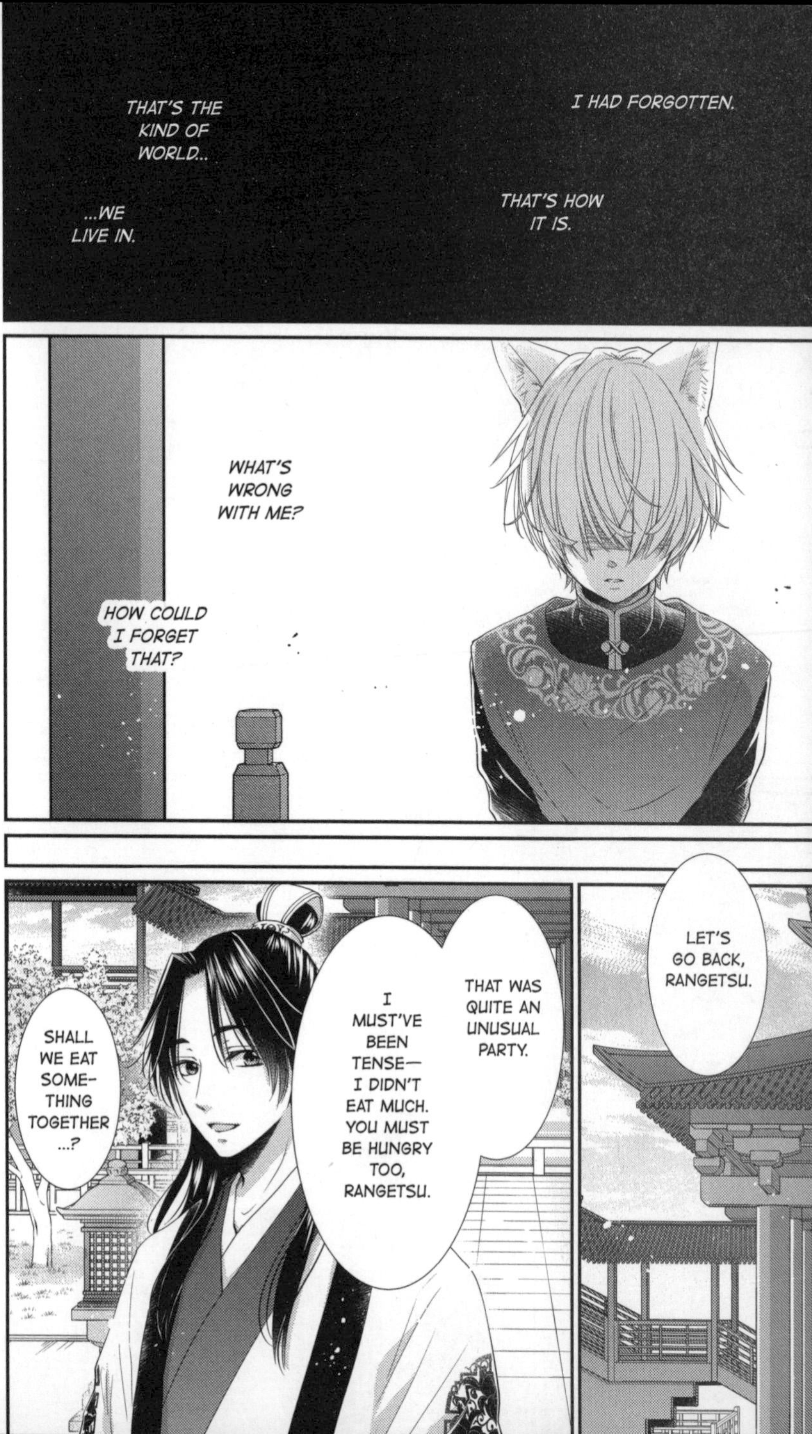
I HAD FORGOTTEN.
THAT'S HOW IT IS.
THAT'S THE KIND OF WORLD...
...WE LIVE IN.
WHAT'S WRONG WITH ME?
HOW COULD I FORGET THAT?
LET'S GO BACK, RANGETSU.
THAT WAS QUITE AN UNUSUAL PARTY.
I MUST'VE BEEN TENSE— I DIDN'T EAT MUCH. YOU MUST BE HUNGRY TOO, RANGETSU.
SHALL WE EAT SOME-THING TOGETHER ...?

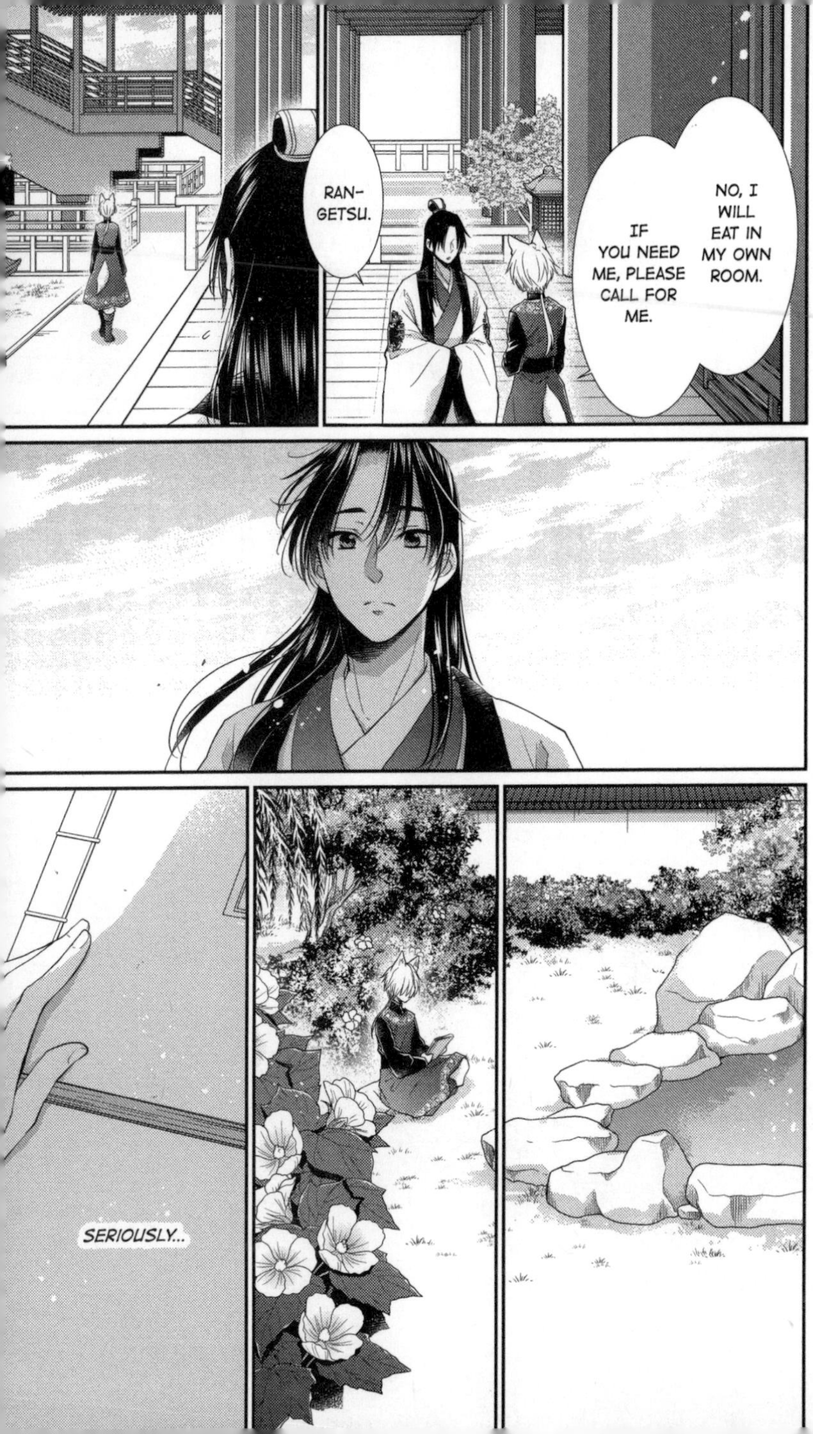
NO, I WILL EAT IN MY OWN ROOM.
IF YOU NEED ME, PLEASE CALL FOR ME.
RAN-GETSU.
SERIOUSLY...

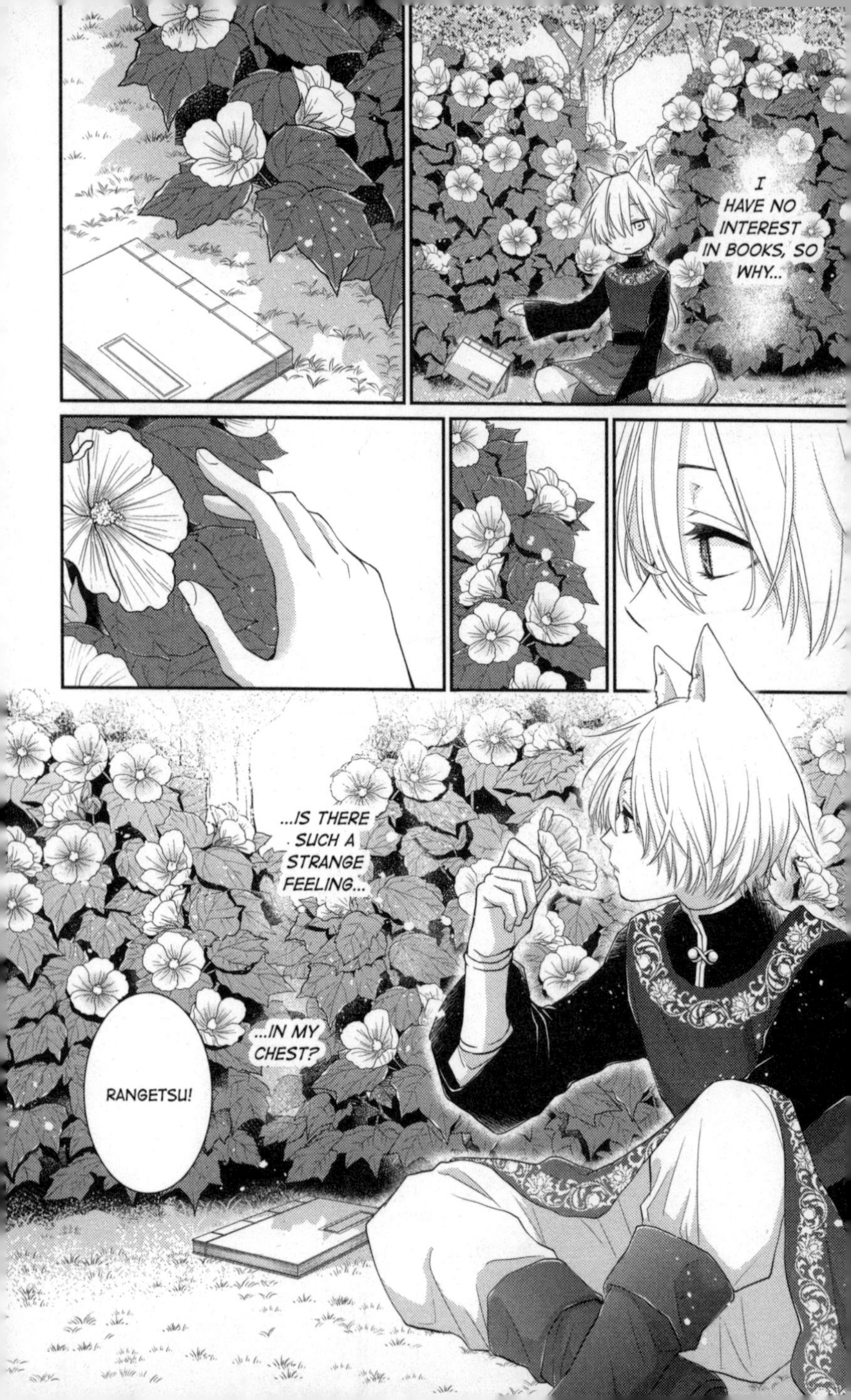
I HAVE NO INTEREST IN BOOKS, SO WHY...
...IS THERE SUCH A STRANGE FEELING...
...IN MY CHEST?
RANGETSU!

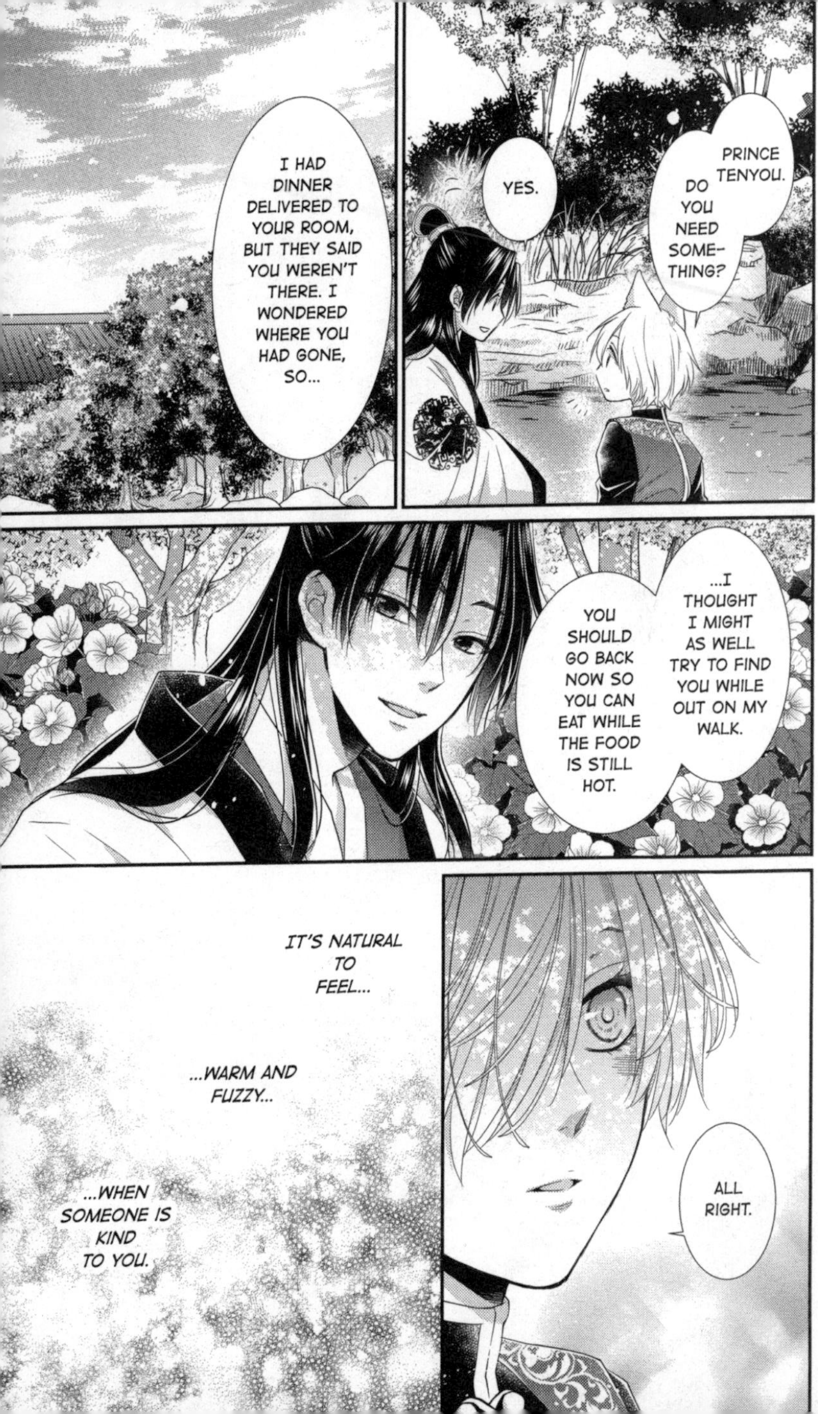
PRINCE TENYOU. DO YOU NEED SOMETHING?
YES.
I HAD DINNER DELIVERED TO YOUR ROOM, BUT THEY SAID YOU WEREN'T THERE. I WONDERED WHERE YOU HAD GONE, SO...
...I THOUGHT I MIGHT AS WELL TRY TO FIND YOU WHILE OUT ON MY WALK.
YOU SHOULD GO BACK NOW SO YOU CAN EAT WHILE THE FOOD IS STILL HOT.
ALL RIGHT.
IT'S NATURAL TO FEEL...
...WARM AND FUZZY...
...WHEN SOMEONE IS KIND TO YOU.

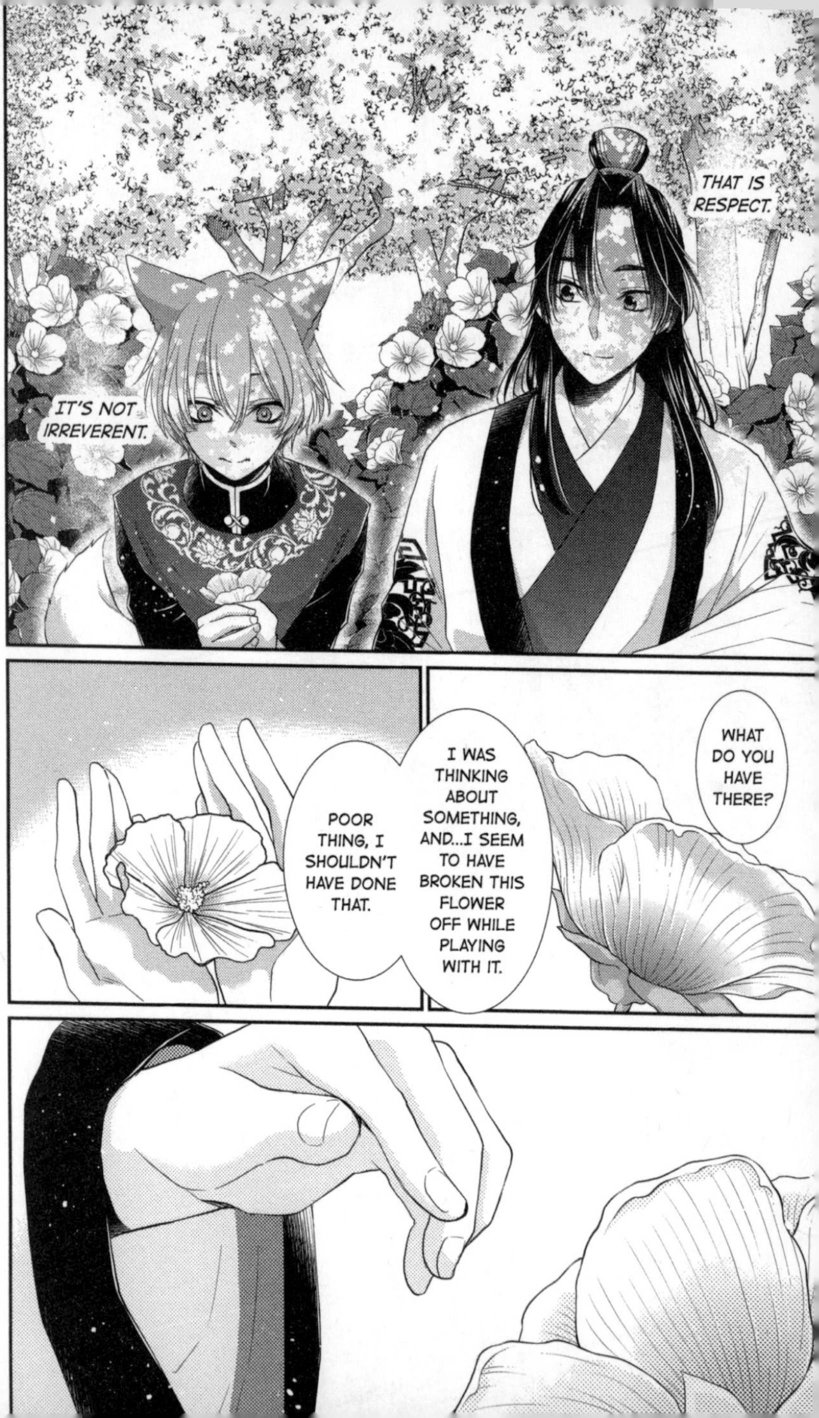
THAT IS RESPECT.
IT'S NOT IRREVERENT.
WHAT DO YOU HAVE THERE?
I WAS THINKING ABOUT SOMETHING, AND...I SEEM TO HAVE BROKEN THIS FLOWER OFF WHILE PLAYING WITH IT.
POOR THING, I SHOULDN'T HAVE DONE THAT.

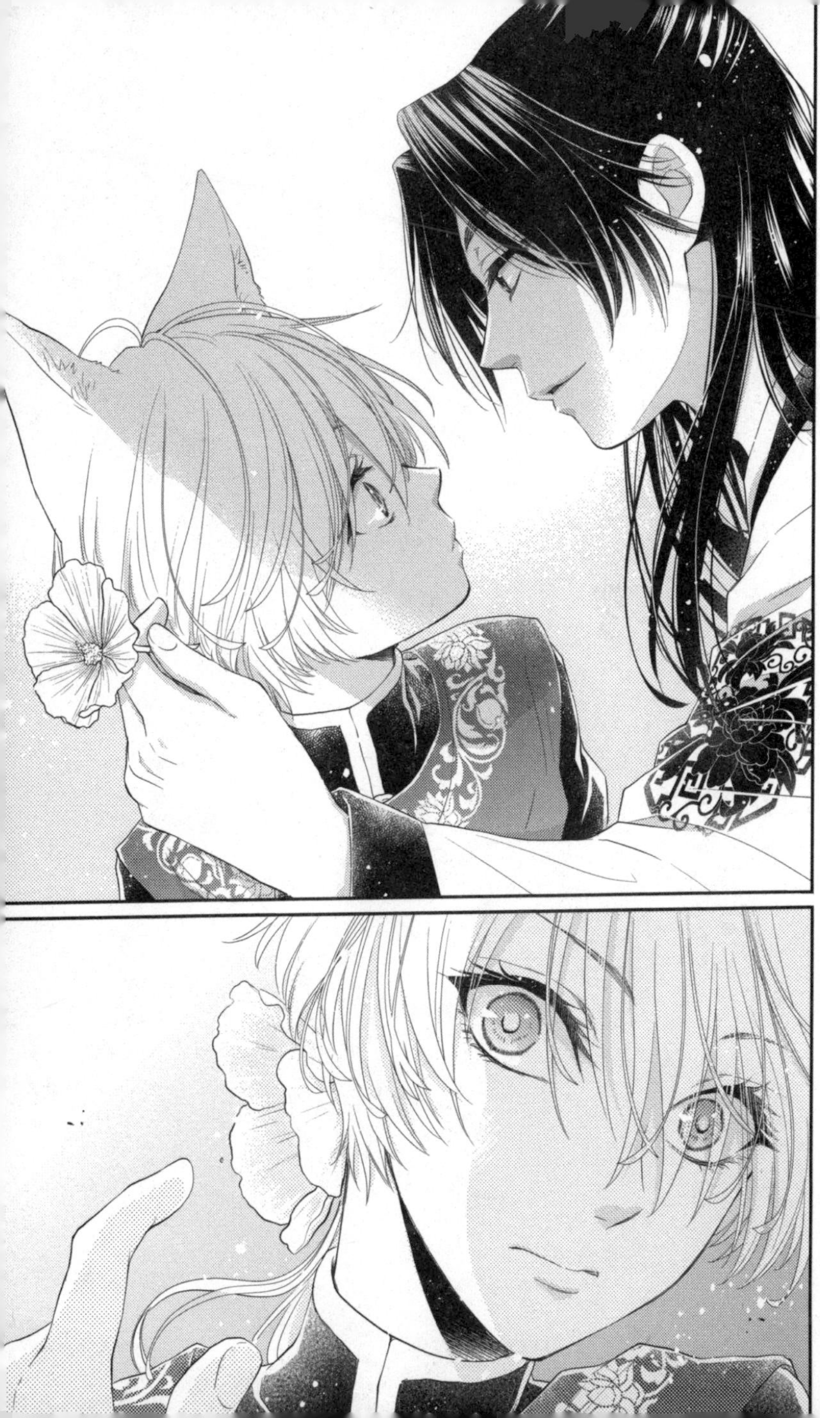

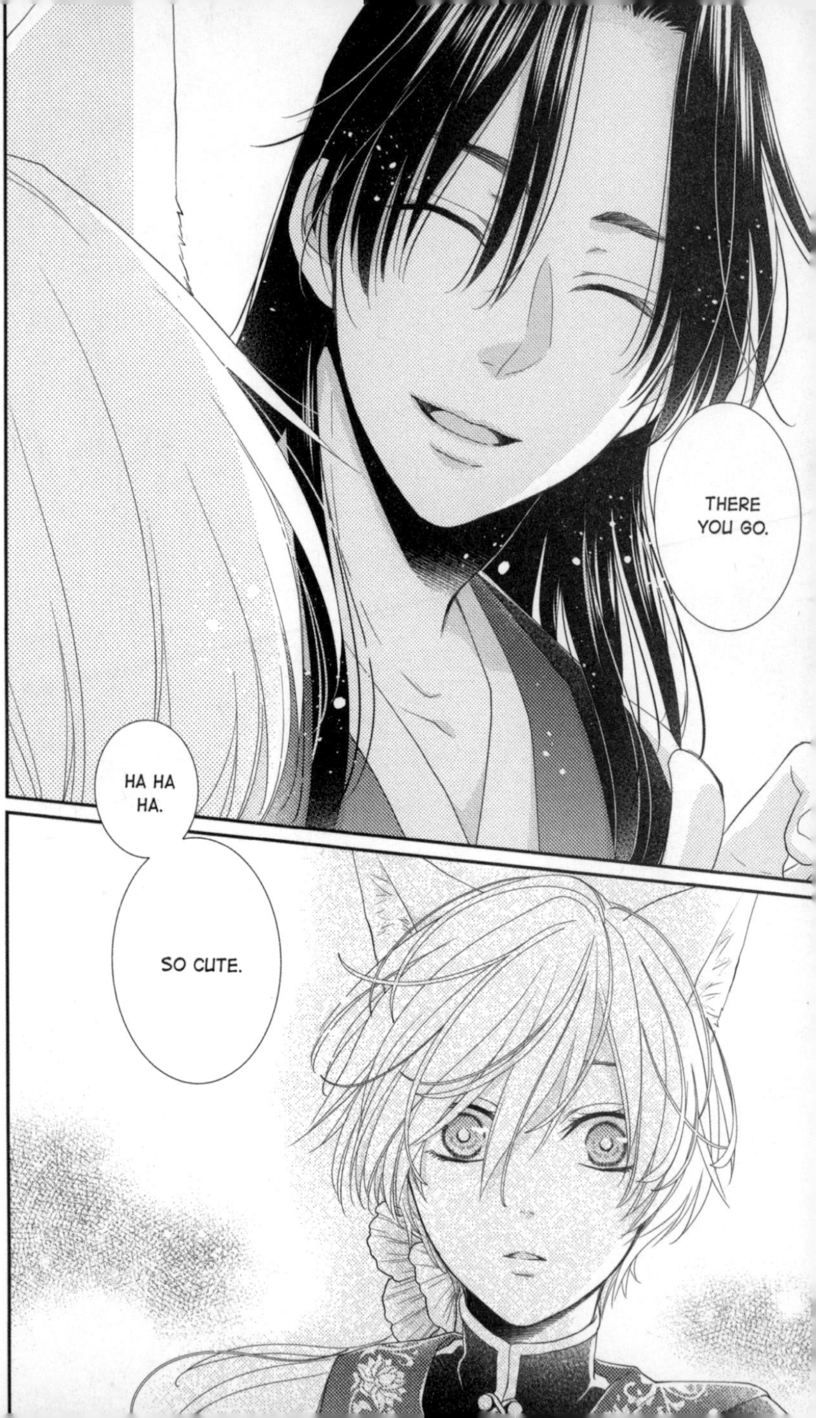
THERE YOU GO.
HA HA HA.
SO CUTE.

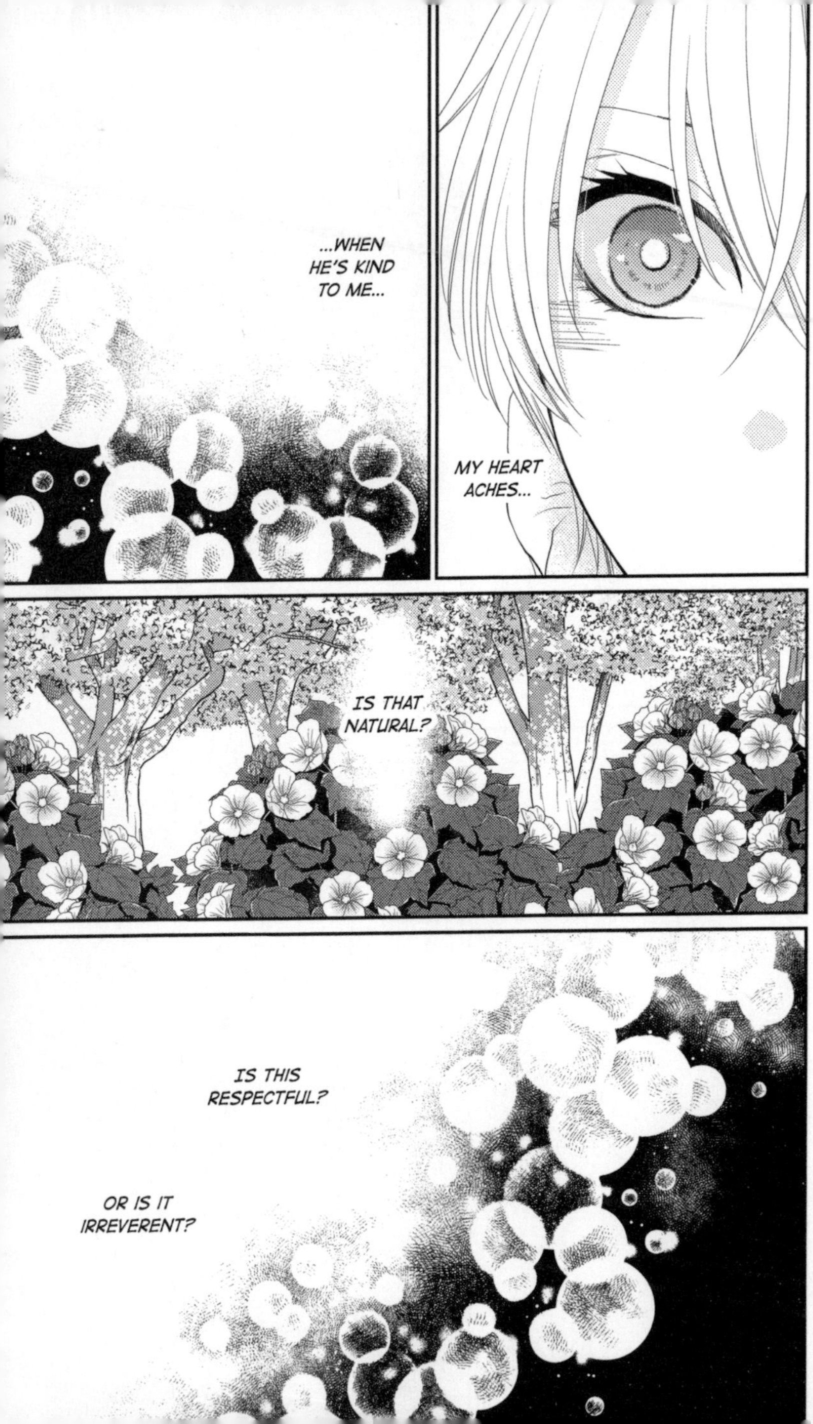
MY HEART ACHES...
...WHEN HE'S KIND TO ME...
IS THAT NATURAL?
IS THIS RESPECTFUL?
OR IS IT IRREVERENT?

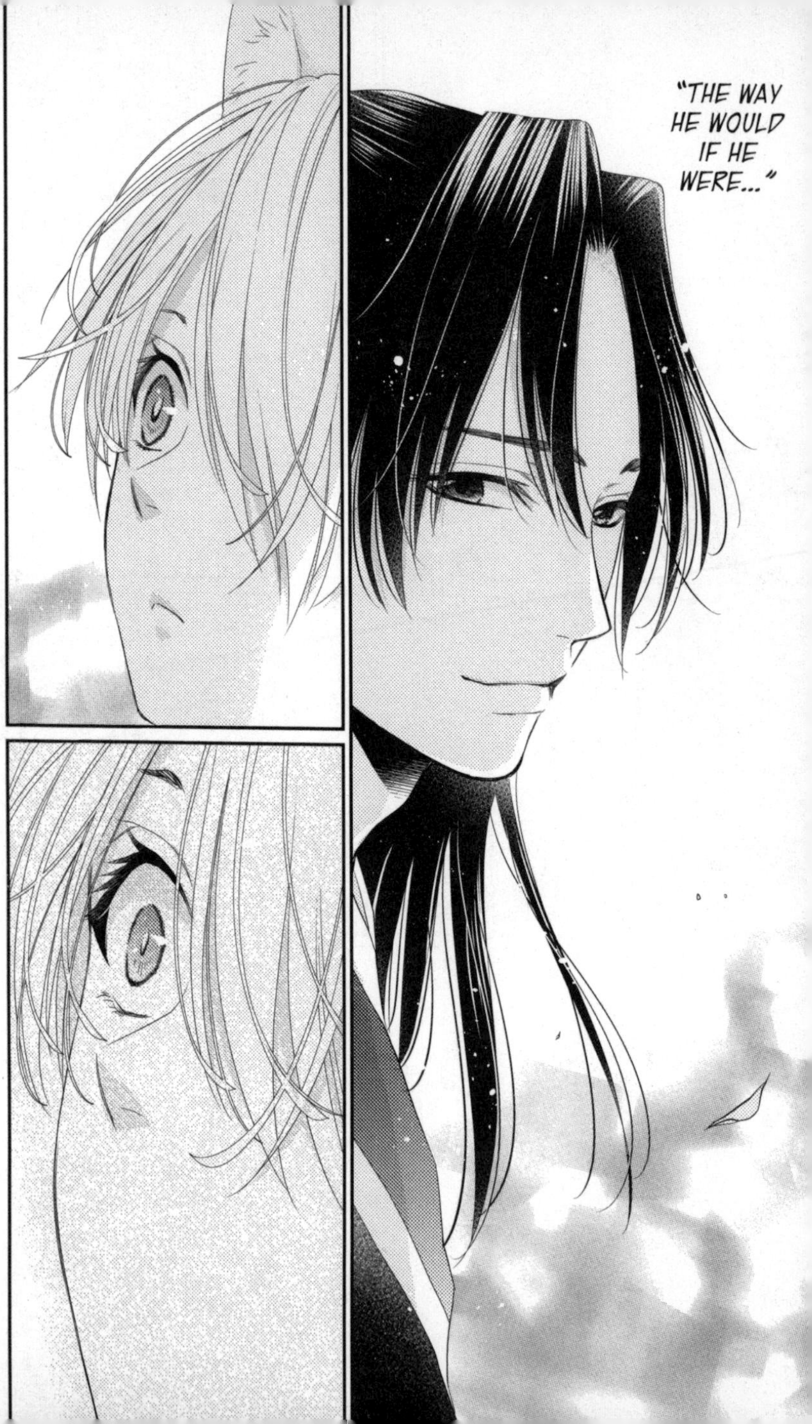
"THE WAY HE WOULD IF HE WERE..."

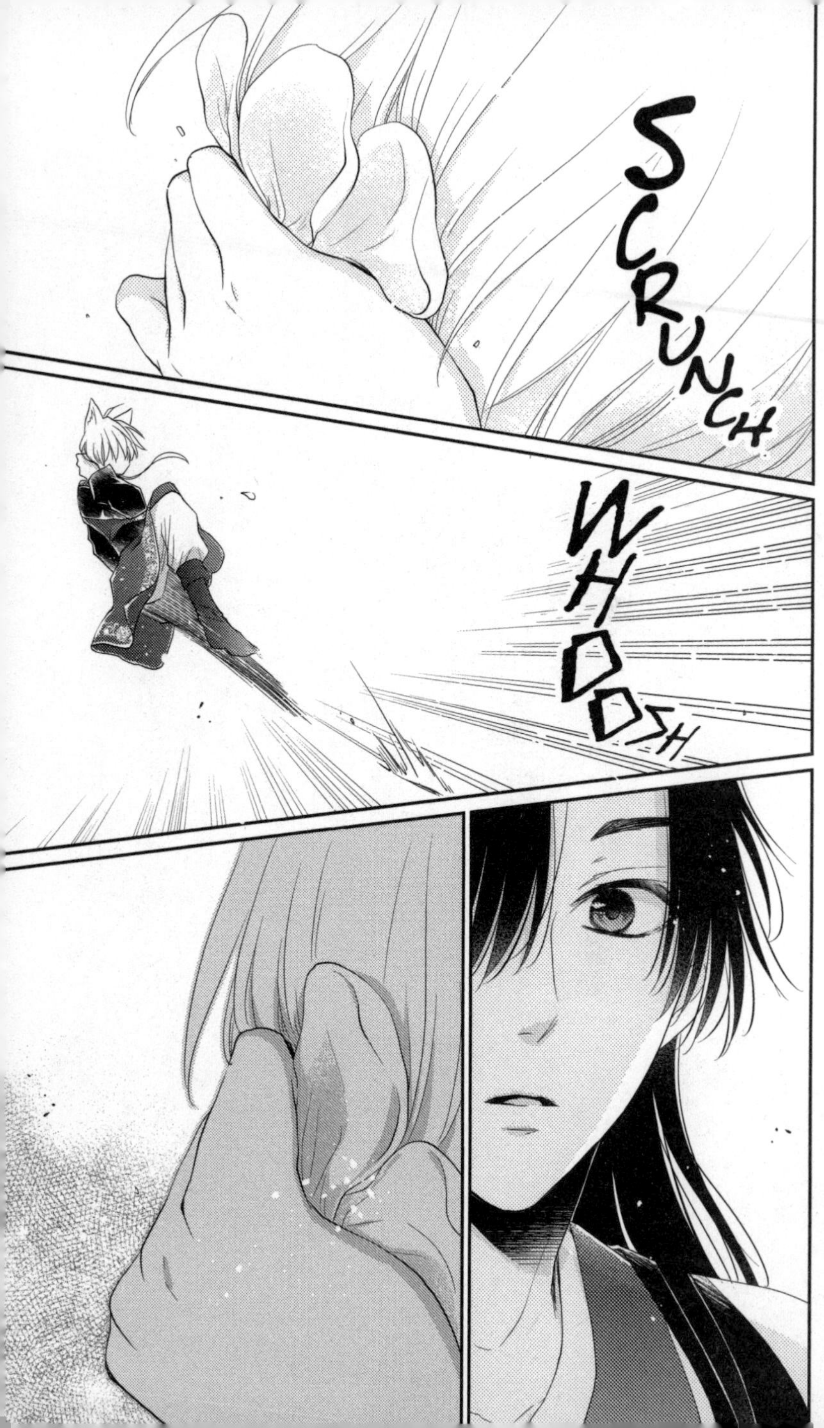
SCRUNCH
WHOOSH

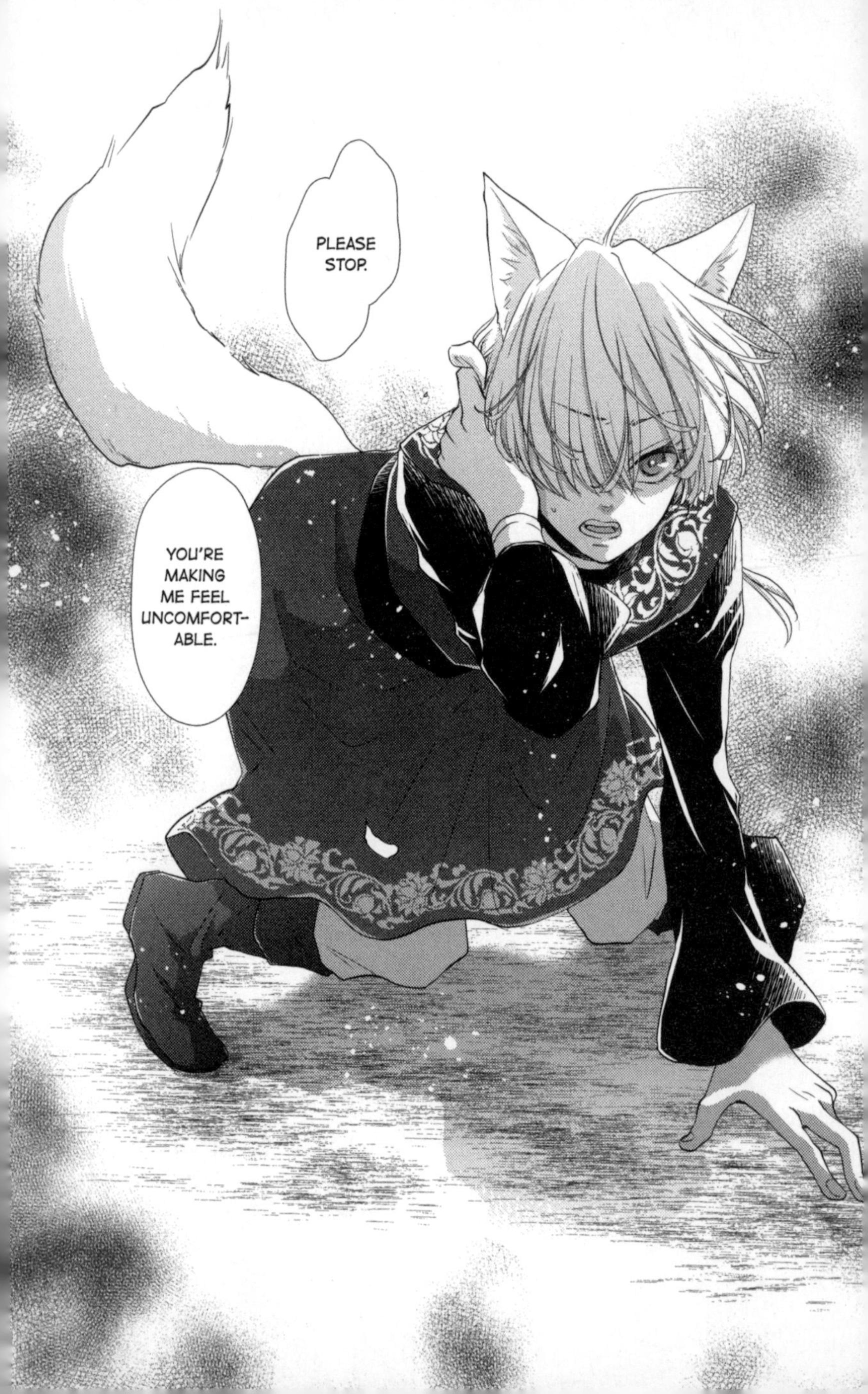
PLEASE STOP.
YOU'RE MAKING ME FEEL UNCOMFORT-ABLE.

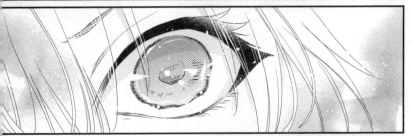

THIS
HEAVINESS...

RANGETSU...

...IN MY
CHEST...

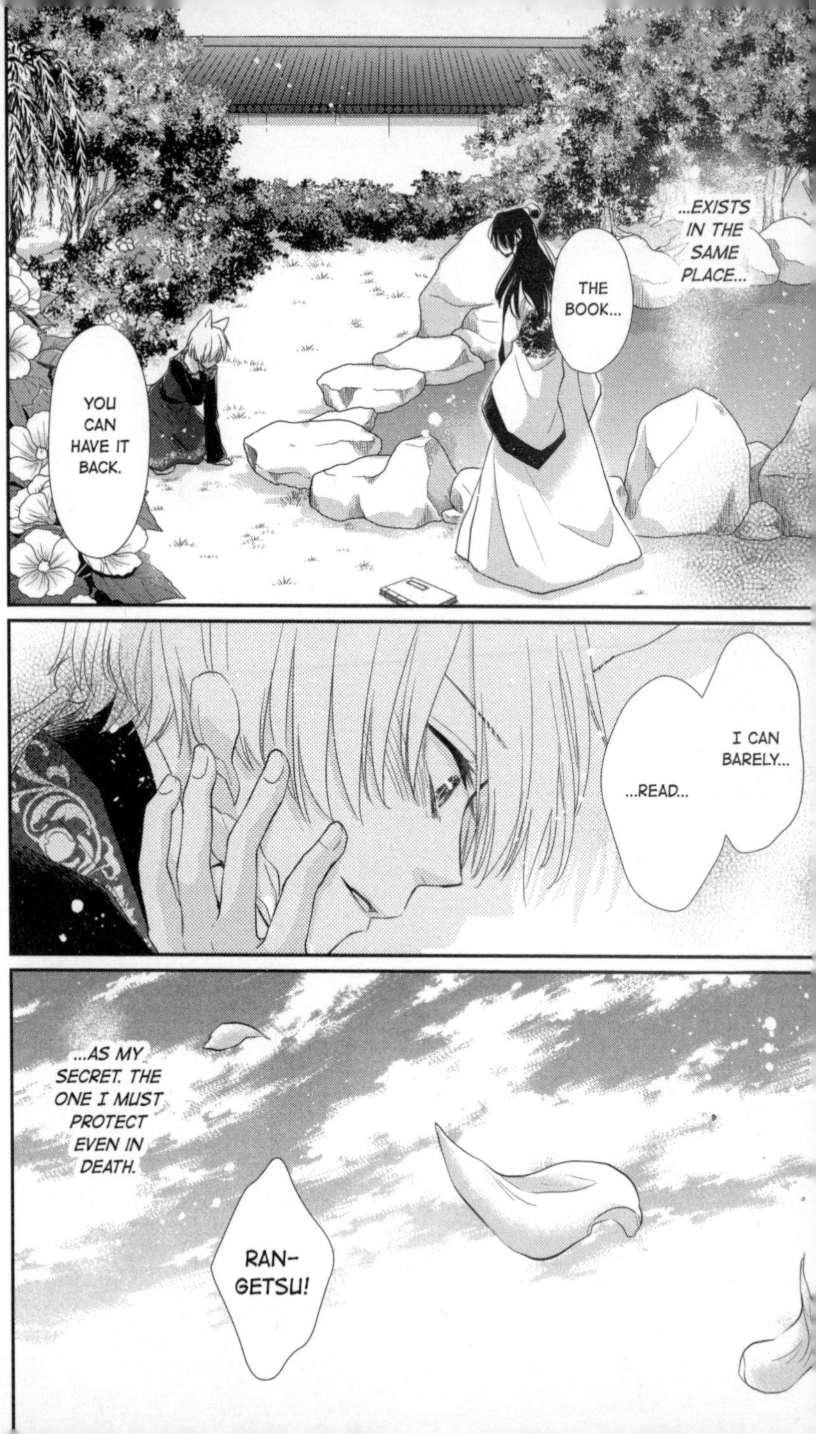
...EXISTS IN THE SAME PLACE...
THE BOOK...
YOU CAN HAVE IT BACK.
I CAN BARELY...
...READ...
...AS MY SECRET. THE ONE I MUST PROTECT EVEN IN DEATH.
RAN-GETSU!

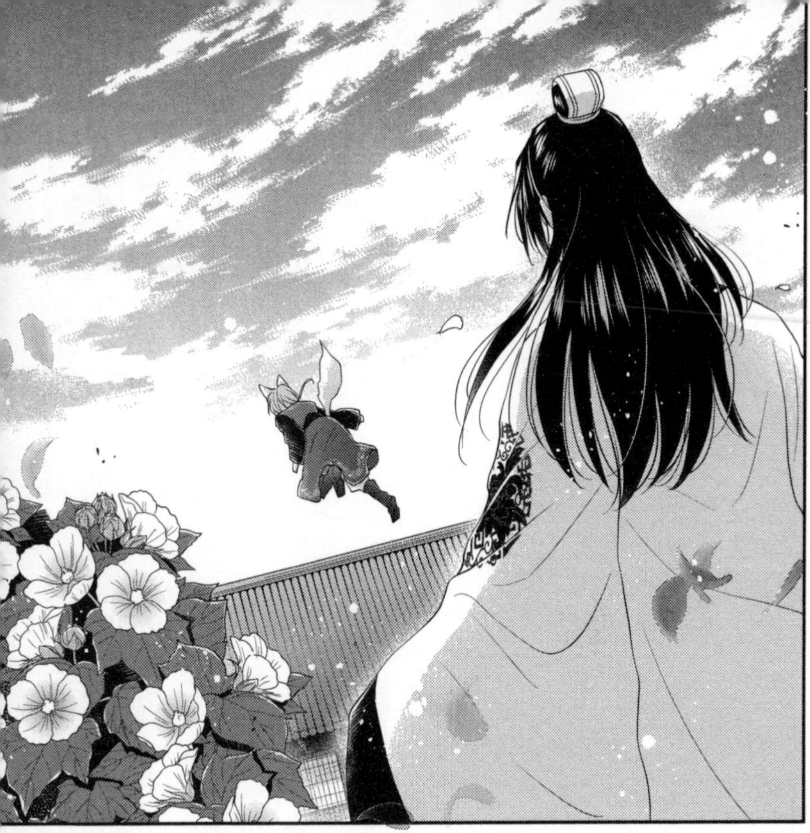

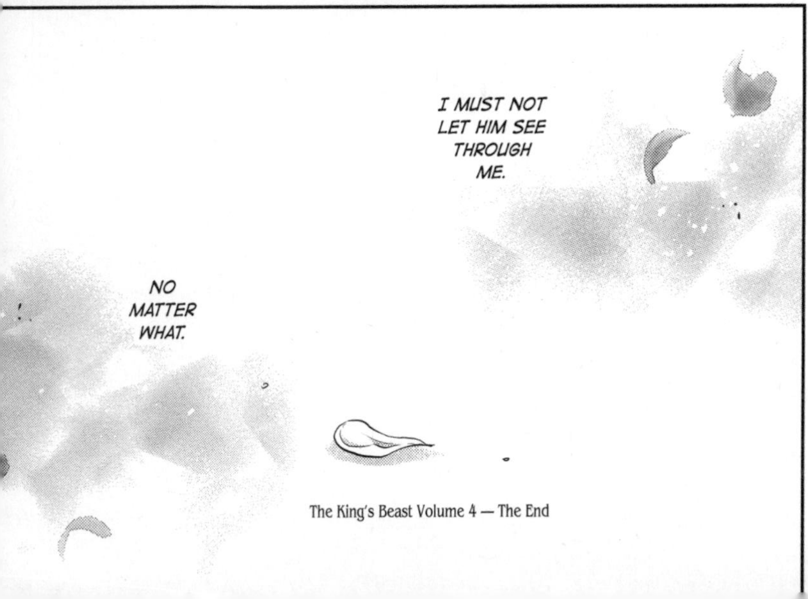
I MUST NOT LET HIM SEE THROUGH ME.
NO MATTER WHAT.
The King's Beast Volume 4 — The End

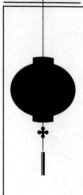

I hope you enjoyed it.

—Rei Toma

Rei Toma has been drawing since childhood, and she created her first complete manga for a graduation project in design school. When she drew the short story manga "Help Me, Dentist," it attracted a publisher's attention and she made her debut right away. After she found success as a manga artist, acclaim in other art fields started to follow as she did illustrations for novels and video game character designs. She is also the creator of *Dawn of the Arcana* and *The Water Dragon's Bride*, both available in English from VIZ Media.

THE KING'S Beast 4

SHOJO BEAT EDITION

STORY AND ART BY **Rei Toma**

ENGLISH TRANSLATION & ADAPTATION **JN Productions**
TOUCH-UP ART & LETTERING **Monaliza De Asis**
DESIGN **Joy Zhang**
EDITOR **Pancha Diaz**

OU NO KEMONO Vol. 4
by Rei TOMA
© 2019 Rei TOMA
All rights reserved.
Original Japanese edition published by SHOGAKUKAN.
English translation rights in the United States of America,
Canada, the United Kingdom, Ireland, Australia and New
Zealand arranged with SHOGAKUKAN.

Original Cover Design: Hibiki CHIKADA (fireworks. vc)

Printed in the U.S.A.

Published by VIZ Media, LLC
P.O. Box 77010
San Francisco, CA 94107

10 9 8 7 6 5 4 3 2 1
First printing, November 2021

viz.com   shojobeat.com

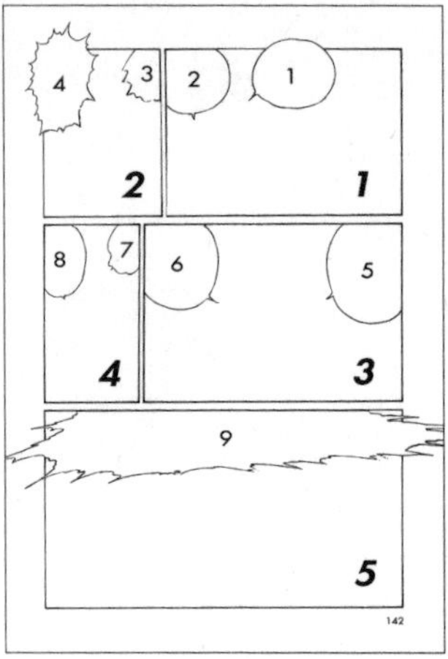

THIS IS THE LAST PAGE.

THE KING'S BEAST has been printed in the original Japanese format to preserve the orientation of the artwork.

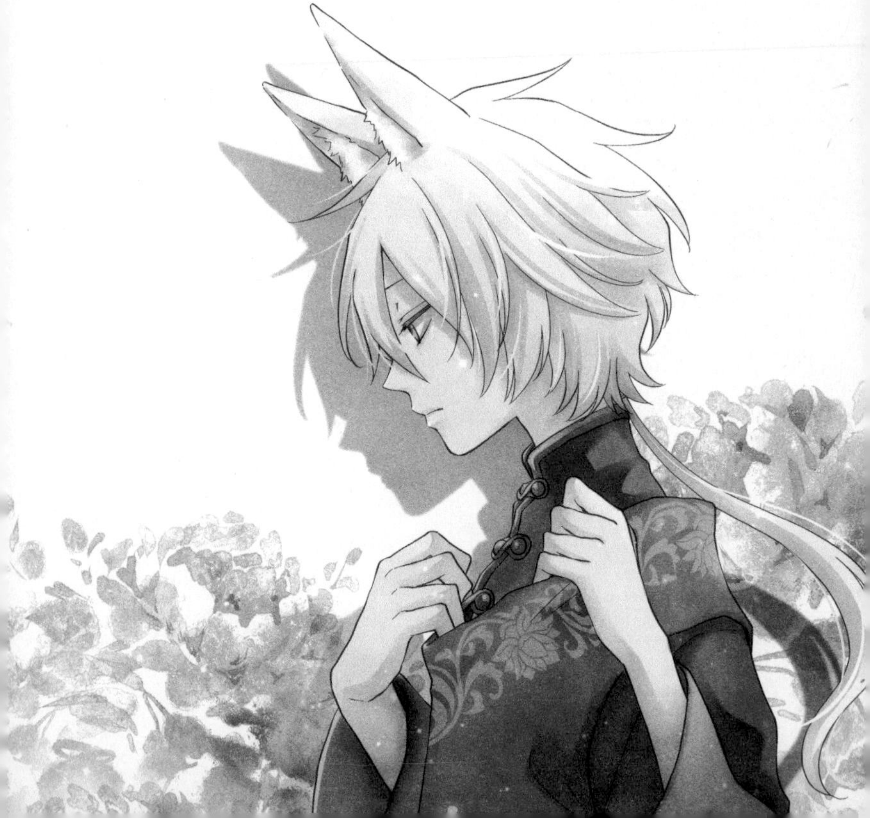